Amy,
thanks for your support!
Karla B. Trippe

# When the
# BIRDS
## *Stopped*
# Singing

Karla A. Trippe

Printed in the United States of America
ISBN 979-8-9916856-0-3 (Hardback)
ISBN 979-8-9916856-1-0 (Paperback)
ISBN 979-8-9916856-2-7 (eBook)

KARLA
TRIPPE
Writer

# Dedications

For

*Scottie & Lin*

*who taught me*

*that friendship is eternal.*

*For the more than 600,000*

*children who are abused in the*

*United States each year.* *

\*     Data from the National Children's Alliance

I have a tale to tell

Sometimes it gets so hard to hide it well

I was not ready for the fall

Too blind to see the writing on the wall

A man can tell a thousand lies

I've learned my lesson well

Hope I live to tell

The secret I have learned, 'til then

It will burn inside of me

"Live to Tell" by Madonna

# Table of Contents

# The Girl with Wings

FALL WAS SERENA'S FAVORITE time of year. The leaves mimicked her wavy golden-red hair, which cascaded down her back, while the forest's browning matches the skins used to create her long dress.

She wore the dress to remain hidden from the people who traipsed in the woods during the daylight hours. When Serena saw herself mirrored in the clear, cold mountain lakes, she knew she didn't look exactly like the humans. Her body was longer and more flexible, so she could hide inside a tree if a human came upon her quickly. Serena knew of other wood nymphs who lived in specific trees, but her body could slip inside any of the trees in the mountains. Her favorite at lower elevations was the cottonwood due to its larger trunk size. But when she was up high, nearer her cave, she went into the lodgepole pine, though it was a tighter squeeze, and her body had to spread out longer. Serena didn't know how many turns of the Earth she had lived in the woods. It was the only home she'd ever known.

The day was warm and sunny. Serena decided to venture farther down the mountain.

She fancied a bath in her favorite lake before it froze over. Upon emerging from the tingling cool water, Serena heard an unusual sound. She grabbed her brown dress, dashed up to the edge of the tree line, and watched as a black 1961 Chevy moved quickly down the hill. As it began turning into the gravel parking lot, one of the car doors flew open. A small child fell out of the car, struggling to maintain her grip on the door with her right hand while desperately reaching for the bottom door frame with her left foot.

Suddenly, Serena saw wings emerge from the child's back, holding her aloft. As the car came to a stop, an older man and woman jumped from the front seats, rushing toward the little, curly-headed, auburn-haired girl. As they drew close, the wings folded in just like a bird's. The petite, pretty woman with short, tightly curled dark hair grabbed ahold of the little girl, yelling, "Caroline, what happened? Are you alright? You could have died if you fell!" Serena heard the girl crying and her mumbled words, "Edward opened the door and pushed me out!" A tall, dark-haired man reached into the car and yanked out a small, brown-haired boy who was yelling, "I didn't do anything! Caroline just had to sit in my place by the door, and then she opened it and fell out!"

Serena, now dressed, inched back farther into the line of trees. There was something about the tall man she didn't like. She felt an ominous darkness permeating from inside him, putting her on edge.

She noticed an older, thinner boy stepping out from the back seat on the other side of the car. He slipped unnoticed toward the lake, looking down on the ground at the stones, ignoring the commotion at the vehicle. By now, the man and younger boy had stopped yelling, and the little girl was no longer crying. The man strolled over to the car's trunk, which he effortlessly popped open to retrieve a handful of fishing poles. With a graceful motion, he distributed one to each of the eager boys, who sprinted toward the tranquil lake and began casting their delicate, translucent lines. The woman pulled out a striped blanket and a wicker basket from the trunk, which she closed with a click. Then, she walked toward a grassy area farther back from the lake.

Serena peered around the cottonwood tree she was hiding behind, stepping on an exposed root to see better. The woman unpacked the basket while the little girl walked up the hill toward Serena, twirling her red pleated skirt and singing. *Like a magical forest bird,* Serena thought, *inside a springy body.* For a moment, Serena was mesmerized, drawn to the girl's voice. But she didn't want the family to notice her, as the tan hides she wore didn't provide full camouflage. Like rainwater seeping into the needles, Serena quickly slipped inside the tree before the girl got any closer.

Serena concealed herself in her hidden spot, discreetly observing the young girl and her endearing features—a dainty face adorned with large, expressive brown eyes, a cherubic button nose, and a delicate, petite mouth. *She doesn't look like a bird,* Serena thought. But something about her differed from the rest of the people in the car. Serena sensed a need to protect this girl, though she wasn't sure why. The girl would soon get into the car and go back to wherever she lived. A sadness descended over Serena. That was even stranger. She wasn't used to these types of feelings regarding humans. Typically, she found them annoying, but this family was different.

Serena continued watching as they finished their afternoon of fishing and picnicking. The family returned to the car, with the little girl sitting in the front seat this time. Her head turned toward Serena, and for just a moment, their eyes locked. Then, the car pulled away, and the connection was broken. A chill of sudden apprehension coursed through Serena's being, causing her to shudder. Slowly, she emerged from the shelter of the ancient tree, her steps hastening as she sought solace in the welcoming embrace of her secluded cave, where the comforting warmth beckoned to her.

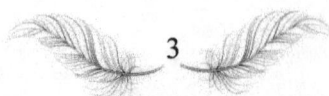

# Little Star

CAROLINE LOVED HER MOTHER, Patsy Howard. Driving home from their fishing trip, Caroline snuggled close to her mother, who tenderly ran her fingertips along Caroline's spine, exploring every delicate vertebra with a gentle touch. Caroline felt safe when her mother was close, as though she covered Caroline with a protective shield as soft as one of her grandma's patchwork quilts.

As they drove in the dark, Caroline wondered about the tree that seemingly looked at her. She asked her mother, "Are trees alive like people?"

Her mother looked down at Caroline and shook her head. "No, a tree is just a large plant. They don't have eyes, and they don't watch people." Caroline felt her mother was correct, but she couldn't let go of the idea that one of the cottonwood trees had been watching her when they drove away from the picnic.

Caroline's mind moved to pondering what was wrong with her and why her brother seemed to hate her. He was always so mean. Like when he tried to catch her fingers in doors, pushing them against her tiny digits until they hurt for days. Or when she begged Edward to take her to the playground at the school on his bike. He finally gave in. Edward instructed her to tuck her legs in as she mounted the rear of the bicycle. However, as he began to rotate the pedals, one of her legs became entangled in the chains. Oblivious to her distress, he continued to pedal, causing her to tumble from the bike in tears. Edward laughed, knowing she wouldn't ask again.

Why didn't people like her? The same predicament plagued her at

school. Caroline loved her kindergarten class, but some girls were mean to her. Thank goodness she had her best friend, Gwynn, a tall, blonde girl who lived down the street in a gray two-story house. They played together every day over the summer, sometimes dressing up in Patsy's old clothes or creating grown-up lives with their Barbies in her dollhouse in the basement. Caroline spent time making bedspreads and pillows from her mother's scrap basket to cover the cardboard furniture. She smiled as she daydreamed about meeting up with Gwynn and talking about their weekend activities as they walked to school on Monday morning. She would ask Gwynn about the tree, as Gwynn was smart like Andrew.

It was dark when the Howards arrived at their small brick home in the leafy-green community of Arvada, a suburb west of Denver. Once inside, her mother helped Caroline get ready for bed. The little girl checked that her dolls were asleep in their little wooden cradle. Caroline and her mother drew back the pink floral bedspread, and Caroline jumped under the covers, arranging the many stuffed animals that kept her safe at night. Her mother sat on a wooden chair and read a fairy tale from Caroline's big book of children's stories. Caroline looked forward to when she could read stories herself. But for now, her mother's soft voice helped Caroline fall asleep.

She found herself trapped within the clutches of one of her recurring nightmares. She dreamed of women dressed in dark, tattered dresses. They walked toward a grove of trees where a small fire was burning. The women joined hands around the fire and began to chant. Caroline didn't understand their words, but she sensed their power. Suddenly, men on horseback galloped into the circle, striking at the women with sharp swords. Caroline was jolted from her slumber by the piercing screams of women, leaving her trembling with fear. Her breath came in rapid, shallow gasps, and she now faced the daunting task of deciding on her course of action: staying in bed, trying to go back to sleep, and hoping the nightmare didn't return, or going to her mother's bed. But reaching her mother was a treacherous journey.

The path to her mother's bed began by creeping past the creatures that lived under the bed. Caroline knew they liked to steal things, chiefly bright, shiny objects. She was careful not to drop anything onto her beige carpet because it might not be there when she reached down to pick it up. That had happened with her favorite bracelet. Her mother had scolded her for losing it, but Caroline knew better. Her most precious treasures were stored safely in boxes in a drawer of her dresser.

After thinking for a short time, Caroline decided to go to her mother. Working up the nerve to step down onto the floor took a few moments. That was the hardest part. She worried the creatures would grab her legs and drag her down to some dark, dank place she couldn't escape. *Stop dawdling, Caroline!* She placed her tiny feet on the floor. Like a rabbit, she was off running from her bedroom and down the small hallway in front of the bathroom. Her bare feet raced across the frigid wooden floor, carrying her to her parent's room. She jumped into their bed and curled against her mother's warm body. *Safe.*

The other place Caroline felt protected was her Grandparent Andersen's' 500-acre farm on the eastern side of Colorado near the Kansas border. Two weeks later, the family made their monthly trek. The moment the car rolled to a stop, Caroline and her brothers leaped out, running behind the white clapboard farmhouse to the screened-in porch to discover what treats Grandmother Andersen had baked. There was typically a cake and, without fail, at least one pie. They couldn't wait to see which of their favorites sat on the big white table. This time, it was Caroline's favorite—a yummy cherry pie cooked from the fruit that grew on the trees in the front yard. From the porch, they headed into the kitchen, where, from the cookie jar, each child grabbed a ginger snap baked especially for this visit. Caroline's brothers shot-out the screen door to play baseball. They wouldn't let Caroline play.

Left to herself, Caroline asked her grandfather if there were any new kittens. He nodded his balding head. "Yes, Caroline, there's a small litter out at the barn. But you know they won't play with you, as they're feral." Caroline wasn't sure what "feral" meant, but it didn't matter. There was a new bunch of kittens! Caroline asked her grandmother if there were any empty cardboard boxes in the garage and if she could have one. Her grandmother nodded yes. Caroline headed for the desk in the living room, opened the top drawer, and grabbed the crayons and scissors she kept there. Then, she ran to the south bedroom through the new door to the garage. She looked at the boxes folded by the wall and picked a smaller one. *Tape!* Back inside she scrambled, grabbing the tape from the drawer.

Arms full of her items, Caroline walked to the grassy area in front of the big red barn. She taped close the bottom of the box and drew a door and windows on all sides. She deftly cut three sides of the cardboard door with scissors and gently bent the fourth side. It opened and closed to her satisfaction. Next, she cut out all the windows. With her crayons, she drew green shutters on all the windows. *Ready!* Now came the hard part: catching a kitty to live in her house.

Quietly, Caroline walked toward the barn door and opened it as noiselessly as possible. But the thick wooden door was heavy, and the hinges

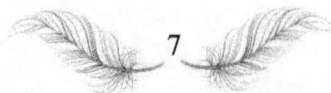

creaked as she pulled the door open and grabbed the metal loop from the entrance to hook it on the outside wooden wall. She took a deep breath and crouched down to wait. She knew from practice that the cats would have run farther under the building when the door opened. She had to remain still until they returned to the small opening below one of the cow pens. Caroline waited for what seemed like an eternity and then got down on her hands and knees on the cold, dusty concrete floor and slid toward the hole. She had learned not to sing out to the cats; they wouldn't come unless they heard Grandpa's heavy boots as he walked in with the battered pan full of gravy with some meat mixed in to feed them each evening.

Suddenly, a tiny black and white kitten poked its head out. Caroline's hand shot out. *Gotcha.* Caroline ran with the kitten, who snarled and scratched her arm. She reached the little house with the green shutters, pushed the cat through the door, and closed it. *Kitty, you'll love this pretty new house. So much nicer than living under the barn.* The cat banged around inside, paws flying through the windows. Suddenly, the cat tipped the box over and dashed madly back to the barn. Caroline plopped down in frustration. *Shoot! Now what?*

Caroline eyed the big hay wagon. She picked up the kitty house, scissors, tape, and crayons and hauled them back to the garage. She slipped inside and went to the cold north bedroom. In the closet were her mother's old tap shoes. Caroline grabbed them and headed back to the hay wagon. While she had never taken a dance class, Caroline loved watching musicals on the black and white TV in her parents' bedroom and imitating the steps. Climbing onto the wagon, slipping off her dirty pink sneakers, and tying on the aged white tap shoes, she thought of a song.

Pack up all my care and woe, Here I go,

Singing low, Bye bye blackbird,

Where somebody waits for me, Sugar's sweet, so is she,

Bye bye Blackbird!

Singing and hitting the taps whenever she could, Caroline danced on top of the wagon. Her high soprano voice soared above her shuffling feet, which picked out the beat on the thick wooden planks.

Caroline's mother walked outside with a metal bowl, planning to pluck some ripe strawberries from the garden. She heard a lilting sound and looked toward the barn. Caroline saw her mother and waved. A smile crossed her mother's face. But then a sadness seemed to sweep in, and her mother's shoulders hunched as if she were carrying a great weight. The quiet woman finished her chores, looking up occasionally at her twirling, tapping child, and then slowly walked back into the farmhouse to help finish dinner.

Once night came, Bill Howard, Caroline's good-looking father, turned to his two sons and said, "Want to go for a ride?" Edward and Andrew jumped up. They knew the signal. Caroline looked at her mother and saw her pursed lips. Caroline knew better than to ask to go along. She got to go once, so she was familiar with what happened and why it upset her mother.

The one time Caroline rode along on a night adventure, she was rather shocked at the activities. There was no liquor allowed in the Andersen household, just as in their house in Arvada, but her father knew where to buy it. He slid into the driver's seat of the old Chevy with Andrew in the front and Edward and Caroline in the back. He drove down the dirt road to the Ten Mile store. It was an old structure built before the Depression. Next door was a windowless building where the farmers played cards. But her father was there for beer. Caroline wondered if her grandparents knew about her father's drinking.

When her father got back inside the car, he said to the group, "Ready?"

"Ready," they cried in unison.

Off they went, driving down the dark roads, her father drinking beer and handing the finished can to one of the boys to see who could throw it the farthest. Edward usually won. He had the better arm. Her father cruised along, smoking cigarettes, drinking cold beer, and listening to country western songs on the radio. He said nothing, just looked out into the dark of the night. Caroline kept feeling that what was happening was wrong, even if everyone else seemed to have fun. She knew her mother wouldn't like it. Why did this happen? What accounted for the disparity in behavior between her father and her mother and grandparents? Why was it that things didn't make sense and were so complicated?

On Sunday, everyone—even Caroline's father—was required to go to church. The Christian church near the farm was a simple one-room building with a rectory upstairs and meeting rooms in the basement. All the Andersen's who had lived in this small town since her great-grandfather came from Denmark lay buried in the graveyard behind the church. The Andersen's took great pride in the little church, as their hands had helped build it.

Caroline preferred attending her grandparents' church as compared to the Southern Baptist church they went to at home. The people at both churches sang the beautiful hymns that Caroline loved, but her parents and grandparents drank grape juice and ate crackers during the service at the Christian church.

Caroline and her brothers weren't allowed to, and she wasn't sure why. The minister at the pulpit spoke of God and his affection for humanity. At the Baptist church, the pastor often preached about the devil and going to hell. These sermons scared Caroline and reminded her of the nightmares.

Following the church service and a delightful afternoon meal featuring Grandma Andersen's special noodles alongside delicious baked chicken, it was time to make their way back home. Grandma Andersen hugged Caroline, drawing the girl to her ample bosom. Caroline whispered, "Love you, Grandma!"

Her grandmother responded, "I love you, too!"

Her grandfather's hug was much different. His strong arms pulled her toward his hard chest, and he gave Caroline a few quick hugs. After the last one, when she was still close enough to smell the chewing tobacco on his breath, Grandpa said, "A little something for you," and slipped a quarter into her palm.

As her father started the drive back to Arvada, Caroline turned her head. Her beloved grandparents were standing on the front porch. The west wind blew her grandpa's bit of hair and her grandma's floral skirt as they waved goodbye. Caroline turned forward, looking at the dirt road that led to the highway. She contemplated the farm and how it seemed enveloped in an aura of happiness. And then she prayed to God to make her home in Arvada just as peaceful.

# Wrestling at the Chase

BILL HOWARD HATED BEING alone. Thoughts of his father often crept in. Small, dusty Kansas towns, one after the other, where the family lived, and his father, Charles "Spec" Howard, published the local newspaper. Life began on a positive note. Bill attended the local school with his younger sisters and brother while his beautiful mother wrote the society page and offered readers some of her favorite recipes. Spec wrote the remaining copy, which was ready when Bill got home from school. He set type and helped his father print and deliver the afternoon news.

But Spec could never hold it together. He started drinking, which often led to him chasing some local skirt. His actions required Bill to stop attending school, burdened with getting the paper out each day to make the family money. At the same time, his mother tried to keep Spec from drinking it away. He would never be like his father. Bill went to his job as a proofreader at the Denver Post every day wearing his short-sleeved white shirt. Because he supervised the afternoon shift, he left home at two o'clock each day. The children were asleep when he returned home after ten o'clock each night. To relax, Bill might take a nip from the pint of whiskey he stashed in the upper kitchen cabinet while talking to Patsy about the day.

Bill looked forward to Sundays. It was his day to do as he pleased. If Patsy nagged him, he joined the family for church in the morning. Then, with a sandwich Patsy made, Bill grabbed a beer from the stores he kept in the garage and settled into his favorite blue chair to watch the Denver Broncos with his sons. He didn't think too much about why he drank beer on those days. He saw it as a way of letting go. The pain in the side of his head went away as the alcohol drifted through his system. He looked out from his big chair at the family he'd built. Andrew, his oldest, was a gifted boy, according to his teachers, destined for a significant medical career. He just needed to toughen up a bit, and Bill would help him with that. Then there was Edward, the child who resembled him the most. That kid concerned Bill, but he'd keep Edward in line by focusing on sports. Edward was amazingly talented. Bill firmly believed he could go all the way to the majors in baseball with his guidance.

He turned his head to consider the small girl. Bill enjoyed the vibrant little girl, but she also made him nervous. She seemed to live in her own world. Even as she sat nearby quietly putting together a puzzle, he got fidgety and started picking at his nails. When she looked at him, it was as if she could somehow see inside him. He didn't want his auburn-haired daughter to know his thoughts. Shaking his head, he popped open a fresh, cold can of beer. "Patsy, dinner on the table at six o'clock?" he asked.

Patsy was sitting at the other end of the room, sewing a red Christmas dress for Caroline. "Yes, Bill. Everything will be on time and just the way you like it. Plenty of gravy for the roast beef and mashed potatoes."

"Don't forget, Dad," piped up Edward. "Tonight, 'Wrestling at the Chase' is on TV. You said we could practice some of the moves afterward." Edward enjoyed any physical activity, while Andrew would rather have his head in a book.

On Sunday nights, a local TV station aired a show called "Wrestling at the Chase." The broadcast came from a hotel in St. Louis called the Chase Park Plaza. It showed live wrestling, and Bill and the boys watched it weekly.

They'd clap and yell for their favorite wrestlers like Dick the Bruiser and King Kong Brody. Afterward, they practiced the different moves in the living room. The boys "tagged in" and piled on Bill, trying to pin him with other movements. He threw them off, wobbling from the alcohol he'd been drinking all day. Caroline observed discreetly from the threshold of the door.

Suddenly, Edward rushed over and grabbed Caroline. He raised the small girl over his head, holding onto her waist. Then, he began spinning her around while yelling, "Look at me! I've got Caroline in the airplane spin."

Caroline raised her voice, shouting at him to set her down. Edward, always showing off, tried to throw her into the air and catch her. Caroline screamed louder, "Edward, please don't drop me!"

Edward started to lower the girl, grabbing her by the legs. "It's King Kong Brody," he said, imitating the announcer. "He's performing the famous pile driver." Edward started pounding Caroline's head into the gold carpeting.

The little girl shouted, "Mom! Make Edward stop."

Patsy rushed into the room from the kitchen, where she was cleaning up from the evening meal. "Edward, stop that!" she yelled. "Bill, don't let the children hurt each other!"

Bill stumbled to his feet, releasing the wrestling hold he had on Andrew, eager to provoke the boy into fighting back. "Aw, Patsy, we're just having some fun."

Patsy grabbed Edward by the arm as he dropped his sister to the floor. "How often do I have to tell you not to hurt your sister?" she asked.

Edward kept stomping around the room with his arms in the air, yelling, "I'm King Kong Brody!"

Patsy shouted above him, "Bill, stop all this now! Edward, Andrew, get ready for bed."

Andrew swept past her and headed upstairs to his room. *Are there tears in his eyes?* his mother wondered. *Oh, I hope Bill didn't get rough with him again.* She knew Bill couldn't always control the strength in his six-foot frame, especially when he'd been drinking. He would start using some of the moves he learned in the Marines on the boys. Should they gain the upper hand, he had the potential to swiftly become hostile.

Once she was certain the boys were safely upstairs in their bedroom and getting into their pajamas, Patsy checked on Caroline. Her bedroom had a deep closet behind the wall where she kept toys she didn't play with regularly. Patsy walked into the pink room but didn't see Caroline. Someone had nearly shut the closet door, but a bit of an old blanket was sticking out. Patsy opened the door, calling softly, "Caroline, come out now. It's bedtime." She waited quietly and soon heard a small shuffling sound inside.

The faint voice of a little girl quivered as it said, "Edward hurt me. He slammed my head on the floor."

"Caroline, come out so I can look at your head and see that it's alright," said Patsy. When Caroline didn't emerge, Patsy bent down and called through the small opening in the door. "Caroline, Edward didn't mean to hurt you. He just got excited pretending he was one of the professional wrestlers."

"Mommy, I don't want to end up like someone he beats up in wrestling," cried Caroline.

Patsy said, as she always did, "I'll talk with him. Now, come out."

The small girl emerged, disheveled from hiding under the mound of pillows and blankets she'd pulled into the closet.

"Oh, Caroline, you're a mess!" her mother complained. She reached for Caroline's frilly white nightgown and handed it to the girl. "Get dressed for bed. Tomorrow, you will have to straighten up your closet." Patsy needed to tell Caroline only once. The girl was surprisingly neat.

Patsy walked over to the little glass dresser she'd found at a garage sale and refinished for Caroline. On the mirror top was a hairbrush with bristles large enough to go through Caroline's thick, wavy hair without hurting her scalp.

"Come on, Caroline, let's brush your hair before you clean your teeth." Caroline and Patsy sat on the twin bed, the mother carefully brushing out the knots in the girl's hair. Caroline began to whistle a tune. Her mother couldn't recall hearing Caroline whistle before. "When did you learn to whistle, sweetie?" she asked.

"Gwynn and I have been practicing before and after school," she replied. "It seemed to come easier to me. While I wait for her to reach our house, I try to mimic the sweet songs of the beautiful bird in our front tree."

"What does the bird look like?" Patsy asked.

Caroline jumped off the bed and ran to her small wooden desk. She grabbed a notebook and skipped back to her mother. Then, she opened the notebook to show Patsy a small grey and white bird with a black throat and cap.

"I believe that's a chickadee," said Patsy.

Caroline looked up at her mother with a big smile. "A chickadee! What a pretty name." Caroline whistled the song of the bird again. *Chick-a-dee-dee.*

Patsy smiled down at the little girl. "Time for little chicks to go to sleep." She tucked in Caroline and turned off the light.

# In the Wintertime

SERENA STOOD INSIDE HER cave high in the mountains, watching the snow flutter down. She sensed a long, cold winter coming to the mountains. She pulled her heavy cloak tighter to keep warm as she began to walk outside through the lightening woods. She was careful not to snag the clothing, which was turned inside out so that the warm fur was close to her body and the cured skin provided protection from the elements. Leather ties Serena had made from strips of animal skin closed the cloak from the wind and snow. Similar to Native Americans, Serena was meticulous in utilizing every part of an animal. The game that lived in the mountains was a gift from the Creator.

Many animals now slept during the long winter, but she watched for the deer and elk herds that moved through the woods. She wanted the animals to find food. Serena didn't eat large animals, though she accepted parts of their hides if she discovered them. She did eat the meat of the smaller creatures. She was out checking the traps she had set for them. She tried to eat sparingly so she needn't ask the Creator to send her animals to kill often. Serena loved the quiet of the woods in the winter. Her cave was just above the ridge line on a mountain not easily reached by humans. She kept the cave warm using a fire she lit with the help of a bit of magic. Serena was alone except for the wildlife. She didn't remember how she had come to live in this forest, but she had resided there for a long time.

In winter, Serena occupied herself with books filled with ancient tales and healing methods. She would have enjoyed having someone to practice her arts with, but wood nymphs typically spent much of their lives alone. However, something was moving in the air. For the past few days, Serena had observed a falcon soaring in the sky above her cave. Falcons were believed to be messengers from the spirit world. She'd received a message that she must be patient and trust her instinct but know that someone was coming her way. Thus, she continued her studies, which helped fill the long, cold days of winter.

The storms came in during these dark days and nights, but when they were over, Serena loved to go outside and see the clean, untouched snow under the bright blue sky. Sometimes, she took the paints she made to the front of the cave and tried to replicate what she saw on the backs of the animal hides. Serena had acquired her painting skills from an elderly nymph who had departed many moons ago. Serena understood that she needed to go back to work with the Creator. She knew she would receive a message to do the same someday, but that time was not now.

A snowy white owl suddenly flew overhead and hooted at Serena. "Yes," she answered aloud. "I know I must be patient. And I will stay busy while I wait for the winter to end. But someone needs my strength." Suddenly a strange feeling overwhelmed her. *I must send energy down to the village on the plains.*

The owl settled into the corner, in a niche high in the rocks, to wait with Serena. She delved into the flames, searching for the one in need of her assistance.

# Seeing the Other Side

*I*T WAS 1969 WHEN Caroline started third grade. She loved the teacher, Mrs. Jennings, a broader, older woman with soft, white hair. She was kind to her students and complimented Caroline whenever she did well in her schoolwork. Caroline loved Mrs. Jennings' praise and worked hard to please her.

On a Saturday night at the beginning of December, Caroline went through her standard ritual: take a bath, wash her hair, and have it rolled in hard brush curlers by her mother so it would be especially curly for church the next day. Usually, Caroline sat under the old hair dryer with the big cap and long hose. She loved Saturday evening TV with "The Carol Burnett Show," which entertained her while her hair dried before she went to bed. But tonight, they had to pick up her brothers, who had gone ice skating at the Arvada rink. It was a chilly night, with the temperature hovering at freezing, and Caroline's hair was still wet. "Mom, can't I stay home and wait for the boys here?" begged Caroline.

Her mother looked at the young girl and shook her head. "No, Caroline, you are too young to be home alone. It would be best if you came with me to the rink. Put on your warm coat and bring a blanket with you." They walked outside to the old black Ford Galaxy her mother drove. It was her grandparents' car, and it had been kind of them to give it to the family when they bought a new one. Her mother needed something to run her many errands. However, because they had a one-car garage, they Galaxy was typically left outside, and it took a long time to warm up. The car wouldn't heat up until they reached the rink.

Caroline sat in the back seat, shivering in her navy quilted coat, but she didn't complain. She could tell her mother wasn't pleased about having to pick up the boys. Still, Caroline understood how much fun it was to go ice skating on Saturday night. She couldn't wait to skate with her friends when she was older.

Her mother pulled up at the rink but didn't see Edward or Andrew. She had made it clear that they should be in front by 8:30 p.m. She idled by the rink door, but other cars were waiting behind her, so she entered the parking lot. "Caroline, stay here while I go find your brothers," her mother said. "Don't leave the car!" The warmth quickly dissipated as the temperature continued to drop. Caroline snuggled into the old wool blanket she'd brought along and fell asleep.

Out of nowhere, the doors were wrenched open. Edward jumped in the back seat behind Andrew, who sat beside their mother. *Uh-oh*, Caroline thought, awakening quickly. *Mom is going to be mad*.

"I told you to be standing outside at eight-thirty sharp," said her mother.

"Mom," complained Andrew, "we were the first to leave! The other kids get to stay until nine o'clock."

You can stay later if someone else drives you home," her mother said in an exasperated voice. "I'm busy with Caroline on Saturday night, and her bedtime is earlier than nine o'clock. Now, everyone will likely get to bed late. I don't want to hear your complaints when it's time to get up for church tomorrow morning."

The boys groaned.

"Don't think you can skip Sunday school and church service," she finished.

Andrew said quietly, "Dad doesn't have to go."

Her mother's voice grew higher-pitched and louder. "I can't tell your father what to do, but you children will follow my rules. Church on Sunday!"

As her mother carefully drove the family home, the old car skidded across the snow-covered roads, Edward started coughing. He turned toward Caroline and coughed on her. Caroline scooted away from her brother. "You're gross, Edward," she yelled.

Everyone was tired when they finally reached home. Caroline was glad her mother didn't make her sit under the hair dryer, but she wished she didn't have to sleep with the hard rollers and pink pins sticking into her head.

Later in the week, Caroline began to feel sick. Her throat was sore, and her body felt achy. Her mother took her temperature. Caroline looked at the thermometer and saw that her temperature was over 100 degrees. "No school for you," instructed her mother. She had Caroline take two aspirin and lie in bed quietly, reading her favorite books. Her mother checked in on Caroline later in the day and found the girl asleep. She placed her hand on Caroline's forehead. It remained quite warm.

The next day, Caroline awoke sensing she was worse. Her throat was very sore, and she was still running a fever. Plus, she started throwing up everything she ate, hurting her throat even more. Her mother called the pediatrician's office to make an appointment.

Fortunately, they could fit Caroline in later in the day. They had to leave the boys home alone, but her mother was strict with her instructions. "Andrew is in charge, Edward. I don't want any horseplay. Do your homework and stay out of trouble, or I'll tell your father, and you know how he'll punish you." The children knew their father could quickly yank off his leather belt. When he whipped them, no crying was allowed. Tears led to a prolonged beating, as they were seen as a display of vulnerability. In this, Caroline's father treated all the children the same.

Caroline shuffled into the doctor's office with her mother. Her entire body hurt, particularly her throat. She hated going outside in the cold, as it made her feel worse. She didn't care for the doctor. He wore a goofy rubber butterfly on his stethoscope as if that made him a nice man. The doctor looked at Caroline's throat and tapped on her chest. His nurse took her temperature. The doctor asked her mother how often she was giving Caroline aspirin. He determined that Caroline's condition was the flu and advised her mother to keep her home until her temperature had stabilized. Back into the cold car they went.

The following day, when Caroline stirred, she had a bad cough. Her dad was still home, so her mom headed to the drugstore for cough medicine. Caroline hated the taste but swallowed, flinching as the strawberry-flavored fluid rolled past her burning throat. She fell asleep and was annoyed every time her mother woke her to check her temperature. Caroline glanced over with blurred vision, attempting to decipher the thermometer's reading. Her mother said aloud, "One hundred and two degrees. Why isn't your temperature going down?" Caroline didn't know and laid back down. She wondered why the doctor couldn't give her something to make her feel better.

Caroline couldn't remember a time when she had been sick this long. Mrs. Jennings had sent home her schoolwork, but she didn't have the energy to work on it, and her mother let it go. Caroline could do homework when she was better. On the following day, Caroline felt extremely unwell. Now, her chest was hurting. She had to get into the cold car again and go back to see the pediatrician. He diagnosed Caroline with a word she had never heard before: tuberculosis. All Caroline knew was that she felt hot, her throat hurt, her body ached, and it was hard to breathe. She wasn't hungry, which was good because she couldn't keep food down, and throwing up pained her throat. She couldn't go to school and see her beloved Mrs. Jennings or Gwynn, and she might miss singing in the church Christmas pageant.

The next day, Caroline's temperature was at 103. Nothing was working, and her mother seemed frantic. She bundled up Caroline in her warmest flannel nightgown with thick socks that barely fit in Caroline's boots. Her mother put her in the thickest coat she could find and had Caroline stay in bed until the car was warm. When her mother informed her father about what she was doing, he offered no objection. Her mother drove Caroline downtown to the Children's Hospital. A doctor whom Caroline had never seen before examined her and told her mother that Caroline was sick pneumonia. He carefully explained the treatment. Using a payphone, her mother called her father and instructed him to buy a humidifier.

Once they returned home, her mother put Caroline back in bed and told her to lie still. She was coughing badly, and her breathing was growing more painful. She could barely focus on her parents as she watched them put a table over her bed. Over the table, her mother placed a white sheet that covered Caroline's head and chest. On the bedside table, her father put a humidifier. The soft, droning sound of the machine helped Caroline fall asleep. In a few hours, her mother woke her and checked her temperature again. It was now 104 degrees. Her mother tried to spoon some chicken broth into Caroline's mouth, but Caroline would take only a few sips. The soup burned her throat and made her nauseated. The little girl laid back down and fell asleep. When she woke up, her mother had her take small sips of cold water to stay hydrated. Caroline took two more aspirin, managing to swallow the pills. She laid her head on the pillow and asked her mother for her favorite doll. As Caroline held Tiny Tears, she told the dolly she would be better soon and they could get dressed up for Christmas. She heard her mother murmuring. It sounded like praying.

Caroline's body trembled uncontrollably even though she was wrapped snugly in numerous quilts and blankets. Her mother woke Caroline every few hours to take her temperature. In the middle of the night, Caroline heard her father come into her room and felt him lying on her bed. She thought she heard him crying.

It was now the fifth day, and when Caroline's eyes opened, she started crying. Her mother rushed in to hear Caroline say she couldn't move her head. Her neck was stiff. She told her mother there was a painful pounding inside her head. Caroline begged her to do something to make her feel better. Caroline's temperature had spiked to a worrisome 105 degrees.

Her mother and father conferred. Caroline's mother wrapped the girl in several blankets and laid her down in the back seat of the warm car. With urgency in her heart, Caroline's mother raced back to the hospital, her hands clenching the wheel tightly as she prayed fervently. The color drained from her knuckles, mirroring the snow-covered yards she hurried past along the way. She stopped at the emergency room and ran in, begging for help. An orderly brought out a wheelchair, and Caroline sat in it while coughing and crying. He took Caroline into an exam room to wait.

After a short time, a young male attending doctor came to examine Caroline. He checked her throat and lungs and then spoke with her mother about the diagnoses and medications she'd been giving the child and how long Caroline had been running a high fever. The young doctor told Caroline that he was going to perform a procedure called a spinal tap. Two nurses came into the room to hold Caroline down. Alarmed, Caroline's mother expressed her concern as the doctor empathetically explained that the spinal tap procedure could be both challenging and painful. Caroline could not move as he slid the needle into her back.

Just then, another white-uniformed nurse stealthily appeared, whispering to the attending doctor that Caroline's pediatrician was on his way. As her mother held Caroline's hot little hand, the doctor paced the room and checked the girl's temperature, which had reached 106 degrees. The doctor decided he couldn't wait any longer and called for the nurses to return to the room. Just as he was about to insert the needle, Caroline's pediatrician walked in, shouting, "What are you doing to my patient?"

The attending doctor replied loudly, "Trying to save her life!"

The pediatrician told the doctor he would take over, but the attending doctor didn't leave the room. He watched as the pediatrician prepared the spinal tap. To Caroline, it looked like the longest needle in the world. Slowly, the doctor inserted the needle into the space between two lumbar vertebrae to remove a sample of cerebrospinal fluid surrounding the brain and spinal cord that protected them from injury. The pediatrician told the lead nurse to have the culture analyzed post haste. A nurse rolled Caroline into an elevator alone with the pediatrician.

They took Caroline to a room empty of other children. There, more needles were inserted into Caroline's right arm and connected to an IV. Her high temperature and lack of food and fluids had severely dehydrated her. Caroline's eyes welled up with tears as the sharp sensation of the needles pricked her skin. The nurses spoke soothingly to Caroline when she asked for her mother.

Charlie Brown's Christmas was showing on the TV as her mother quietly walked into the hospital room. She leaned over Caroline and asked if she was watching the show. She knew how much the girl loved seeing this program annually. Slowly, Caroline opened her eyes and noticed her mother wearing a green gown, hat, gloves, and mask. Fear overtook Caroline. Why was her mother dressed this way? She could barely see her face. The nurse walked in and whispered to her gowned mother that they were pumping as many antibiotics into Caroline as her body could stand. Her mother nodded. The nurse explained they were focusing on the spinal meningitis that was killing her daughter. Caroline also had pneumonia, which they were treating as best they could. Caroline no longer felt the pain that had racked her body. Now, she felt nothing at all.

The hospital room was silent and colorless. With difficulty, Caroline turned her head to the left, noticing there was no wall. Instead, it looked as if the room was draped with a pale curtain, which moved as if pushed by a slight breeze. Shadows passed behind the curtain, fascinating Caroline. Everything felt calm and weightless. The other side of the curtain looked warm and safe—a different kind of warmth than the burning feeling that had consumed her body. This warmth was like floating in a bathtub. She wondered what it was like on the other side. Could she visit it and then return to this side? She tried reaching her hand toward the figure closest to the curtain. She couldn't feel her mother stroking her feverish head. As Caroline watched the figures behind the curtain, she heard them say, "Close your eyes and sleep." For once, she peacefully drifted into a deep and dreamless sleep.

Caroline had now been in the hospital for more than eight days. Her mother came to see her before the boys got home from school. They couldn't go into the room because Caroline was still in quarantine. She mustn't catch any more germs. One day, her dad stopped in on his way to work. Caroline was surprised to see him. He didn't say much, which wasn't like him. Then, he began to talk about her birth. Caroline knew the story: She had been born in a car on the way to the hospital. But this time, her father shared a different portion of the story. He talked to Caroline about how she was born in the birth sac. He explained that babies lived inside a nourishing sac that protected them while they grew. When a baby was ready to be born, the sac broke. Though her father looked at her as he told the story, he seemed far away.

"When you were born, the sac didn't break," said her father. "You emerged still inside it, and it immediately began collapsing. You were turning blue as I ran to get someone to help before you suffocated. An old nurse saved you. When I got home that night, I told your Grandmother Howard about your birth. She said you were born under the 'sign of the veil,' which meant you would have a life of wealth. She mentioned the existence of other folklore surrounding being born in the caul, which is another term for the birth sac. Caulbearers were considered capable of seeing ghosts and spirits and communicating with the dead."

He stared at Caroline for a long time and then told her she must stay well and not cause any more problems. Caroline told her father she would try hard and asked if she could go home by Christmas. Her father reassured her that he would consult with the doctors about it.

Caroline was still weak when she arrived home. People from church dropped off dishes to feed the family. Caroline could eat only soft food, as she easily got nauseated. Her mother fed her soup and Jell-O—lots of Jell-O. Also, her mother told everyone to stay quiet so Caroline could continue to rest. Sleep was the best medicine to heal her traumatized body. Caroline didn't mind. It was easier than swallowing the many pills each day. Her dear friend Gwynn was sick with pneumonia, too. Tragically, another young girl from their church had contracted spinal meningitis at the age of three and lost her life.

Caroline sometimes thought about the people behind the curtain in her hospital room. She didn't believe she knew any of them, even if some felt familiar, but they emanated kindness. None had approached her. They kept their distance, patiently anticipating her approach. But even though the place seemed nice, like the farm, Caroline wanted to be with her mother and Gwynn. And Mrs. Jennings. She looked forward to going back to school once she was finally well.

# The Fishing Trip

*T*HE HOWARDS SPENT THE winter watching over Caroline. In January, the third-grader tried returning to school but got pneumonia again.

Many people from the church and her school worried about the sick little girl. Caroline received numerous cards, prompting her mother to give her a scrapbook to keep her engaged by creating a collage of the cards and notes. Caroline enjoyed this project so much that she continued saving items to make another scrapbook at the end of the school year.

Caroline was unbelievably happy when she finally returned to school and saw sweet Mrs. Jennings' face again. She had caught up on her schoolwork with the help of her mother and teacher. However, Caroline's life had changed irrevocably. She had lost significant strength in her arms and could no longer climb the rope to the ceiling in gym class. She had to eat strange foods full of protein and take many large vitamin pills daily. Her mother watched her constantly. Strangely, some girls at school were mean to her because Caroline got more attention from grownups, as she got sick easily. Caroline was always afraid when she got a sore throat and had to tell her mother. She didn't want to go back to the hospital. Caroline exhibited a sore throat as the initial symptom, regardless of the ailment. It remained that way for the rest of her life.

Spring arrived, and her father decided to take the family on a fishing trip up in Summit County. Her mother was afraid to take Caroline. Even though the snow had stopped, it was still cold outside. Her father thought the fresh air and sunshine would help Caroline. Everyone was tired of being cooped up in the house.

Caroline wasn't excited about the trip. She didn't care for fishing and generally spent her time reading. But Caroline was bored of books. Her mother suggested taking nature walks down by the river. Perhaps they could look for birds that Caroline could draw. Also, she promised to get Caroline a new puzzle, a harder one that they could work on together.

Caroline told her mother that she would prefer to visit a warm location, such as the beach. Her mother's smile was filled with longing. "Yes, Caroline, that would be fun," she said. "But those trips cost money." Her parents still had bills to pay for Caroline's medical care. She had heard her parents arguing about money. Her father thought the fishing trip would be fun, particularly for Caroline's brothers. They had been shunted to the side over the winter and forced to stay indoors because Caroline's mother didn't have extra time to drive them places and didn't want to keep asking other parents for favors. The family would go on the fishing trip and have a good time.

The Blue River was a beautiful, clear mountain stream full of rainbow trout. Landing one of these magnificent fish took skill, and Caroline's brothers enjoyed the challenge. They arrived at the cabin early in the morning. Her father immediately took the boys out for a day of fishing. Caroline's mother set out to organize the cabin, and Caroline tried to help. But the small girl still tired quickly. Her mother suggested making chocolate chip cookies, and Caroline tried to show excitement about the suggestion. Together, they mixed the batter and dropped scoops of dough onto the greased cookie sheets. Then, they popped the trays into the old oven. Her mother set up a folding table so that Caroline could start on the new puzzle while watching the cookies bake. Her mother was relieved by Caroline's healing. Still, the doctors warned her that the girl's immune system was highly compromised and she would be susceptible to germs for many years. They had come too close to losing Caroline, and her mother couldn't help but be overbearing.

Caroline's mother suggested walking a nearby trail after her father and brothers left to fish a different part of the river the following morning. Caroline nodded and pulled on her shiny red boots and navy wool jacket. They shuffled outside, with her mother taking the lead. There was a path beside their cabin. Caroline loved exploring the deep woods, especially enjoying the fragrance of pine and mimicking the songs of various birds. Caroline wanted to go farther into the woods than before. However, her mother didn't want too much cold air entering Caroline's still-healing lungs.

They returned to the dark green cabin, and her mother insisted that Caroline lay down for a nap on the metal bed while she made a salad and shucked ears of corn to go with the fish she hoped the men would bring home. Late in the afternoon, the men returned, stomping their boots on the wooden floor and roaring about their success. Caroline's father handed her mother a wire basket containing six large fish. She began preparing the flour and cornmeal mixture to fry the trout.

Caroline hated eating fish. She had to carefully pick out the bones before she could chew the meat, and the work tired her out. Her father was in a good mood, bragging about who had landed the largest fish. He was drinking beer, and Caroline watched him closely, unsure which direction he would turn. Would he be fun or strict? Caroline liked the father who came to the hospital to see her, but that father seemed to have melted away. The drinking father said cruel things to everyone, and he chose particularly mean things to say, each designed to hurt a family member. He told Caroline that he wished she had been born a boy. Why couldn't he be happy about having a daughter? Her dad also grabbed her mother's buttocks, which Caroline thought was disrespectful. Patsy always told Caroline to ignore what her father said or did, but Caroline found this harder to do as she got older.

The next day, her dad and brothers fought over who would use which fishing pole and what part of the Blue River they would fish. Her brothers' voices grew louder as they quarreled, and her dad grabbed Andrew, causing her mother to react. Caroline felt her mother was most protective of Andrew, even if she did hover over Caroline. Chaos erupted as everyone yelled, with Caroline's mother trying to persuade her father to release his grip on Andrew.

Caroline found all the loud noise triggering and didn't have a closet to hide in. She grabbed her coat and ran outside. She started moving up the same trail she'd taken with her mother the day before. Now sobbing, Caroline began making a keening sound that, due to her strong vocal cords, carried high into the woods.

Serena was down low today, searching for herbs and sprouts that came up in the early spring days. As she heard the sound, the vibration in the air started to intensify, causing Serena to feel its presence. Suddenly, the noise stopped moving and settled in one location. Serena walked toward it and saw a large rock next to a stream of trickling water. Sitting on top of the rock was a small wailing girl. Serena moved close to a pine tree, peeking through the branches, trying to decide whether to move inside it. But there was something familiar about this human that Serena couldn't quite pinpoint. She began to wonder if this girl was part of the message she had received from the falcon during the winter. As Serena waited in the deepest shadow of the tree, Caroline's crying began to slow. Given her father's insistence that Howards didn't cry, Caroline made every effort to stifle her tears, even when subjected to the painful lashings of his belt. In contrast, while Caroline and Edward strived to maintain a tough exterior, Andrew never held back his emotions.

As her breathing gradually steadied and her vision cleared, Caroline caught a glimpse of a figure that appeared to be a woman lurking in the depths of the forest. She was a unique creature, as if from a fairy tale, very tall with beautiful long, wavy, golden-red hair. Her dress looked like shades of white and brown animal fur that reminded Caroline of rabbits. She longed to touch the dress and feel its softness. The woman was carrying a woven basket over her arm, and Caroline could tell it was full of plants. Caroline stared, knowing it was impolite, but she couldn't help it. She had never seen a person such as this.

Serena stood as still as the rabbits she wore, debating whether to slip into a tree. The little girl who had spotted her showed no fear. Serena could see the cylinder of golden color that went up into the sky and down into the ground. It surrounded the girl. She immediately understood the unique meaning of the color. The spirit world guarded the girl.

Several minutes passed, and the birds in the trees had resumed their songs. A hummingbird flashed up by Serena's face and flew down to the girl. Caroline noticed the tiny dancing bird and said, "I love to watch hummingbirds. I have a feeder outside my window at home."

Then, Serena received a message from the bird confirming this was the person she was waiting for. Serena continued standing mutely by the tree, watching the girl closely.

Caroline bravely called out, "I'm Caroline Howard. What's your name?"

The woman answered in a high tone that Caroline couldn't understand. The young girl gazed at her with confusion, wondering who this stranger was.

Serena spoke again in a lower tone. "I am Serena of the White Mountain Forest."

Caroline asked, "Do you live here all the time?"

"Yes," responded Serena. "This has been my home for a long time."

"Have I seen you before when my family stopped at a lake on the way home from Aspen? You seemed to watch me from inside a tree."

"Yes, that is possible," replied Serena.

'You don't look like other women," observed Caroline. "Why are you so tall?"

"I am a wood nymph," Serena explained.

Caroline was intrigued. "What's a wood nymph?" she asked.

Serena thought about how best to answer this human's question. "We are creatures of God who live a long time and help guard the forest from harm."

"What kind of harm?" Caroline continued questioning the nymph, hoping she would stay.

"Some people make fires and leave them. These can burn down the trees. We keep watch and put them out. We watch the animals and ensure they have an easy death if they are shot but escape from the hunters."

"You seem very kind," said Caroline.

They both turned toward the sound of her mother's voice; she was calling Caroline's name.

The little girl sighed. "Just when something interesting happens," she said. "I must go, as my mother worries about me all the time. Can I see you again?" she asked excitedly.

"Perhaps," Serena replied. "Visit this stone alone. I will find you if I have time."

Caroline leaped off the rock and headed back down the path. She stopped and turned around. The forest looked the same, with no sign of the beautiful nymph. Then, she saw a basket sitting next to a pine tree. She swore she could see eyes looking back at her. But her mother's voice came closer, and Caroline didn't want to scare the nymph, so she hurried back down the trail.

As she lay in bed that night, Caroline told her mother about the unusual woman she had met in the forest. At first, her mother was alarmed and was about to interrupt the girl to remind her about talking to strangers. However, when Caroline described the woman's clothing, her mother realized Caroline had made up a story to cover up the fact that she'd run up the trail alone. While her mother generally found Caroline's imaginative stories enjoyable, she was tired and longed for bed. She asked Caroline to keep the story to herself and turned off the light.

In the darkness, Caroline sat up to look out the window. As she gazed at the starry night, she thought of the beautiful woman or nymph (she was a woman, right?). Caroline had never seen anything like her, even in her dreams. It was exciting and perhaps a bit dangerous. She couldn't wait for tomorrow. Then, sleep took over, and she closed her eyes.

The next morning, Caroline was roused by the boisterous commotion of the men departing for another day of fishing. It was a relief they were gone, as quiet overtook the cabin again. Caroline stretched in bed and suddenly sat up. Serena! Was it possible to see the enchanting nymph again? The girl jumped out of bed, and her feet hit the cold cabin floor. She reached for her socks and yanked them on while yelling to her mom about breakfast. As she headed to the tiny kitchen, her mother smiled upon seeing her daughter's good mood. Her mom was drinking coffee with the skillet on the stove. "Pancakes?" she asked.

Caroline nodded enthusiastically as she pulled a chair to the kitchen table. Her mother mentioned juice, and Caroline jumped up to pour a glass. Before long, her mother had set a plate with two pancakes before the girl.

"I never know if you like pancakes or French toast more," she said as Caroline covered the cakes with butter and her mother's homemade syrup. "My, you're in a good mood this morning."

"I want to go back into the woods today. I want to search for . . . some pinecones and learn the different songs sung by the birds. Can I hike by myself?" asked Caroline.

Her mother's eyes grew wide. "No, Caroline. You are too young to go alone."

"I hate never getting to do anything by myself," Caroline complained.

Her mother sighed. She understood the girl was tired of the constant supervision, but she couldn't risk losing Caroline again. "How about we walk down by the river? We haven't gone there yet," her mother suggested.

"Oh, alright," said Caroline unenthusiastically.

After they got dressed for their walk, her mother headed to the river. Caroline trudged behind. The girl looked at the trees, wondering if she would see any eyes. Was there a way to call the nymph? Caroline thought of yesterday's loud, high crying, which had seemed to bring the nymph to her. She began singing a song she heard regularly on the radio.

When the moon is in the Seventh House
And Jupiter aligns with Mars
Then peace will guide the planets
And love will steer the stars

She sang the words loudly in a higher key until her mother cast a disapproving look over her shoulder. Caroline softened her voice so as not to disturb nature.

They reached the Blue River and watched it rapidly pour over the rocks, with whitecaps of water splashing by. They walked on the west side of the river, and Caroline kept humming, her gaze searching the trees. Suddenly, a warm breeze passed her face, and she turned around, staring intensely into the trees. A smile crossed her face. One cottonwood looked more expansive than the others. A hand came up as if from the tree. Caroline whistled her chickadee imitation, and the hand waved.

Her mother said, "Caroline, I don't think there are any chickadees around here."

Caroline stopped but kept staring at the cottonwood, which was now the same width as the other trees. She looked again and saw a tree closer to her had expanded. Caroline realized Serena could quickly move into trees without detection by humans.

"What bird should we be listening for?" asked Caroline.

Suddenly, they heard a rapid knocking sound. "Well, how about a woodpecker?" her mother asked with a laugh.

Caroline looked at the cottonwood and saw a woodpecker knocking on Serena's tree! She wondered if the nymph could call birds. She burst out laughing.

"Come along, Caroline, it's time to be getting back to the cabin. It's growing chilly by the river," said her mother.

"OK. But this was fun, lots of fun," she said, turning back toward the little cabin. The sound of the woodpecker followed them practically all the way home.

# Music in Me

AS SUMMER EMERGED IN Colorado, Caroline graduated from Mrs. Jennings' class, but that wasn't her only heartbreak. Her beloved friend Gwynn was moving away. Gwynn's father's company had transferred him to California. Caroline and Gwynn spent the summer packing boxes and finding spare hours to play their favorite games.

As the departure date approached, Caroline faced the task of finding a new best friend—a first for the young girl. Caroline tended toward competitiveness, particularly in athletics, whether it was getting her president's badge in gym class, playing jump rope, or practicing gymnastics in the field behind the school. But after her illness, Caroline's body wasn't as strong as it had once been; thus, she wasn't as good at sports. Caroline's introverted nature made her more inclined toward having a single best friend rather than a group of friends.

The new school year brought another first—the opportunity to play an instrument. Caroline begged her mother to let her play the drums like Andrew did, but her mother said, "No." Caroline refused to back down, and mother and daughter had their first big fight. After a few days, her mother suggested the flute. Caroline said, "No." Caroline mentioned the clarinet for no reason other than that her mother didn't suggest it. The two reached an agreement.

The band was a graded class, so Caroline had to learn to play the clarinet and perform in the school concert. As Caroline opened the dented leather case, she was greeted by the sight of shiny black wood accompanied by silver keys. It was smooth as silk. Blowing through the reed was complicated and required quite a bit of spit. Ick! The excess rolled out the bottom of the clarinet and dripped onto the floor. She always tried to hide it.

The music teacher was a big, balding man with thin black hair. He was firm, and Caroline worked hard to learn to play the first assigned song. Due to her tiny hands, Caroline found it easier to play the clarinet than to play the piano. However, though she diligently practiced, her progress was not as swift as that of other kids playing the same instrument.

What was wrong? Music came easy to her. She loved singing in the children's choir at church, and she'd surprised her mother when she was offered a solo in the Christmas concert. But the verbal encouragement Caroline craved never came. Her mother's way of showing pride in Caroline was to sew her a pretty new dress.

They chose a particular Saturday, when the trees changed colors, to shop for fabric. Fall was wildly colorful in Arvada due to the many different trees there. They drove to the store and walked among the various colored materials, selecting based on texture and drape. To complement Caroline's skin tone and hair color, her mother suggested a navy velvet dress with a cream lace collar and golden buttons. She emphasized how the combination would beautifully enhance Caroline's appearance. Caroline loved the softness of the velvet, rubbing her fingers against it. She thought, *I'll look like an angel singing to the heavens*. She asked her mother for cream tights, and they decided her black shoes would finish the outfit. Caroline couldn't wait for concert day.

For the first time, Caroline experienced nerves. She wanted to sing perfectly, just as the birds in the forest did, and she practiced constantly, to the annoyance of everyone in the house. She still took piano lessons, which helped her read the different music. However, all this practice began to inflame Caroline's throat, which became sore. Her mother panicked. Her father yelled about Caroline costing him more money. He said having a sick girl trying to learn music was a waste. Caroline hid in the closet every time her father screamed. She began to daydream of a different life. She closed her eyes and let her mind wander. Suddenly, she was back in the forest. But it wasn't the same as it had been in the spring. There was snow everywhere, and it was quite cold.

Caroline shivered in her closet and pulled the blankets closer. She heard a crunching sound as if someone were walking in the snow. The scene expanded to include a large dark spot on a mountainside with a bright yellow glow. She was moving toward it.

Not far from the opening sat a woman she recognized. "Serena!" Caroline cried.

The nymph turned and saw Caroline's image at the cave entrance. *This one is strong enough to bring her spirit self so far from her body.* "Come in by the fire," Serena said.

Caroline felt her body move toward the fire, and she reached her arm out. *It's hot! How can that be?*

Serena watched the spirit move about the cave, looking at the books and drawings she had set out. "Is this where you live?" Caroline asked.

"Yes, this is my home," Serena replied. "Do you know why you are here?"

Caroline looked at Serena and slowly shook her head. "Sometimes, when the fighting overwhelms me, I climb deep into the back of my closet and pretend I'm someone else, somewhere else. Usually, I like to live in shows on TV. But I went farther away this time because my dad was so mad at me."

"Did you do something wrong?" Serena asked.

"I don't think so, but I have been practicing my music a lot, and I guess I strained my throat. I get sick rather easily, and it costs money to go to the doctor. My dad doesn't like to waste money. Paying for my music lessons and doctor's appointments made him angry."

Serena kept looking at the spirit who could transport herself to a cave to escape an angry father. The child did not know her gifts. Serena realized she must protect her. But she had never taught a human, let alone one so young.

"Caroline," Serena said firmly.

The spirit looked up.

"You must listen closely to what I tell you. You are a special little girl, and I will help you learn all about the gifts the Creator has bestowed upon you. I will teach you how to keep yourself safe. But it would be best if you kept these teachings a secret. You cannot tell anyone about how to learn from me."

The little spirit girl nodded. "That won't be a problem. I don't have any friends because Gwynn moved away. I enjoy singing and playing the piano and clarinet, though I'm not very good at it yet."

"Music is a wonderful gift," said Serena. "Continue to practice it as much as you can despite your father's anger." She saw that the spirit self was beginning to flicker. "It's time for you to return to your body," said Serena.

"I don't understand," Caroline replied.

"You will remember your body waiting for you where you left it. Rejoin it now!" Serena clapped her hands.

Suddenly, Caroline looked up and saw that she was in her closet. She heard her mother calling her for dinner. Slowly, Caroline got up, her legs stiff, her body cold. As she emerged into her bedroom, she looked at her image in the mirror. Although there was no apparent transformation, she sensed a shift within herself. Serena's words lingered in her mind as she recognized a subtle transformation in her perspective. She was excited to have a friend, even a secret one.

Her mother's call became harsher, and Caroline ran to the kitchen. Everyone was gathered around the table, waiting to eat. She slid into her chair and folded her hands for prayer. Silently, grateful to have found a special someone to confide in, she expressed her appreciation to God. And then she picked up her fork, as she suddenly felt hungry.

Caroline managed to play well. She received many compliments for her solo at church and enjoyed playing the clarinet in the school concert. Afterward, her mother took Caroline to the ice cream shop—a rare treat. Caroline asked to do this after every show. Her mother nodded with a smile. Caroline wished her father and brothers had come, but they stayed home. Their comment was that, after hearing her practice so much, they'd had enough. It hurt her that she always went with just her mother. But what good would it do to force her brothers to come? Edward would mock her.

Edward and Andrew were now in junior high school at West Woods. Andrew still played the drums in the band and was learning the electric guitar. He continued excelling in all his classes. Edward struggled some with schoolwork but loved sports. He now played on a league football team, learning the quarterback position, as his arm was so strong.

When summer arrived, the Howard family was consumed by baseball. Andrew was pitching, and Edward played catcher. They made quite a team. But for Caroline, the summer was lonely. She was bored with baseball, as there were rarely any girls to play with at the field, and it was hot and dirty. The family spent a few weeks up at the farm helping with the summer work. Caroline picked peaches, which she ate from the vine, but she hated having to can them all. She picked corn and strawberries from the big garden for dinner. And, at long last, Caroline found a cat that liked her! It was a gray kitten, a few months old, friendlier than the other barn cats. She loved sitting in Caroline's lap and being petted. The cat purred loudly, to Caroline's glee. She begged her mother to let her take the cat home. For once, her mother finally relented, and Caroline named her new pet Smokey.

Caroline continued practicing the clarinet. She was bothered, as she wasn't improving as quickly as the other kids in her class. Without telling her father, due to the cost, her mother signed up Caroline for a course at the high school. Her mother talked about how much she had loved playing the French horn in her high school band, and she wanted Caroline to have a similar experience. When Caroline learned she would be practicing at the high school, she grew nervous. One of the boys in the class was older than Andrew! The high school band teacher, who stressed the importance of playing scales expeditiously, instructed it. Every day at the start of class, they were required to perform a scale as swiftly and accurately as possible. Although Caroline was not the poorest performer, she was nowhere near the top of the class. Consequently, she devoted considerable time to practicing the scales and the ensemble's new composition, which they were scheduled to play on the last day of class. Caroline's mother expressed her admiration for her efforts and progress. Moreover, she approached the boys, urging them to stop teasing Caroline. Caroline still hadn't found a friend since Gwynn moved, which worried her mother. She preferred that Caroline not spend so much time alone.

On the last day of class, Caroline was scared but intent. She wanted to do well in the scale competition. When the teacher said, "Begin!", Caroline played her best. When she finished, she was in shock. She had tied for first with the high school boy! He looked at her and said, "Wow." He had never spoken to her before. Then, they played the music, and Caroline performed it at her finest. As she was packing up to leave, the teacher said she had done a respectable job in the class, and he hoped to see her in the high school band. Caroline couldn't wait to tell her mother. But she didn't know if she would play the clarinet in high school. Singing still mattered most.

August arrived, signifying the beginning of the yearly fishing trip. They went up to the mountain cabin, leaving Smokey at home with a big bowl of water and a pan of dry food.

# Summertime in the Mountains

SERENA LOVED PICKING THE flowers that bloomed in the mountains during the warm summer months. The blue columbines and red-orange Indian paintbrushes created a beautiful contrast against the green lodgepole pines and aspen trees.

She walked along, seeking to refill her stock of herbs, including rosemary, dill, and basil, to improve the taste of the fish and greens she regularly ate. More importantly, Serena wanted the fresh healing herbs. She found peppermint for stomach ailments and grindelia for a sore throat. She enjoyed brewing tea from the chamomile plant, which she sipped while sitting at the entrance of the cave in the chilly evenings.

Today, Serena was down on her favorite section of the Blue River, fishing for her dinner in the clear, chilly water. She had a spot unknown to humans, so she wasn't bothered by them. As was part of her practice, Serena prayed to the Creator to give her the life of a fish that would nourish her body. Even though she was deep in meditation, a sound came through to her conscious mind: "Serreena," sang a voice downriver. Serena quickly finished her prayer and began walking toward the musical sound.

Caroline was wearing red rubber boots and a big smile while dancing around a rock. The young girl watched Serena as the nymph moved with a floating effect.

Caroline walked cautiously toward her. She called out, "Do you remember me? I'm Caroline!"

Serena stopped moving, remaining perfectly still. In response, Caroline also stopped. Serena saw the girl was surrounded by a bluish hue as though she had gathered up the color of the river. The color indicated Caroline could speak in more ways than just words. Softly folding her mouth as if blowing the slightest breath, Serena said, "Hello." The word was carried on the wind and touched Caroline's forehead like a slight push. Caroline felt the expression in her body as a tingle rather than a sound in her ear. She had never felt a word in such a way, and she laughed, which garnered a slight smile on Serena's face.

Slowly, the two of them moved toward each other like animals, sensing a presence and determining whether it was a safe creature or a predatory one. When they were almost a foot apart, they instinctively stopped again and gazed. Serena was not wearing her cloak. Her dress was made from a woven fabric in different shades of the forest trees. Her hair carried most of the color. Even her eyes were a muted green. Caroline thought she was the most beautiful woman she had ever seen. "I was hoping you would come," said Caroline.

Again, Serena seemed to breathe the words: "And I thought you would come," she replied.

"Why is it that you talk differently?" Caroline asked.

"I speak the language of whatever animal I am communicating with," Serena replied.

"So, how do you speak to a bird? Do you tweet?" asked Caroline.

"No, I sing like you," she responded. "Your voice is musical in the way of the birds."

Caroline excitedly asked, "Can you teach me to sing to the birds?"

"Yes. But there are other, more important things I can teach you."

"Really? Can we start today?" asked Caroline.

Serena made a trilling sort of laugh. "You are an anxious one. I will need to understand your skills better before I decide how best to teach you."

"Will I come to you from the closet like before? Except there's no good closet at the fishing cabin."

"No, you won't have enough strength to learn from me in spirit form. We should gauge the strength of your human  body. Can you come to this spot again tomorrow? I need to fish for my dinner right now," said Serena as she began to move away.

"Do you eat fish? I hate to eat fish," babbled Caroline, trying to continue talking to the mystical creature.

"The Creator provides the fish for our nourishment," replied Serena.

"Who's the Creator?" asked Caroline.

"He created everything you see," explained Serena.

"Oh, like God," responded Caroline.

Serena sighed, "He who goes by a thousand names. When you come tomorrow, sing out my name like you did today, only a bit more quietly. I can hear for a long way. Then, I will come and meet you," said Serena. She turned and walked away in her ethereal manner. Caroline intuitively grasped that she should not pursue her. She headed back to the cabin and decided to wait for the next day.

Caroline wasn't sure how she would get away from her mother to meet up with Serena. Her mother still hovered over her, and Caroline couldn't imagine her mother letting her go off into the woods alone, but she must figure out how! While she was lying in bed that night, an idea suddenly came to her. Caroline's thoughts went to Serena's basket, and she knew what she wanted to do. She would ask her mother for permission to collect a variety of blossoms and craft gorgeous bouquets to adorn their cabin. She would promise to stay within a certain distance. That way, her mother could work on her quilting without worry.

In the morning, Caroline was unusually helpful around the house. Then, she pulled out an old basket, telling her mother she was off to pick flowers. Her mother wasn't sure she liked the idea. Caroline promised to stay on the trail, and her mother could call for her anytime to come back. She hoped Serena's hearing was as good as she claimed.

With her mother's reluctant approval, Caroline dashed out to the rock. She quickly reached the place where she was supposed to meet Serena. Unable to contain her excitement, she called out to her friend, perhaps a little louder than the nymph had advised. Trying to remain still like Serena, Caroline closed her eyes and listened to the movement around the forest. She heard a sound to her right and turned her head. There stood Serena! "Very good," Serena cooed with the voice that poked into Caroline's forehead. "You must learn to be quiet if you want to hear the magic in the forest."

"Magic!" Caroline responded excitedly. "Can you do magic?"

"Yes, I practice the white arts," said Serena.

"White art?" asked Caroline. "What does that mean?"

"The white arts are a form of casting spells that do not harm others. They are designed only to help, such as healing a sick or injured animal. I will not teach you any black arts, as there is already too much darkness in the world."

"I don't understand," said Caroline.

"You are too young to understand all that I say. Just listen, and don't ask so many questions! Follow me," Serena said.

Caroline didn't move, and Serena looked hard at the little girl. "I need to hear my mother call," Caroline said. "Otherwise, I can't get away to spend time with you."

Serena's look softened. "I understand. I will listen to your mother's voice and teach you how to hear from deep in the forest. Now, follow."

Serena walked for a way to a small clearing surrounded by aspen trees. It was a lovely spot.

"Sit down," she said. "First, you must understand the directions and what each one signifies. This knowledge will help you should you ever become confused or lost in the forest." Serena walked in a circle. "Follow my path with your eyes. I walk in the direction the Earth moves each day. The directions have significant meaning and power. We begin with the south. Look down the Blue River. It flows from north to south. There are three practices of the south. The first is non-attachment. Attachment causes suffering. Have you ever been attached to someone who left you?" Serena asked.

"Gwynn," Caroline replied.

"This caused you great pain due to your attachment," Serena said. "We choose our pain. To lose the pain, you must lose the attachment. This emotion will occur throughout your life. Next, you must learn to be non-judgmental.

Humans are programmed to judge people, which is wrong. Only the Creator can judge. If we try to judge, we become attached to the outcome. People try to control outcomes. But these are often pre-ordained by the contracts we have signed. Last, you must understand non-suffering. Pain is insignificant. Suffering is a choice. When we practice non-suffering, we come into the moment. Do you remember when you came to my cave? Your spirit form arrived here when you were in a state of distress. It had separated from your physical body and sought refuge by sitting beside my fire for healing. That was a sign of power given to you by the Creator. But it also showed that you have chosen a life full of pain. You must learn how to separate from the pain. Now, come and bring your basket."

Caroline stood, grabbed the handle of her basket, and followed Serena, who moved as quickly as she did quietly. They went to the river. Facing south, Serena moved her hands over the water. She called Caroline and told her to look into the water and see which stones spoke to her. Caroline knew she wasn't to ask questions, but how was she to know whether the rocks would "speak?" She slowly moved her hand over the water, imitating Serena. The water was chilly, as it came from the melting snow draining from higher elevations.

Serena explained, "The rocks come from the mountains made during ancient times. Look for smooth rocks. They have been in the river gaining energy for a longer time."

Caroline reached her hand into the frigid water.

"Feel for the heat. That means the rock is still living and breathing and gathering energy. Pick three stones."

Caroline leaned over the river, feeling for rocks. She decided to look at the stones and see if any were "breathing." She picked up a few larger pebbles, but they felt cold. Then, she sensed something warm to her touch and pulled it out. She looked the rock over closely and saw different colors in the stone. As she peered deep within, she caught a glimpse of an otherworldly hue—a mesmerizing shade of dark green that stirred something wild and unknown within her. Gazing back at the glistening riverbed, she reached down to retrieve a smooth, reddish stone that seemed to radiate a fiery heat. With a gasp of surprise, she barely managed to hold onto it. After she placed it in her basket, Caroline searched the river and noticed a black stone. She was sure it would feel icy from the river, but still, it drew her attention. As she brushed it with her fingers, she felt warmth. How strange. She picked up the rock and added it to her basket.

"Now we will search for sweet grass and sage. They should dry out before becoming part of your mesa." Serena directed Caroline to where sweet grass was sprouting. "Do you have a knife?" Caroline shook her head.

Reaching down and carefully guiding her hand, Serena showed Caroline how to pull the plant without damaging the roots. "We must always help the plants continue to grow. Our goal is not to destroy but to continue creation." Suddenly, Serena stopped her movements and looked up toward the north. "Your mother is calling. It is time for you to go home." As Serena showed Caroline the way back to her cabin, she told the girl to ask her mother for cornmeal. Now, Caroline could hear her mother. She began running toward the little house. She stopped to turn around and wave goodbye, but Serena was gone.

Caroline walked back into the house. Her mother relaxed, seeing the girl was unhurt. She told Caroline to remove her muddy boots and looked into the basket. "Grass and rocks. Not certain how pretty that will look in a vase." Caroline took the basket into her room and placed it by her stack of clothes. She came back out to explain she didn't find any flowers to pick, but she was trying to learn about the different plants that grew near the river.

"Caroline, I didn't permit you to go by the water. The current is swift, and you can't risk falling in!"

Caroline decided she shouldn't let her mother know where the rocks came from. "Hey, Mom, do we have any cornmeal?" asked Caroline.

Her mother looked at her with surprise. "Yes. I roll the fish in it before frying or baking it. Why do you ask?"

"Just wondering if it was something you had on hand. No big deal."

After dinner that night, Caroline picked up a handful and placed it in a plastic sandwich bag. She added it to her basket under her clothes. decided to hide the items to prevent her mother from asking questions.

Caroline waited at the rock with her basket in hand the next day. Serena silently glided through the trees. She stood, waiting to see if Caroline felt her presence. Caroline looked west and spotted Serena.

"Very good," Serena said. "Follow me."

They walked back to the grove of aspens. Once Caroline was seated on the grass, Serena began. "There are four elements on Earth: wind, fire, water, and air. Our lives revolve around the wheel, turning in four different directions. Its clockwise movement is dictated by the planet's rotation. Thus, we begin our training in the east, where the sun starts each day just as you begin the stages of human life, including birth and early childhood. That stage is a time of innocence and purity.

"You must understand that when we choose to start a new life, we sign a contract. This contract contains the purpose for this life and what you must learn before life ends. During our lives, we create karma, defined as the sum of a person's actions in this and previous states of existence, believed to determine one's destiny in future lives.

"Life is based on energy. You are components of energy that break off from the Creator. Because you are energy-based, the essentials of cause and effect take place. You have thoughts, say words, and take action throughout your life. You need to understand that for every action, there must be an equal and opposite reaction, which is the basic cosmic principle. You must live consciously on this principle. Do you understand?"

"I signed a contract before I was born?" stammered Caroline.

"Yes, you sign a contract for each life you live," explained Serena.

"I've lived more than one life?" Caroline burst out.

"You are too young to understand what I am saying fully, but I will try to make this easy for you. To help, I will take you on a journey to visit a life before this one. Lie down, close your eyes, and listen to my voice. Imagine yourself being carried deep into the earth, just like when you first came to my cave. Let go of your body and surrender to the journey.

"Look for a tree. Do you see it? Now, look at the tree's roots and see if you can find an opening. Did you find it? If so, nod your head."

Caroline slowly nodded.

"Now go to the hole and climb down the roots. Follow the roots to the very bottom. You should now be inside a cave. Walk toward the lighter part of the cave. Look for water like an underground pond. Again, nod if you see it."

Caroline nodded.

"Walk over to the pool and sit by the water. Wait quietly, and a friend will meet you."

Caroline tried not to be scared. She didn't know where she was, but she understood to trust Serena, and naturally, she was intrigued. As she sat by the pool, she heard heavy breathing. Then came a large thud. She looked over and saw a bear. His coat was brown with white tips. He looked at her with deep,

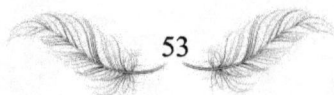

dark eyes. What kind of bear was he? She wasn't sure, but it didn't seem like the bear wanted to eat her. She drew her hand out and touched the bear's fur. He growled and stretched more comfortably. Then, she felt something warm in her lap, and when she looked down, she saw a black and white hare with a pink nose. Caroline giggled and touched its nose.

She heard Serena's voice: "Have you met your power animals? If you wish to proceed, kindly introduce yourself. Please note that whoever you encounter will remain with you throughout your journey. Once you have completed your task, retrace your steps through the cave, ascend through the roots, and exit the tree. When you are sitting across from me again, open your eyes."

Caroline was full of wonder. It was as if the forest had changed since she'd gone below the earth. The colors were brighter. The grass was softer. And she had touched a bear. She began to speak excitedly about the bear, the intricate texture of his fur, and the little hare's warm, soft body.

Serena gave her a small smile and motioned with her hands for Caroline to calm down. "Now that you have met your power animals, you will start to build a relationship with them. They will protect you throughout your life.

"Caroline!" The girl heard her mother calling. She didn't want to go back but she must. She looked at her empty basket. What would she tell her mother this time?

"The truth is always the best," said Serena. "Tell your mother you couldn't find any flowers today, but you will look again tomorrow. We can continue our work at the same time in the future. Remember to communicate with your power animals before you sleep so they can convey important messages to you during your slumber."

When Caroline returned to the cabin, her mother asked for her help making iced tea for dinner. While Caroline poured cold water over the tea bags, she asked her mother if she believed in past lives.

Her mother looked at her sharply. "No, we only live one life. We come into this world and try to live a life as Jesus did, and when we die, our soul goes to heaven or hell."

"Do we meet other souls in heaven?" asked Caroline.

"Well, yes," her mother stammered, clearly uncomfortable with the direction of the conversation. "We meet the souls of our family members who have died."

"Like Grandpa Howard?" asked Caroline.

"Now, Caroline, you know you are never to mention your grandfather, particularly to your dad," her mother said firmly.

"Do you know why Daddy doesn't like him?" asked Caroline. "Yes, but that is not something I will talk about with you," said her mother. "And don't ask your father!"

As she lay on her cot that night listening to her father snore, Caroline thought about her power animals. She asked them to visit her and explain more about different lives.

The following day, Caroline discovered the serene grove of aspen trees. She quietly awaited Serena's arrival while ruminating on the numerous questions she had to ask her. Suddenly, Serena was standing above her. "Are you ready to get to work?" asked Serena.

"Yes!" replied Caroline.

"We will continue with the east today," said Serena. "Now that you have met your power animals, I want to take you on a different journey. Lay down and close your eyes. Think about your power animals, then go down to the pool and sit beside them."

Caroline was surprised at how quickly she could reach the place she had left yesterday. Sitting curled up next to her animals, she heard Serena saying to go back to when she was in her mother's belly. Because of her father's stories about her birth, Caroline was able to think about the time she had lived in her mother. She heard Serena say, "Next, we will go to a time before this life and this birth. Breathe in and out slowly and relax your mind. Let yourself float backward until you see someone. Nod when you do."

Caroline felt herself transforming into a bird. She flew high, searching the ground until a small group of people came into view. As Caroline touched the ground, a transformation took place, and she reverted to the form of a young Native American girl. Glancing down at her slender, boyish frame and long, black tresses, she took in the realization of her appearance. With new-found confidence, she strode toward a group seated near a glowing campfire. They spoke to her in a language Caroline hadn't heard before, but she immediately understood the Algonquian words. Someone told her to grab a basket. Caroline walked inside a teepee and looked around. There were furs on the ground and paintings on the walls. It was beautiful and warm. She saw a basket, picked it up, and carried it to a white-haired woman.

"Thank you, Kanaka. It is good to see you again."

Caroline was surprised by the statement.

"Sit next to me, and let's work on braiding baskets for fishing," the woman said.

Caroline's hands began to perform work she didn't remember ever doing. Then, she heard yelling in the distance and jumped up with the rest of the tribe. Men riding horses bareback were crying, and suddenly, Caroline saw men in military uniforms. When they spotted Caroline, fear surged through her veins, and she found herself pursued by the relentless soldiers. Panic lingered in her eyes as she frantically searched for a place to conceal herself, unable to find a safe haven from their fiery onslaught.

Suddenly, she fell to the ground and was back with Serena. Caroline breathed heavily. "No, no!" she yelled.

Serena stroked her hand and told her to breathe slowly through her nose. As Caroline's nerves settled, Serena shared with her a startling revelation: In a past life, Caroline had lived as a plains Indian.

"My name was Kanaka," said Caroline. "I loved being with my grandmother just as I do in this life."

"Yes, that is common. We often ask for certain people to live with us in many lives. These people may be members of our soul family," explained Serena.

"Are they relatives like our grandparents in this life?" Caroline asked.

Serena responded, "This is often true. We love certain souls over many lives." Then, she told Caroline to get up and follow her. "Let's look for some flowers so your mother won't be suspicious."

"Serena, my mother says we only live one life and must be very good so that we can go to heaven rather than hell when we die. Is this true?" Caroline asked.

Serena sighed. "This is what the Christians believe, and they have a book that supports their beliefs. However, that is a religion that came about to destroy older religions that had different teachings and different gods. Sadly, these religions give certain men power and control. But that is not what the

Creator wants. He wants humans to learn all the good and positive qualities so souls can reach their highest state. Remember, when discussing the east, we speak of love and purity. This state is the highest goal for a soul.

"In the next turn of the wheel, we go south, which is the summer season. This direction is also the season of youth when you begin to question, 'Who am I? What is my purpose?' For this reason, you receive the gift of power animals. They are intended to help with this journey. In this direction, we must seek balance within ourselves as we listen to our spirit guides. Do you have the rocks you gathered?" asked Serena.

Caroline nodded.

"Place a rock in each direction. You must choose the rock and the direction. Now, sit in the middle of the wheel. Close your eyes and listen to Spirit. Bring your spirit animals next to you and hear the message from the universe."

Caroline sat quietly. She didn't know what she was supposed to hear. A voice?

Serena could tell she was struggling. "Don't try to force anything. Just relax. You may not hear anything. You may get a feeling. That's called 'intuition.' Just breathe slowly and evenly."

Caroline focused on her breathing. She called her spirit animals, and they came. Then, she asked for guidance from the universe. As she listened to her intuition, Caroline picked up a rock and placed it in each of the directions. One direction had no rock.

In her mind, a tall Native American man appeared. He seemed old due to the creases on his face, but he stood very straight. She asked if he was her guide. He replied, "Yes. I will walk with you throughout this life. I will be here to protect you and give you guidance."

"Have I met you before?" asked Caroline.

"Yes, you were a member of my tribe. We died on the same day," he said.

"I saw this when I went on a journey with Serena," cried Caroline.

"Yes, we were together then and have been together at other times. I have served this role for you many times physically and spiritually," he explained.

Caroline didn't know what else to say to this man. So, she simply said, "Thank you." She watched him take a seat by the east quadrant's reddish stone, which she had arranged.

The next person she saw was a woman dressed in clothes from the late 1800s: a long, dark skirt and a starched white blouse with Battenburg lace. Caroline said, "Hello. Who are you?"

"I am Anne. I have been with you for a long time, in many lives."

"Why are you dressed like that?" asked Caroline.

"Because I like this clothing and thought you would like it, too," she replied.

"I do!" cried Caroline.

Anne said no more and just sat by the black rock.

Caroline waited, but no one else showed up. Then Serena said, "We are done," and clapped her hands. Anne and the chief disappeared. Caroline opened her eyes.

Serena went on, "Let us see what we have learned." Caroline moved to the rock where the chief had sat. It was the reddish rock, and it was in the east quadrant. "The person is from your past. He will help you understand what happened in your earlier lives." Caroline headed toward the black stone at the south quadrant, where Anne had rested. "She came to help you understand the purpose of this life."

Caroline looked at the third dark green rock she had placed in the north quadrant. "No one came and sat there," she said.

"That's because this guide has yet to appear. Your council is not yet complete. Just as you will look for other rocks, you will look for other guides to help you. I believe that is enough for today. Pick up your rocks and go back home. Tonight, hold each rock and speak to it. Listen to what it tells you."

That night, after everyone had drifted off to sleep, Caroline tiptoed into the living room. She rummaged through her basket and picked out each rock, placing them in their respective directional quadrants. Anne came from the east, where she had placed the black stone. This direction meant the beginning. Caroline concentrated on the figure of the woman. She saw a flash for a moment, and it frightened her because it was the black-robed women from her dreams. What did this mean? She quickly put down the stone.

As she retrieved the reddish stone from the south, the noble visage of the chief sprang to mind. A feeling of fortitude surged forth within her as she held the stone, certain his presence would imbue her with strength. Serena said she would need this because she had picked a hard life. Why hadn't she picked an easy one? She would have to ask Serena about that.

There was no rock or guide for the west. That was what was to come, the future. She thought Serena had said it was yet unwritten. Last was the north, where she had placed the dark green stone, but no one had come to sit in her council. Who was this person from the past? Again, the flash of dark women.

Caroline beat Serena to their meeting spot the following day. She proceeded to form the circle, carefully positioning the rocks in each quadrant where she had left them the day before. Once the preparations were complete, Caroline took her place in the center of the circle and closed her eyes, directing all her attention to her breath. Shortly, she heard Serena speaking. "We now go to the west, the time of autumn and the setting sun.

At this point, we return to the cave, which is like returning to the womb. Go inside as if you were going back inside your mother as we did before."

Caroline followed the path. When she arrived at the pool, she saw her spirit animals waiting for her.

"This is when we prepare for what is to come," said Serena. "Your spirit animal is the bear. The totem of the west is the Dancing Bear. The cave is a powerful place. It is the place of becoming. Dance with the bear to celebrate what you will be."

Caroline jumped up and looked at her bear. He got up and began to dance, and she danced with him. The rabbit joined in the dance, and it was magical.

When the bear stopped dancing and laid back down, so did Caroline. She placed her head on his great body and fell asleep. While in a dream, she heard Serena's voice: "Awaken, and we shall make the final journey. We will go to the north, the place of winter. This quadrant represents the space for your grandparents and elders, both those who are physically present and those who have passed on to the spiritual realm. It is the place of the hummingbird and the ancient ones who have stepped outside of time but can slip through the curtain to help us remember the ancient ways. Do you remember seeing the curtain?"

"Yes, when I was sick and in the hospital," replied Caroline.

"You went to the north but only looked and did not cross," explained Serena. "You were not ready to shed what you were and transform into what you will be. You did not have a guide in your north quadrant, as this person is yet to come. Are you close to your grandparents?"

Caroline sat up and saw Serena, the woods, and the medicine wheel she had made. "I am very close to my Andersen grandparents," said Caroline. "Those are my mother's parents. I don't know my father's mother very well, and his father is dead. My father hates him."

"Then you have your quest," replied Serena firmly. "You are to build a relationship with your father's mother and ask her about your grandfather. In this direction lies a dark corner that requires your immediate attention and change in this lifetime.

"Caroline, it is time for you to depart. You have absorbed enough knowledge for someone of your youth. Until we meet again during the next full cycle of the planet. But know that you can always call on me. You learned how."

Caroline was afraid. She didn't know how to meet her Grandmother Howard, and she suddenly felt very lonely. She didn't want to leave Serena.

"You are strong, Caroline," said Serena. "You are gifted and can succeed at whatever challenge you meet. Now, go and start your quest!"

Caroline picked up her things and placed them in her basket. She started down the path she now knew so well. As she walked toward the cabin, it seemed as if the flowers had bloomed. She picked the prettiest ones to create an arrangement when she returned to the little house. Caroline turned to look at Serena one last time, but the nymph was gone.

# Kansas City

WHEN CAROLINE RETURNED HOME, she was excited about the idea of a quest. It made her think of Arthurian legends, so she went to the school library to check out a book that would help her understand this new idea. Of course, back during the time of King Arthur, his knights rode horses to reach their destinations. To reach her Grandmother Howard's home in Kansas City, Caroline had to come up with a plan that her parents would agree to. Caroline didn't even have her grandmother's address! But she was determined.

"Mom, do you think I could write Grandmother Howard about coming to visit? Do you think she might say no?" asked Caroline.

This topic made Patsy nervous. She didn't know how Bill would react to the idea of Caroline spending time alone with his mother and what she might say. Why was Caroline so obsessed with this idea? "Caroline, why don't you go to the farm for spring break? We could start a new quilt," her mother suggested.

"No!" Caroline responded emphatically. "I want to go to Kansas City and spend time with Grandmother Howard."

"Alright," said her mother. "I will write her a letter and see what she says."

Her mother put pen to paper the following week and started the letter. "Dear Mother Howard," she wrote, "It has been a while since we have seen you. We hope you are well.

Caroline is now in fifth grade and becoming curious about the Howard

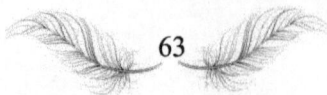

family. She would like to visit you during her spring break next year. Would that be possible?" Once her mother had finished the letter, she put it in the mail.

Patsy was surprised to receive a response within two weeks. "Dear Patsy, I have long wanted a closer relationship with Caroline. I would relish the opportunity to spend some quality time getting to know her better. Aunt Peggy has offered to help by picking Caroline up at the train or bus station and bringing her to my apartment. Once you have worked on the details for the trip, please post the information to me. With love, Kathryn Howard." So, she wanted to see Caroline. Patsy wished they didn't have to involve Bill's opinionated youngest sister, but Grandmother Howard didn't drive.

"Caroline, I've heard back from your grandmother. She is pleased to have you visit. But, as we discussed, you will need to raise money for your travel expenses," Patsy said.

Caroline leaped with glee. She'd done it! The first step in her quest was complete. She posted flyers looking to rake leaves that fall and picked up a few jobs. Caroline worked constantly, and one yard was far too big. Her mother sent Edward over to help. Neither of the children was happy about it. Still, their mother wouldn't run the risk of Caroline over-tiring herself and getting sick just before the start of the winter season.

While Caroline raked, she pondered the conversations she would have with her enigmatic grandmother. She yearned to learn more about Grandmother Howard from her father, but his displeasure at discussing the topic of his kin still lingered.

The following Sunday, when the football game was over and her father was in a good mood due to the Broncos' win, Caroline asked him about his mother. "Daddy, where did your mother grow up?"

Her father responded without thinking. "I remember the big white house in Washington, Iowa, where Mother and her two sisters lived. They had the best of everything. But Grandmother was a bit of a wild girl and always out with her latest beau."

"Did you like going to Iowa?" Caroline asked.

"Yes. Everything was nice there. Always plenty of food. And no work!" he replied. But as her father thought about the trips to Iowa, he began to see his father's face. It was not his favorite image. He'd hated returning to Kansas from Iowa and always wanted to stay. However, despite his yearning to remain, he had to help with the paper, while his mother persistently called him back home.

"I'm going to see her," Caroline told her father.

"What!" he yelled.

Caroline held her ground. "I want to get to know her. I am a Howard and I want to know about my grandmother and her life."

"No," yelled her father. "There is nothing about your grandmother you need to know. Patsy, what is going on here?"

"Bill, Caroline wants to visit her grandmother. I have written to your mother, and she is excited Caroline wants to come."

"You did this without my permission," Bill exploded. "I don't want that girl anywhere near my family."

"Bill, that is silly. Your mother is a lovely woman. It will be good for Caroline to learn how to behave like a lady. No one can teach her better than your mother."

"Daddy, it's important for me to see Grandmother Howard," Caroline explained. However, before she could express herself completely, she saw her father's hand reach back. In a sudden motion, she found herself on the floor. The side of her face was throbbing.

"Bill!" screamed Patsy. "What have you done?" Her mother helped her up, but Caroline's head was swimming. She couldn't get her balance.

Bill stood still. He couldn't believe what had just happened. *Damn that girl!* he thought. *Why did she have to push me so far? Everything always goes wrong when my family is involved.* "She's not going!" Bill cried and stormed from the room.

Caroline remained seated on her bed with a cold cloth pressed against her cheek. Despite her shocking encounter with her father, she was determined. Having been warned by Serena that her father's family was shrouded in darkness, Caroline was resolute in her quest to unravel the secrets that lay hidden within. She felt her responsibility was to bring light to this place of darkness. Nothing her father did would stop her. But how could she protect herself? The rocks! She went to her basket and looked inside. The reddish stone was associated with the chief. He was a protector. Perhaps she could call on him. Now, what had Serena said? Oh, yes. *Hold the rock in your hand and then blow your request into the stone three times.* "Chief, protect me from my father and help me reach my Grandmother Howard." Caroline blew in the wish. This process helped settle her, and a dream came after she went to bed.

She was standing on the rise in a large field. Far off, she saw tall buildings. As she looked, the chief walked up beside her. "This is the place on the plains called Kansas City. You will go there to seek the truth about your ancestors of the north. You must inquire about the ancestral gift of power that has been bestowed upon your lineage. The answers you seek lie within that realm, waiting for your discovery.

"Remember, too, that this is a place of safety. The people there will protect you from what you are afraid of. They will understand your fears." Then, the chief walked away.

For weeks afterward, Caroline clearly remembered what the chief had told her in the dream. But she grew curious. These people were to protect her. But what did she need protection from?

Winter came, and Caroline focused on the Christmas concerts at her church and school. She had earned another vocal solo in the church concert, which thrilled her. Also, she was sitting in the first chair in the row of clarinet players in her school band. The teacher had even come to her about playing in the district orchestra. Although Caroline was flattered, she couldn't help but notice that there weren't as many clarinet players, as all the emphasis was placed on string instruments. Was this a less critical role? Her mother was always excited about the band. What should she do?

A thought came to her: That would be an excellent way to start talking to her Grandmother Howard. She could send her a Christmas card and ask some of these questions. Grandmother Howard was supposedly a lady of refinement. She would know the difference between the band and orchestra for a clarinet player. Then, another thought came to her: Anne! She wasn't sure what role this person was to play in her life. Maybe it was time to find out.

# Training Day

BILL SAT IN HIS chair at the kitchen table with a beer in front of him. He had just returned from watching Edward's baseball practice. Though Edward was doing well, he was not getting enough attention from the coach. Edward would need the coach's endorsement to earn a tryout with a Major League scout.

The side of Bill's head started to hurt. He drank and found that, as usual, the cold liquid eased the pain. It wasn't just the pain he needed to stop. It was the memories that might seep through—memories of an angry, drunken father yelling at him for making a mistake when laying out type or wasting time with his younger sister Josephine instead of cleaning the print shop. How he hated that man! His stepbrothers didn't work as he had. He'd felt like a male Cinderella. *Just drink and don't think about him*, Bill said to himself.

As he continued forcing memories from his mind, Caroline walked in from her piano lesson. She hummed a tune he hadn't heard before and then added a whistling sound like a bird. She seemed to enjoy making up music. But he had noticed his little girl was growing up. He didn't like that. He'd overheard her talking on the phone with another girl about boys at school. At his home, there would be a strict no-boyfriend and no-touching policy. Bill was concerned that Patsy wasn't being strict enough with Caroline, so he felt the need to take matters into his own hands.

More of the relaxing liquid ran down his throat. He would ensure that Caroline understood precisely how he expected her to behave. That evening, during dinner, he brought up the topic of virginity. His daughter stared into her lap. Patsy began to say this wasn't an appropriate dinner conversation, but he held up his hand. "Caroline, you know what it means to be a virgin, don't you? As Jesus' mother was a virgin when she married, I expect the same from you," he said. "There is to be no dating, no boys touching you. You are to remain pure until you are married."

Caroline said nothing.

"Do you hear me, Caroline?" he asked.

"Yes, Father. I will do as you ask," Caroline said quietly.

"Now, can we change the subject?" begged Patsy. The boys had become used to their dad's strange conversations, and if the spotlight was off them, they ignored what was going on. Bill was satisfied but needed to be firmer and more diligent with Caroline. What if she was only placating him? That would not be sufficient!

The next day, Caroline came home right after school. Bill hadn't gone to watch practice. Patsy had started a new secretarial job at a real estate agency, so he had the house to himself. Caroline went straight into her room. Bill sat at the kitchen table with a beer. The phone rang. "I'll get it," she cried.

As the girl ran past him, something snapped inside, and he grabbed her. She struggled to get free. "Daddy, let go of me," Caroline cried. But the more she fought, the more he tightened his grip. He pulled the girl against his chest with one arm. With the other hand, he began rubbing his finger over her growing breasts. He whispered into her ear, "This is what boys will do to you. But you are not to let them. They are not to touch you!" Before he realized it, his hand had gone under her blouse and onto her bare skin. "And this is even worse!" he snarled. "You are never to let them touch you here." He moved his hand down between her legs.

Caroline stopped moving momentarily and then frantically tried to pull away. "Stop it, Daddy! Stop it." Her voice was barely above a whisper.

Suddenly, he realized what was happening and threw Caroline to the floor. "Go to your room!" he ordered.

She ran, and the last sound he heard was the door slamming. Quickly, he gulped down the rest of the beer and got up, stumbling to retrieve another can from the garage. Images of what had just happened ran through his head. *Oh, God, what have I done? Did I touch my girl? No, I just ensured she understood what boys aren't to do. She must know so she doesn't make mistakes and get talked into something like her mother did!*

More of the cold beer blotted out the new images in his head. *I'm just teaching Caroline as a father should. She's never to let a boy touch her. She's to remain pure!* Pain throbbed in his head. *Drink more!* Slowly, the images began to disappear, the pain stopped, and as he looked up, everything was softer. He waited. Patsy should be home soon to make dinner. He got up, stumbled to the family room, and turned on the TV. A baseball game was on. *That will kill time.* And then he dozed off.

# The Golden Shield

CAROLINE SAT DEEP INSIDE her closet, crying with great, heaving breaths. She was frantic, and thoughts ran through her head. *Should I run away from home? Where would I go? Should I go to the farm? I'll be safe there. But will Mother make me come back? I don't want to be here! I don't want to be touched like that ever again!*

How could her father do that to her? Did all fathers do that, or just hers? Was it because of the alcohol? If her father hadn't been drinking, would he have touched her that way? Thoughts swirled around Caroline's head. Her father rarely came into her room and never to her closet. She felt safe in there, but what if he came? What would she do? Who could protect her?

She kept her eyes closed and began to move her soul from inside the closet westward across the mountains. She did not know where to look for Serena's cave. She focused on finding the rock and telepathically called, "Serena! I need your help!"

Caroline searched desperately until she heard a voice calling, "Come this way." She floated along on the sound of Serena's voice until she saw the mouth of the cave and the fire inside it. She passed through the opening and sat close to Serena. "What is wrong, child?" Serena asked.

With a halting voice, Caroline told her what had just happened.

Serena understood that the child was so frightened that she had left her body to come here. But it was not good for the girl to keep separating.

She must learn that her strength was keeping her soul with her body.

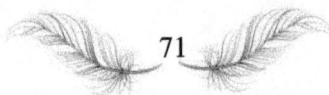

71

Also, she must learn how to protect herself. Serena resolved that it was time for Caroline to master the art of shielding.

"Caroline, I know you are scared, but I want you to return to your body. I will teach you a technique that you will do every morning before you leave your bedroom and see your father."

"Will this stop him from touching me?" she asked.

"No, you must get your mother or some other adult to explain to your father that his actions are wrong. Shielding will make you stronger, so any attacks won't hurt your mind and reach your soul. You must learn to stand in your power to withstand any assault in the human world."

Caroline remained afraid. She didn't know if she wanted to learn shielding if it wouldn't stop her father. She sat there silently.

Serena then asked, "How are you doing with your quest?"

Caroline's heart skipped a beat. "I have permission from Grandmother Howard to visit her over spring break," she cried.

"Very good," Serena said. "Remember that life is a journey with many twists and turns. Your purpose has not yet revealed itself. You must embrace both positives and negatives as you journey forward. If you feel uncertain about your choices, seek counsel from your guides and discuss your concerns. And when you are hurt, ask your spirit animals to wrap themselves around you in a loving embrace. Now, return to your body, but listen to my voice, and I will explain shielding."

Caroline slowly removed herself from beside the woman and returned to her closet. Once she had settled inside her body, she could feel the blankets she had wrapped around herself for protection. Then, she said, "I am here."

"Good. Now, think of a kite floating in the air. That kite is your soul.

I want you to pull the kite down into your body. Pull the kite strings down into the earth where your spirit animals lie. Have them wrap the strings around the bottom of the tree. Tell me when you have completed this."

Caroline struggled to find the path, climb down, and move toward the pool. Her animals were there as if they'd sensed her needs. She handed them the strings, and the bear tied them around the tree. Caroline went back up to wait in her closet.

"Now, I want you to sit barefoot with your feet on the ground so you can feel Mother Earth. Then, you will reach out your arms and create an egg shape surrounding your body. Can you do that?" asked Serena.

Caroline struggled to move her arms in the cramped closet, but eventually, she managed to follow Serena's instructions.

"Imagine there is a beautiful pitcher filled with golden, liquid light above your head, above your crown chakras," said Serena.

"What's a 'chakra'?" asked Caroline.

"Don't worry. I will teach you about those another time. Just trust me," commanded Serena. "Slowly and gently invite your crown chakra to open a little more. Open your crown chakra to receive this beautiful, high-vibrational energy. It is the highest and best energy you can hold now.

"This golden, liquid light pours into your crown, flowing down to your feet, filling your feet and toes, going up your ankles, up your legs, filling them with golden energy, moving, clearing, releasing anything that does not belong in your space, moving anyone and anything out that isn't in the highest and best resonance of you. And the golden, liquid light fills your torso, moving through every area of your body. It even goes to the tips of your fingers, filling and clearing your fingers, hands, and arms solidly up. It continues up into your neck and throat and, finally, into your head."

Caroline looked up and thought about how the gold light might feel as it splashed inside her egg. She thought it was warm and soothing.

"The golden liquid light moves and clears people out of your telepathic system and out of your sinuses, out of your eyes and ears. You're owning and claiming all of this space in your body. The golden liquid light fills up to the top of your head, spilling over and around your body. It goes almost a foot below your physical feet, filling your whole auric field and the beautiful, egg-shaped aura around you. And the light rises all around your body, three hundred and sixty degrees in every direction around you. As your aura fills, your feet and legs slip under this golden, liquid light."

"An aura . . ." Caroline began to ask.

"Shush," ordered Serena. "The liquid light rises over your torso, filling all around your body, around your physical body, around your neck and around your head, all the way until it reaches about a foot above the top of your head.

"Now, see yourself as a beautiful, golden egg. The golden, liquid light stops pouring. You are now solid, with this high-energy vibration, the highest energy you can hold. You are complete from the inside, moving to the edge of your aura. We have evacuated the entire area for your safety. And now, to enhance the security measures, we will add another layer of protection.

"Imagine this as a seven-layered rainbow. It's all the colors of your chakras, from red to orange, yellow, a layer of green, and then blue, indigo, to the final layer, a beautiful violet. The seven layers of the rainbow cover your entire auric field. They are the natural auric layers that have been with you since birth. So, now your beautiful golden egg is covered in this fantastic rainbow protection. Make sure you see the rainbow going out, filling out the back. It should be a foot around your whole body.

"You are solid golden light from your core to the edge of your aura, encased in the seven layers of your rainbow. The final step is to activate and empower your protection by saying these words: Nothing can enter my energy field and body without my permission, and nothing can leave my energy field and body without my permission."

Caroline repeated what Serena had said. Suddenly, the golden light hardened around the walls of her egg, just like a protective shield. "I get it! I feel it," Caroline cried out.

"Good. Now, do this every morning just as I've instructed," said Serena.

"Caroline!" The girl heard her mother pounding on the closet door. "Are you in there?"

Caroline sat there momentarily and realized she could no longer feel Serena. But she could feel her shield. "Yes, Mother, I am in her," said now-stronger girl.

"Please come out. Dinner is ready."

Caroline realized she had no choice but to exit the closet. Although she knew she couldn't face her father alone, she had her golden shield at hand, ready to help her in the battle ahead.

Caroline dutifully wrapped herself in the golden shield every morning, as instructed. However, to avoid her father, she had to distance herself from her school friends, which made her long for a best friend like Gwynn. Caroline was in sixth grade, and it had been several lonely years since Gwynn had left.

There was a pretty new girl in her class named Sarah. She was in the band and had been a cheerleader at her last school. Caroline was fascinated by cheerleaders. She saw them at her brother's games and loved watching them lead the spectators in rallying the team while flying through the air in splits and back handsprings.

One day, Caroline mustered up the courage to approach Sarah after class and inquire about cheerleading. Sarah's enthusiastic response filled Caroline's heart with joy. The two agreed to meet during lunch the next day. While eating, Caroline and Sarah had a chat. Then, they proceeded to the field to start their first cheerleading practice. It was still cold and snowy, and Sarah explained that they would have to wait until spring to work on the jumps, but they could start by learning cheers. Sarah taught Caroline how to hold her hands (thumbs in!) and the different beats with clapping hands and stomping feet. Caroline immediately responded to the musicality of the sport.

Sarah asked Caroline if she had any gymnastics experience. Caroline knew how to do summersaults and cartwheels. Sarah said she needed to work on side and center splits. Knowing how to do front and back walkovers and a back handspring was the best of all. Sarah then asked if Caroline would like to practice after school. "Do you have a room that's large enough?" Sarah asked.

The living room was the only place because it had carpeting, but Caroline's mother was very particular about that room. It was always ready for guests. Still, they could try.

Caroline and Sarah decided to meet at Caroline's house the next day after school. Caroline hoped her father would be at one of Edward's practices or games. It was basketball season, and her father didn't attend as often.

The next afternoon, Sarah walked home with Caroline. Although Sarah lived in the opposite direction, she had arranged for her mother to pick her up after her mother was done with work. Caroline felt comforted by the fact that Sarah's mother also worked; it made her feel less alone in her family's financial struggles.

When they arrived at Caroline's home, her heart sank when she saw her father sitting in his usual spot in the kitchen. *Remember your shield*, she told herself.

"Sarah, would you like a snack? My mother usually has cookies or a cake for us to eat after school," Caroline asked. "Or sometimes I eat cereal."

"Cereal?" Sarah laughed. "I eat that for breakfast. But cookies sound nice."

The girls headed toward the kitchen, but Caroline realized that could be a problem. "Why don't I grab us something, and we can eat in my bedroom?" she suggested.

"OK, that sounds fun. Where's your bedroom?" Sarah asked.

"This way," Caroline said.

Sarah seemed to like Caroline's room, though Caroline wondered if it looked like a little girl's room. Perhaps she could get Sarah's advice. Sarah sat on her bed while Caroline went to the kitchen. As she walked past her father, he asked, "Who's your friend with the big boobs?"

Caroline blanched. Oh god, she couldn't believe her father had said something like that. It was so inappropriate. "It's my new friend Sarah. We're going to have a snack and then practice gymnastics in the living room."

"I might like to watch that," her father said.

Appalled, Caroline looked him in the eyes. "I would prefer you to stay

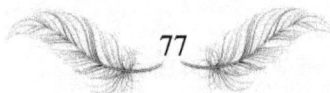

in the kitchen and leave us alone. Isn't there a game you could watch on TV?" she asked.

Her father picked up his can of beer and drank slowly, saying nothing in response.

Caroline put some cookies on a plate and poured a glass of milk. She decided the two of them could share the glass, as Caroline didn't want to return to the kitchen for a second one. As she walked past her father with her hands full, he reached over as if to squeeze her buttocks.

*Shield!* She tried to imagine the space outside her body, keeping her father's hand away. She watched as his hand seemed to encounter a shock and stopped.

Satisfied, Caroline went to her bedroom. After finishing their snack, the girls changed into comfortable shorts and T-shirts as Sarah had instructed, then made their way to the living room. Sarah began showing Caroline a series of stretches that would help loosen up her muscles enough to eventually master the splits. It was hard! Sarah explained that Caroline would need to do these exercises daily if she wanted to do the splits. Then, Sarah spotted Caroline and showed her how to bend back and raise.

Again, Sarah explained that Caroline would need to strengthen her stomach muscles for a backbend. Finally, Sarah demonstrated to Caroline the technique of jumps. The toe touch was the most important one, Sarah explained. Caroline watched in amazement as Sarah leaped into the air and raised her legs to touch her hands." Some people call this a Russian jump, but what matters is that your legs must be parallel, and you must point your toes," Sarah said.

Caroline tried and fell on her bottom with a big thud. "Ow," she said.

Sarah giggled when her father yelled, "What is going on in there?"

Caroline jumped up and went to the doorway. "We're practicing our cheerleading jumps. We need to be in the living room where there is soft carpeting to land on."

"Are you sure your mother will like this?" her father asked.

Caroline lied, saying, "I already have her permission." Then, she turned back to Sarah. "We should probably take it easy on the jumps."

"I understand. We can practice at my house, though we don't have a room this big," said Sarah. "But my mom is used to it. You need to practice regularly to get good at it, especially as a beginner." The girls practiced backbends and cartwheels until Sarah's mother honked the horn. When Sarah left, Caroline thanked her for the enjoyable afternoon. Sarah responded with a big smile. "Yeah, it was fun, and your mom's cookies were great!"

Caroline tidied up the living room until it was as flawless as her mother preferred, then proceeded to her room. "Caroline," her father sang out. "Come here."

She slowly walked toward the kitchen, remaining an arm's length from her father.

"It was very rude of you not to introduce me to your friend with the great figure."

"Ugh, Daddy, don't speak that way about my girlfriends," she said. "You sound gross. That's why I didn't introduce you. What if you said that to her face? How embarrassing." Caroline turned and stomped into her room. She didn't care about being proper if she had to worry about her father speaking this way to her friends. Was this how people acted in Grandmother Howard's house? How could her grandmother be proper when her father was so indecent? It was all so strange and confusing.

When her mother got home, Caroline rushed to the kitchen door and maintained a distance from her father. She then asked her mother to speak privately with her in her bedroom. Caroline's brothers were already complaining of hunger, and her mother seemed to be preparing dinner. However, Caroline's mother looked into her eyes and then accompanied her to the bedroom.

Her mother sat on the bed while Caroline faced her. "I had a new friend over today named Sarah. She's nice and pretty and a cheerleader! She was showing me different jumps and moves in the living room."

"Now, Caroline," her mother said. "You know I don't like the living room used that way."

"I know, Mom, but we had to have the carpeting. We were careful not to touch anything. And it was so much fun!"

Her mother knew how lonely Caroline had been, and she was glad to see the girl making a new friend. Could she relent on the rules?

Then Caroline said something that made her very uncomfortable. "Mom, Daddy spoke about Sarah's breasts. She's mature in that way, and hers have already come in." She looked down at her still-flat chest. "I don't want Daddy to say something like this to my friends. That would be so embarrassing. And you know it's not appropriate."

Caroline couldn't read what was going on inside her mother's head. But she saw the stern look on her face as she said. "It's alright to practice in the living room. But try to pick days when your father isn't around." Then, her mother headed back to the kitchen.

Later that night, after the children had completed their dinner and retired to their respective rooms, Patsy quietly made her way to the family room. There, she found Bill, who was comfortably settled in his chair, seemingly on the brink of drifting into slumber. "Bill, Caroline said you mentioned the size of her friend's breasts. Why would you say such a thing?" she asked.

"Hey, the girl has nice tits, better than anything Caroline will ever have. Or you."

"Bill, that's an awful thing to say. No wonder Caroline is upset," Patsy said. She got up and headed back to the kitchen. As she walked by Bill, he lowered his hand and flicked her bottom. She tensed up but kept walking, saying nothing.

Caroline tried to go to Sarah's house to practice cheerleading as often as she could and minimized how frequently they went to her house. She would even sneak out extra dessert to take to Sarah's, as her mom didn't bake regularly. Caroline remained apprehensive whenever she was alone in the house with her father. She kept to her room even when the phone rang. Her father never picked it up. He just sat in the kitchen chair and drank.

# The Quest

SPRING BREAK WAS NOW just a month away. Patsy decided Caroline would take the bus to Kansas City, as it would be safer. It was a long ride, but it was an express bus. Her father had retrieved a large, old suitcase from the basement, and Caroline had cleaned it inside and out. She constantly thought about what to pack and had Sarah over to consult. Caroline decided to take one nice dress for church (she wasn't sure where her grandmother went to church), while the rest would be comfortable pants and tops. Caroline kept asking her mother if there was something else she needed. Caroline usually packed her bags with the expectation of spending time at the farm or going on fishing trips. She wasn't quite sure about the daily attire her grandmother and aunt preferred. In light of this uncertainty, her mother decided to sew her a smart pair of pants and a matching blouse, believing it would suffice for any occasion.

The night before Caroline was to leave, her mother came in with some cash. She said that Caroline was to use it for emergencies and told Caroline to hide it in her shoe. Caroline thought this was strange. Her mother explained that someone might try to steal her purse, which she was to keep clutched to her side at all times. Caroline's mother also prepared a selection of sandwiches and packed bags filled with cookies, potato chips, and a juicy apple. "Try to spread it out," her mother said. Caroline could use her money to get a Coke when the bus stopped for breaks.

Caroline had three books in her bag. She was reading the *Little House on the Prairie* series by Laura Ingalls Wilder, and she loved the stories. Caroline identified with young, courageous Laura.

The bus left early. Caroline got a seat next to an older woman, as her mother instructed. The woman asked Caroline some questions about where she was going and why. Caroline was nervous, but the woman said not to worry. She made the trip often to see her daughter. Caroline opened her book and began to read. Before she knew it, she was asleep. The woman shook her when the bus stopped for the lunch break. Caroline looked around frantically, but everything seemed OK, and then she remembered: She hadn't shielded that morning because she was leaving her father and didn't think she would need it! That was dumb. But where could she do her work?

The older woman gestured for Caroline to accompany her, and they entered the restaurant. Caroline needed to retrieve her money discreetly, without anyone noticing. She slipped into the restroom and carefully peeled off a dollar bill. It felt slightly damp and had an unpleasant, musty odor. Why did her mother have her do this? She finished peeing, washed her hands, and returned to the restaurant. The older woman had saved her a seat. Caroline ordered a Coke and ate her sandwich and some chips. The cold soda tasted good, though it sometimes made her belch. When she finished paying, the woman looked at her and said, "It's always nice if you leave a tip for the waitresses."

"Oh," said Caroline. "I didn't know. How much?" The Coke was ten cents. The lady suggested she leave another dime, mainly as Caroline hadn't ordered food.

When they returned to the coach, Caroline asked the woman if she should have eaten her sandwich on the bus. "It would have been more polite than eating something you didn't buy in the restaurant," she said. There was a lot to learn about traveling on the road!

Then, Caroline remembered about shielding. She thought she could do it in the bathroom. She was just about done when someone started pounding on the door. Caroline quickly finished her prayers and came out. A man was standing outside. "You was in there a long time," he said, glaring. Caroline didn't respond.

When she returned to her seat, the older woman asked if she was feeling alright. "Is your tummy upset?" she inquired.

"No," Caroline responded. "Sometimes it just takes a while."

"I understand," said the woman, who then patted Caroline's hand. Caroline picked up her book and started to read.

It was dark by the time the bus pulled into the station. It had taken over twelve hours to make the trip. Caroline was yawning as she stood waiting for her bag. The older woman tapped her arm. "Make certain you wait inside for your aunt," she said.

Caroline nodded, too tired to speak. When she had her bag, she walked inside and looked around. She tried remembering Aunt Peggy. She recalled a beautiful woman with long silvery-grey hair and a darker complexion than Caroline's pale skin.

Standing in the middle of the terminal, Caroline saw a woman with striking hair, full of confidence. "Caroline?" the woman asked as she walked up to the girl.

Caroline nodded vigorously.

Aunt Peggy reached out her hand. "Hello, and welcome to Kansas City," she said, still holding out her hand. Caroline realized she was to shake it.

Her aunt stood there momentarily, then turned and asked, "Is that your bag? It looks a bit big for a week. Let's go. Your grandmother is waiting in the car, and it's getting toward her bedtime." Caroline's aunt, being considerably taller, walked with long strides while Caroline hurried to keep up.

When they reached her aunt's car, Caroline stared. It was so sharp-looking. The auto was red on the outside, with a soft white top and a white interior. They put Caroline's suitcase in the trunk, and then Aunt Peggy told Caroline to get in the back behind her. Sitting in the front seat was Caroline's grandmother. She had practically no lines on her face, just one age spot.

Her hair was white and fluffy, and it looked as if it was soft. Her voice was high and soft, without a trace of an accent. "Hello, Caroline," she said. "Welcome to Kansas City."

Though tired, Caroline remembered what her mother had told her to say. "Hello, Grandmother Howard. Thank you so much for allowing me to visit you. I'm so looking forward to spending time with you." She heard her Aunt Peggy make a sound like a snort. "Oh, and I can't wait to see your beautiful home, Aunt Peggy," Caroline finished lamely.

"Time to get home and settled in for bed," said Aunt Peggy as she lit a cigarette and put the car into gear.

They drove to Johnson County, on the Kansas side of the border. Caroline's grandmother resided in a beautifully furnished apartment adorned in various shades of pink. It had a spacious dining room with a mural on the wall—something Caroline had never encountered before. The bedroom had two double beds. It was perfect and so elegant. "Do you need to unpack?" her grandmother asked.

Caroline opened her suitcase, and Aunt Peggy walked over to look inside. "I see Patsy is still making all your clothes," said Aunt Peggy. Caroline didn't feel this was a compliment.

"Yes, Mother and I love to go to the fabric store and design outfits," she replied.

"What did you bring that's nice?" Aunt Peggy asked.

Caroline pulled out the dress and the new pants and blouse her mother had made. "Those are very nice," said her grandmother. "Let's hang them up to get the wrinkles out." Caroline watched as her grandmother slid open the door to her closet and pulled out some hangers for Caroline to use. The closet was full of beautiful clothing.

"Do you like to shop?" asked Aunt Peggy.

"Shop? Usually, I only shop for presents. I want to get my new friend Sarah something," said Caroline.

"We'll go down to Harzfeld's one day to shop and have lunch," said Aunt Peggy. She turned to her mother. "Mama, have you taken all your medication? Get that done so I can be on my way."

While the in the kitchen, Caroline changed into her pajamas (made by her mother) and got her toothbrush, then went into the bathroom. The room smelled so good. There was something puffy with a beautiful smell and lots of bottles and jars. It was nothing like her parents' bathroom. Caroline brushed her teeth and went to slide under the sheets. They were so perfect! Not a wrinkle anywhere. Her grandmother spent a brief period in the bathroom, and upon emerging, she was toothless. Ah, she wore dentures like Caroline's other grandmother. "We have lots of time to talk and get to know each other, so let's just try to get a good night's sleep," her grandmother said.

Caroline nodded as she turned and looked at the window covered with beautiful thick curtains. She suddenly realized they were gold. *I'm in an entirely gold room!* Caroline smiled and knew she was safe. She drifted off to sleep.

When Caroline awoke the next morning, her grandmother was already up and about. Still groggy and yawning, Caroline shuffled into the kitchen. Her grandmother was seated there, dressed in a pink quilted robe and sipping coffee from a delicate china cup. Grandmother Howard looked at Caroline and smiled. "I thought you might be tired today from your long trip," she said. "We shall have an easy day here. Is that OK with you?"

"Sounds great," Caroline responded enthusiastically.

"Would you like some coffee?" she asked.

"I don't drink coffee," Caroline replied.

"I understand, but would you like to try some? It's always nice to have your morning coffee with someone else."

Caroline realized this was the beginning of learning how different Grandmother Howard was from her mother and Grandma Andersen. She wasn't offered coffee at the farm. "OK, I'll try it," she said. Her grandmother got her a matching cup and saucer from the cabinet and asked her how she liked her coffee. "I don't know," Caroline said, feeling unsophisticated.

"It can be bitter at first, so let's add cream and sugar to make it tasty." Her grandmother carefully prepared Caroline's cup and set the coffee before her. Caroline reached down to pick up the cup, knowing only one finger would fit in the handle. "Placing your other hand on the cup is fine to help balance. You want to minimize using your hands, as it warms up the liquid faster." Caroline slid her middle finger through the handle, carefully raised the cup to her lips, and took a sip. It tasted nice! She unknowingly raised her pinky finger.

"Always keep your pinky down, and if you do not take another sip quickly, place the cup back on the saucer."

Caroline was lifting and sipping, feeling like a sophisticated lady.

"What would you like for breakfast?" Grandmother asked.

Caroline thought for a moment and realized it was Sunday. Church! She should be getting ready for church! "Grandmother, we usually have donuts or some coffee cake before leaving for church. What time is it? What time do I need to be ready?"

"Calm down, Caroline," said her grandmother. "We aren't attending church today. I don't go too often anymore. I have learned everything I need to know from a church. Sundays should be for relaxing. Do you like to read the paper?"

Caroline wasn't quite sure how to answer. No church! She was still trying to grasp this when her grandmother slid the front page of the Kansas City Star over to her. She pointed to the masthead. "You know, your grandfather retired from the *Star*, but when he was still working there, editorial would often have him write funny sayings for the top of the paper. Peggy might still have some copies you can see."

Spec! This was the first information about her notorious grandfather. Could she now start asking questions? "My father doesn't speak about Grandfather often, and when he does, it isn't nice. I feel I don't know anything about him."

Her grandmother let out a long sigh. "I loved your grandfather very much, but he was not the easiest man to live with. He was rather old when we married, a long-time bachelor. He hadn't planned to have a big family with lots of responsibilities. He enjoyed freedom."

"Kind of like a bird," Caroline said.

"Very much like a bird." Her grandmother smiled. "He had a pet parrot always sitting on his shoulder or head. His name was Ike."

"I love birds," cried Caroline. "I try to practice their songs."

Watch out that window." Her grandmother pointed. "There's a cardinal that usually comes to visit every day. They have a lovely song." Then, she changed the subject. "Do you like pancakes?"

"Yes, very much," Caroline responded.

"I'll get started on those for our breakfast." As her grandmother cooked in the kitchen, Caroline looked over the paper her father and grandfather had worked on. When her grandmother set a plate full of pancakes in front of her, Caroline started to ask questions. "Remember not to talk with your mouth full," her grandmother instructed. "And put a napkin in your lap."

Caroline chose to remain silent, savoring her pancakes while discreetly observing her grandmother's elegant dining manners. Her grandmother displayed a remarkable level of delicacy and refinement in her eating, prompting Caroline to emulate her by taking smaller bites and chewing with a gentler, more effortless grace. When she finished, Caroline put her elbows on the table, to which her grandmother responded, "No elbows on the table, Caroline. And if you are finished, place your knife and fork diagonally across the plate. That indicates you're done. Now, pick up the plates and carry them into the kitchen."

Caroline hesitated, uncertain whether to tackle one at a time or make an attempt to pick up both.

"Do what feels most comfortable. What is important is that all the pieces arrive safely to the sink."

Once Caroline had moved all the breakfast dishes into the kitchen, her grandmother came in. She placed certain pieces in the dishwasher and filled the sink with warm, soapy water to wash the china.

"These pieces are rather old and delicate. They were my mother's," her grandmother said.

"Did you enjoy growing up in Iowa?" Caroline asked.

"Washington is a nice town, but we lived on a large farm, which could get lonely. I have two younger sisters, and they could be bothersome. I was glad when I got married and left Washington." Caroline was a bit confused. Her grandmother had indicated that she was young when she left home, but the timing wasn't working out in her head. "There are certain things I am happy to share, but I know that your father doesn't want me to convey all of my history to you, so I hope you understand that some topics are off-limits," her grandmother continued. Could this have to do with the darkness she was to uncover?

Out of nowhere, Caroline's attention was captured by a sudden flash of crimson. Perched gracefully on a branch was a stunning red bird. He started his song, and Grandmother Howard exclaimed, "There he is! Isn't he a beauty? Only the males have the beautiful red color. Typical." She laughed. "They can be such show-offs like your dad and grandfather." There was some new information. But for the moment, Caroline was obsessed with the cardinal. She was trying to absorb his song so she could repeat it. His voice was a bit lower and more robust than that of some birds. She tried to imitate it. "That's very good," her grandmother said. "That will get our beauty to come back regularly. Keep practicing. Do you like to sing?"

"Oh, yes," Caroline said.

"Let's go into the living room and sit and chat," her grandmother said. Grandmother occupied a mauve Queen Anne chair adorned with a subtle floral pattern. Caroline sat on the sizeable mauve sofa. "Tell me about your singing," her grandmother said. Caroline told her about the different concerts and her solos. She also told her grandmother about playing the clarinet and how she had moved up the row to first chair. Her grandmother listened intently.

"Can you sing one of your solos without an accompanist?" she asked.

"Oh, yes," Caroline replied. "Would you like me to do that now?" she asked.

Her grandmother nodded.

Caroline stood in the middle of the room and sang beautifully for her grandmother, who beamed at her. When she finished, her grandmother clapped her hands. "I can't wait for Peggy to hear you sing! Perhaps she can accompany you on the piano. Peggy plays beautifully."

Caroline's head hung a bit lower.

"What's wrong?" her grandmother asked.

"I don't play the piano very well," she said.

"Well. That's alright. God doesn't give us all the talents. Just the ones he wants you to have."

"What are your special talents, Grandmother?" Caroline asked.

"Oh, my talents aren't necessarily ones you can show on a stage like yours. I was a pretty girl. Not a talent. That can be a problem, as it was for me." She looked off into space as if seeing a place in the past. Caroline waited. Eventually, her grandmother came back, and the two talked about dinner. Peggy and Josephine, another aunt, would be picking them up to go to their favorite Italian restaurant. Her grandmother suggested they go pick out what to wear. Caroline thought that would be lots of fun. They spent the afternoon looking through her grandmother's wardrobe of beautiful clothing. Her grandmother showed her how to put together different pieces. Caroline followed her grandmother's instructions, hanging the clothes neatly by item and color. It was a novel closet organization method she couldn't wait to replicate at home. After selecting her grandmother's outfit, they moved to her jewelry case, where her grandmother introduced her collection. While most pieces were costume jewelry, she shared the precious ones, including her cherished emerald pin from her grandfather. Caroline studied it intently as if trying to find traces of her grandfather's story within its design.

Caroline wore her pretty church dress, and her grandmother took her hairbrush, gliding it through Caroline's hair. "Your hair is so lovely, Caroline. It comes from your grandfather's side. My hair was never this pretty. Peggy and Josephine will be very jealous of it." And her grandmother laughed. There was a knock on the door. "Time to go," said her grandmother.

Aunt Josephine was at the door. She had a big smile and a hug for Caroline. "We are so glad you are here," she said, making Caroline feel good. They got to her aunt's beautiful car. Caroline and Josephine climbed in the back, and off they went.

The restaurant, called Tangolini's, was an old family favorite. The maître d' greeted them by name and led them to their customary table. He then presented Caroline with a comprehensive menu. There were so many items on it. Caroline's family didn't eat out much, so this dining experience was overwhelming. Aunt Peggy asked about her favorites. "We don't eat much Italian food, I don't think," Caroline said. "Mom makes a weekly dish called 'goulash' that my dad likes,"

"Oh, she got that recipe from Tim's wife," said Aunt Peggy. "She's an excellent cook, but there's lots of Hungarian dishes."

"Why is that?" Caroline asked.

"It's where she's from," said Aunt Peggy. "If you aren't familiar with Italian food, you might want to order the spaghetti. The sauce here is delicious and will be a good way for you to start."

Caroline nodded, happy to have the decision made.

When the waiter came and asked for drinks, the women gave their order. When it was Caroline's turn, she wasn't sure what to say. She always had milk, but that didn't seem right. Aunt Peggy asked, "Would you like a Shirley Temple?" Caroline certainly knew who Shirley Temple was, but she didn't know there was a drink named after her. "Just bring her one," said Aunt Josephine to the waiter. "We're celebrating having our niece with us." Caroline smiled at her. It was clear to her why Josephine was her father's favorite sister.

Caroline's drink came, and she gave it a sip. It was sweeter than expected but very good. The women waited in anticipation for her verdict. "It's terrific," she said. "Thank you for ordering it for me." The women nodded. This response seemed like the correct answer.

Her grandmother said," Oh, girls, Caroline sang for me today. Wait until you hear her voice! It's beautiful. Prettier than a bird. I even listened to her trying to imitate my cardinal. When we go to your house, Peggy, you'll have to practice a duet with her."

Caroline wasn't sure if Aunt Peggy was pleased about this, but Aunt Josephine said, "Oh, I'm so sorry I'll miss that." Caroline wasn't sure when she would be seeing this favorite aunt again. She didn't want to ask many questions, as they all seemed to have finalized the itinerary for her stay in advance. She felt it was best to go along but stay open to any opportunity to learn about "the darkness."

The spaghetti came, and it was delicious, very different from the goulash her mother made. Caroline watched how her aunts ate their pasta dishes. She paid particular attention to her grandmother, who rolled up the long noodles with a spoon. Caroline had never seen that before and wasn't sure whether to try it. She might make a mess, and that wouldn't be good. These relatives were exact with their eating.

"It's OK to cut your noodles with a fork," aunt Peggy said, noticing Caroline's hesitation. "Just don't slurp them." Her mother and sister laughed. Caroline felt her shoulders beginning to loosen, not realizing how tense she had been. There was a lot of teaching, but it was nice, and they were trying to help her be comfortable in these new settings. After dinner, when the aunts dropped them off, Peggy said, "Don't forget, we're going to the Plaza on Tuesday." And off she drove.

As they got into bed, Caroline realized she had forgotten to shield that day. Was it because she felt safe here in her grandmother's golden room? She asked, "Grandmother, why did you pick gold for your bedroom?"

"It's not the highest color in the rainbow. That belongs to violet, but I don't like that color in my bedroom. Gold is a color that comes from the higher levels and is a good color to wrap yourself in for protection."

Caroline stared at her for a moment. She sounded like Serena!

"My mother's line is Celtic, and we have the special skills of a wise woman," her grandmother continued. "Have you been exposed to people who think this way, Caroline?"

"Yes, Grandmother."

"Good. Perhaps we can talk about that more tomorrow. Now it is time for sleep."

Caroline couldn't believe it. She would learn more about the great mysteries from her grandmother. Serena had been right in sending her here on a quest. It took her a while to fall asleep, as she was so excited about the next day.

It was bright and a bit cold the following morning. Grandmother was drinking her coffee when Caroline walked into the kitchen. "Want a cup?" Grandmother asked. Caroline nodded, and her grandmother fixed it just how she liked it. As Caroline sat at the table to enjoy the warm beverage, her grandmother said, "I thought I might show you some photos of my family and tell you a bit about us. Would you like that?"

"Very much," said Caroline.

"Let's have some breakfast and get started. Today, I'll make one of your grandfather's favorite breakfasts. He always made this for the kids when I was in the hospital." She fried an egg and placed it on top of a piece of toast. Next, she delicately folded the egg, carefully slicing it without piercing the bread. Finally, she spread the egg over the toast and cut it into even squares.

Caroline said it was delicious. Then, she put on some comfortable clothes and read a book in the living room while her grandmother dressed. Grandmother emerged from the bedroom, approached a secretary, and opened its lower doors, revealing photo albums and boxes filled with pictures. She chose the oldest among them and settled down beside Caroline on the sofa.

"I told you that I grew up in Washington, Iowa," she said, showing Caroline a large two-story white clapboard farmhouse, much bigger than the Anderson farm. "We lived in Iowa since before the Civil War. But we have been in America for a long time. My mother's line is the Pritchard's, and we are Welsh. Did you know that?"

Caroline shook her head.

"I didn't think so. It's an ancient name. In Wales, they use a system like John ap Richard, signifying John, the son of Richard, to trace the male lineage. We became Pritchard when we moved to America. Do you know much about Wales, Caroline?"

Again, Caroline shook her head.

"It is an ancient part of Britain and is where the legend of King Arthur was born."

"Yes," cried Caroline. "He sent his knights out on quests!"

"Correct," said her grandmother. "They fought many great battles to keep the Saxons from taking over the land. Eventually, they had to retreat to their corner of Britain, but they took with them all the land's mysteries. Welsh women are Celtic and typically born with spiritual gifts such as the ability to see the future. You know, you were born in the caul, a significant sign. It means you can speak with those beyond the veil and typically generate great wealth. Are you familiar with tarot cards?"

Once again, Caroline shook her head.

"I'm not surprised. Your mother would probably think they are evil, but they are a widespread form of fortune-telling. I used to relish reading the cards when I was younger. However, the challenge with clairvoyance is that you cannot dictate what you perceive. It reveals both joyous glimpses, like meeting the love of your life, and distressing images, like witnessing someone harm their own children." Her grandmother seemed to gaze off into the distance. Then, she got up, returned to the secretary, and pulled out something wrapped in a beautiful silk cloth. "These are my tarot cards," she said. "I will explain them to you, and we will see what you can do with them. However, I strongly encourage you not to tell your mother, and particularly your father, about this. I will keep the cards here, and you can work with them when you visit."

Her grandmother spent the rest of the day explaining the major and minor arcana and the different symbols on each card. She also pulled out a regular deck of cards to show Caroline how playing cards had evolved from tarot cards and how to use them in a pinch. It was fascinating but tiring, as there was so much to know. It was almost 5:00 when there was a knock on the door.

"Oh, that will be Peggy with our dinner. Take all of this into the bedroom. It's best if she doesn't see us with it," her grandmother said.

Peggy brought in hamburgers, onion rings, and milkshakes from Winstead's. Everything was delicious. Aunt Peggy asked what they had been doing all day. Caroline looked at her grandmother.

"I showed Caroline my photo albums and talked about family history," her grandmother said.

"Did she tell you about the old Celtic lore?" asked Peggy.

"I learned a bit about it. I found it very interesting," Caroline replied.

Peggy continued. "Mother knows I don't go along with all that witchcraft. The church is against it."

"What church is that?" Caroline asked.

"The Catholic Church, of course," she replied.

"Oh, said Caroline, turning to her grandmother. "I didn't realize you were Catholic."

"I'm not," she said, "but I sent the younger girls to Catholic schools when we lived in downtown Kansas City. I felt it was safer for them."

"So, you don't all go to the same church," Caroline said.

"No," they replied together.

Caroline refrained from further questions, enjoying her excellent dinner in silence. She remembered to thank Aunt Peggy for bringing it. Her aunt expected acknowledgment for anything, big or small.

As she was leaving, Aunt Peggy reminded them tomorrow was shopping day. "I'll pick you up around ten-thirty.

Look sharp," she said, directing the comment to Caroline.

After she left, Grandmother Howard told Caroline to retrieve the tarot cards. "Now that we have more energy, I can show you some simple spreads. Whenever you work with someone for the first time, you typically lay out the tree of life, which involves ten cards. But that is too advanced for you. I'll show you a typical three-card spread for quick answers. Think of a question you have."

Immediately, questions about the family's darkness, particularly surrounding her father and grandfather, leaped into her mind. Despite her arthritic hands, her grandmother managed to shuffle the cards. She expertly squared them up and placed the deck in front of Caroline.

"Cut the deck and pick out three cards."

Caroline did as directed.

"Keep the cards face down. Now, turn over the first card on the left." It was the Knight of Swords. Her grandmother stared at it for a few moments, then said, "Knights are typically sons. The swords are fighters, and this particular knight is the most aggressive. Turn over the next card." This card was the Tower, which Caroline knew was not a good sign. "My, the cards are a bit dark tonight," her grandmother said, trying to bring some fun to the exercise.

"Something big is coming your way. It could be a catastrophe or cleansing action, which is a positive. Most cards have a negative message and a positive one. Generally, it's the other cards that are with it that make the difference. Turn over the last one." It was the High Priestess. Her grandmother drew in her breath. "Caroline, has someone significant entered your life? Someone with great knowledge of things spiritual?"

Caroline looked at her grandmother, thought momentarily, and then told her about Serena and the quest. It was late when she finished. Her grandmother hadn't said much.

As they got into bed, her grandmother said, "What you have told me is significant and powerful. You must perform an important task. But I am afraid it will be a hard one. I am an old woman now, but I will do anything to help you with this."

"Grandmother, will you explain the darkness?"

"Honestly, I don't want to. You are still so young, and there are things I would like to leave in the past. Let me think about this. Let's enjoy our shopping day tomorrow."

The next morning, Grandmother woke them early. They had a simple breakfast of toast, and Caroline skipped her usual coffee. She felt anxious, wanting to make a good impression on Aunt Peggy. Caroline donned her best outfit and meticulously styled her hair. Grandmother looked elegant in pink attire with small gold earrings and a pleasant fragrance. In the bathroom, Grandmother applied soft pink lipstick to Caroline's lips and suggested she ask Peggy for makeup tips. "She's very good at it. But you are so young and pretty, and you don't need much of anything." Caroline gave her grandmother a big hug. This woman had become so dear to her in such a short time. Then, there was a knock on the door.

Caroline had never been to the Plaza in Kansas City. Aunt Peggy told her it was built in 1923 in a Baroque Revival and Moorish Revival style, echoing the architecture of Seville, Spain. She said the area was also notable for all the beautiful fountains. She drove Caroline on a short tour before they parked at Harzfeld's, Aunt Peggy's favorite store. First, they went to the cosmetic counter, where Peggy had her particular salesperson. Her grandmother took Caroline over to the perfumes so that she could smell them. When Caroline found one she liked, Grandmother explained that it had gardenias in the top notes and sprayed a bit on her. Caroline loved it.

"Did you enjoy working in the department stores, Grandmother?" Caroline asked.

"I would have preferred not to work, but that wasn't an option. I love beautiful things, and working in china is the best department. Some girls and their mothers were snooty, but for the most part, it was pleasant."

Aunt Peggy called to them and said she was ready to move on. They went up the next floor to women's clothing. Caroline loved touching the different fabrics.

The colors were rich, and the silk and cashmere felt lovely against her skin. Caroline noticed her aunt admiring a stunning grey coat that perfectly matched her hair. When she saw the price tag—a whopping $700.00—she was utterly taken aback. Her mother could never spend money like that. It made Caroline feel sad for her.

The last department they went into was lingerie. Aunt Peggy walked over to a pretty white nightgown with lovely blue lace. "Do you like this?" she asked Caroline.

"It's beautiful," she replied.

"It's not silk, but it's more practical that way. Would you like it?" she asked.

Caroline was shocked.

"Close your mouth, Caroline," Aunt Peggy said. "A simple yes or no will suffice."

"Yes, I would like it very much," said Caroline. "But you don't need to buy me anything."

"No, I don't need to. I want to."

"Thank you very much," said Caroline.

Aunt Peggy handed the nightgown to the saleswoman and asked her to wrap it up. Then, she gave the beautiful bag to Caroline. "Let's get some lunch," Aunt Peggy said. And off they went.

That evening, Caroline sensed her grandmother's fatigue. She chose to keep her exquisite gift in its packaging, not wanting to diminish its flawless appearance just yet. While she tried to read her book, thoughts of the impending darkness kept intruding upon the words on the page. The cards had shown that something terrible was coming. Serena would be there to help. Would her grandmother? Caroline picked up the deck of cards and studied each one as her grandmother had instructed, looking for all the different messages on each card and thinking about how to interpret them based on the spread. Her eyes were beginning to close when her grandmother walked in. "It's been a big day. Tomorrow, we will go to Aunt Josephine's for lasagna. It would be best if you asked her about your father. Just make sure her husband doesn't hear you talking. They don't like each other at all."

*Is there anyone who likes my father?* Caroline thought.

Aunt Peggy picked them up for the drive to Josephine's house. Caroline finally had to ask, "Is there some reason the women in this family don't drive?"

Aunt Peggy roared with laughter. "It would make my life easier, but Mama always took the streetcar, and Jo was afraid of driving. So, I'm stuck as the family chauffeur."

Upon entering Aunt Josephine's house, Caroline sensed that she was an excellent cook, as the aroma surpassed even that of the Italian restaurant. While exploring, Caroline ventured into the kitchen and noticed a man seated at a table, leisurely enjoying a beer. He was wearing a T-shirt without a shirt over it, and he didn't look happy. "So, you're Bill's kid, huh?"

"Yes, sir," Caroline stammered.

"Is he still the same asshole he always was?"

Caroline assumed this man was her Uncle Larry.

"Larry," Aunt Josephine said sharply. "Caroline has nothing to do with how her father acts. She is my niece, and you will treat her kindly."

Suddenly, Caroline heard a sharp bark, and then a cold nose was on her leg. "Who is this?" Caroline cried as she bent down.

Larry's voice softened. "That's Geraldine."

"What kind of dog is she?" Caroline asked.

"A schnauzer," said Uncle Larry.

"Oh, she's darling. May I hold her?" Caroline asked Uncle Larry.

"Sure," he said.

Caroline sat in the chair opposite Uncle Larry and petted Geraldine until dinner was ready.

Aunt Josephine had set a beautiful table. She, too, had wonderful china and crystal. Everyone sat down and ate a delicious salad with the best lasagna Caroline had ever tasted. There was lemon pie for dessert, followed by coffee. After dinner, Larry left the table to watch TV, and Josephine started to get up to clear and wash the dishes.

"Oh, here, let me help you," Caroline offered.

Aunt Josephine smiled as they went into the kitchen. "I'll wash, and you dry," she said, handing Caroline a clean dish towel.

As she was drying, Caroline said, "Aunt Josephine, I know you and my dad were close. Can you tell me anything about him and my grandfather?"

A melancholic expression washed over Josephine's features. "Those are the two men I loved the most," she said. "Unfortunately, your dad liked to have fun and was always getting into trouble, whether at home or at school. He would dream up these crazy ideas and get me to do them with him. And he always took the blame if we got caught. My father doled out tough punishments."

"Like what?" asked Caroline.

"Oh, your dad would have to clean the printing machines all night. Sometimes, he made my dad so mad that he would hit him with a board."

"That's awful," said Caroline.

"Yes, it was," said Aunt Josephine. "And it wasn't right. But Bill makes it hard to love him."

Caroline didn't ask any more questions.

When they returned to her grandmother's apartment, her grandmother said, "I can't believe how quickly the week has flown by. I hope you've had a nice time, Caroline."

"Oh, Grandmother, it was better than I could imagine."

"You are a charming girl, Caroline. And if it's not too boring, I hope you will return to visit again."

Caroline rushed to her grandmother, embracing her tightly and planting a warm kiss on her lips. "I can't wait to visit again," she said longingly.

On Friday, they spent the day with Aunt Peggy. She had decorated her home in a French provincial style with many tons of white and blue combined with cane furniture. She had the biggest bed Caroline had ever seen, and she even had chandeliers in her bathroom! Her home wasn't huge, but it was very elegant. She even had a beautiful white Persian cat named Miss Prissy. And her lively white West Highland Terrier was named Wise Guy. Caroline ran after him in the backyard until they were both pooped.

Aunt Peggy thanked her for playing with Wise Guy. "He needs the exercise, and I don't get him out as much as I should. You are a good helper, Caroline." That might have been the best compliment she could get from Aunt Peggy.

Grandmother clapped her hands and said, "Music! It's time I hear you two perform together."

Caroline followed Aunt Peggy to her lovely baby grand piano. Aunt Peggy warmed up her hands and then pulled out some sheet music. "Can you sight read, Caroline?" she asked.

"Pretty well. I pick up a tune fast."

"OK," she said, "Let's try this one. It's from the musical 'Camelot.'" Aunt Peggy began to play the notes to "Before I Gaze at You Again." Caroline hesitantly began to sing the words:

Before I gaze at you again
I'll need a time for tears
Before I gaze at you again
Let hours turn to years

I have so much forgetting to do
Before I try to gaze again at you

With each note, Caroline's voice grew stronger. By the time they got to the end, Caroline showed confidence in her singing. Aunt Peggy finished playing, and there was a moment of silence before Grandmother Howard began clapping furiously. "That was better than I imagined, "she said. "Caroline, you have a beautiful voice!"

Even Aunt Peggy remarked, "Caroline, you are much better than I thought you would be. Are you taking lessons?"

"No," Caroline responded. "But the choir director at church works with me after practice when he gives me a solo."

Her grandmother said, "Church music is nice and all, but you need to be training in classical music."

Aunt Peggy agreed. Then, she asked, "Can you accompany yourself on the piano?"

Caroline looked down at her small hands with their short but slim fingers. Aunt Peggy stared at her hands as well.

"Oh, dear. Those are not the hands of a pianist. And why are your nails so short? You always want to have beautiful hands." Aunt Peggy showed Caroline her hands, whose long fingers were accentuated with long, perfectly polished fingernails. It made Caroline feel worse about her hands.

"I take piano lessons, but it gets harder as my teacher gives me more difficult pieces to play," said Caroline. "I would rather take singing lessons, but my mother says no." Everyone was quiet for a moment. "I believe the only way Mom would pay for singing lessons is if they were with the church choir director," Caroline continued. that," said Grandmother Howard. "Peggy and I will keep thinking about this. Peggy, I believe it's time we got everything ready for our cookout."

Aunt Peggy had a beautiful backyard with yellow wrought iron furniture. Grandmother Howard showed Caroline the proper way to set the table. Aunt Peggy made green rice, a family dish Caroline had never eaten. She also made deviled eggs to go with the hamburgers she was grilling. Grandmother Howard made potato salad. It was different than Caroline's mother's but still good.

Caroline kept thinking about this being her last night. She was sad to leave and didn't know when she would see them all again. Grandmother Howard noticed how quiet Caroline had become. As they sat outside enjoying the sunset and watching fireflies, her grandmother said, "Caroline, we hope you will come to see us again soon. Perhaps this summer, if possible. I have a pool at my apartment that you will enjoy. And we can continue our discussions."

"Grandmother, is there anything else you can tell me about my father and grandfather's relationship and why it was so negative?" Caroline asked.

Aunt Peggy piped in, "Your father was always a troublemaker and teased us girls mercilessly. No one could get him to shape up. He didn't respond to anything."

"Peggy, try not to be so hard on your brother. It was difficult being the oldest, particularly during the Depression," said Grandmother Howard. "I always wondered how much came from his broken legs. He was so young when that happened."

"What are you talking about, Grandmother?" Caroline asked with a puzzled look.

Her grandmother sighed and said, "Your father was born pigeon-toed. The doctor fractured both of his legs when he was only two years old, and to correct them, he had to reset your father's legs with the feet positioned correctly. Unfortunately, due to financial constraints, we were unable to remain in Kansas City during his recovery, so we had to leave him at the hospital for the healing process. I will never know how much this might have affected him. To leave him like that, in pain." Tears came to Grandmother Howard's eyes.

Caroline didn't say anything. She felt like there were many things to discuss with Serena and was anxious to see her.

Early the following day, Caroline boarded the bus to head home. She had kept out one book to read during the long return trip, and her grandmother had made her lunch to eat. Caroline waved furiously as the bus pulled out. Her grandmother and Aunt Peggy waved back.

Caroline had a small notebook in her purse dedicated to capturing ideas that popped into her mind and that she intended to discuss with Serena later. She diligently recorded everything her grandmother and aunts had shared. She was relieved that she had remembered to shield herself that morning in the bathroom.

She knew there would be a significant wait before she could retreat to the closet, engage in conversation with Serena, and share the insights she had gained on their quest.

# Darkness Descending

**B**ILL HEARD HIS DAUGHTER'S voice as she entered the house, calling for her cat. It was then that he realized how much he had appreciated her absence. Her presence tended to heighten his stress because, as a female, she demanded more effort to manage. Moreover, he had no clue what she might have picked up from that group of women in Kansas City. "Caroline, come here," he bellowed.

His daughter walked into the kitchen, holding the cat in her arms.

"What did you talk about with your grandmother?" he asked.

Caroline seemed to stiffen. He would drag everything out of her.

"Oh, nothing special, Daddy," she responded.

*Daddy, eh*? He knew when a con was on. "Sit down," he ordered. "I want to know everything you did and what was said."

"Good lord, Dad, I can't remember everything we discussed. We went out to dinner at a delicious Italian restaurant. We went shopping down at the Plaza, and we had lasagna at Aunt Jo's . . ." Caroline trailed off.

"You went over to Josephine's house," he exploded. "Your grandmother knows that is forbidden!"

"Dad, nothing bad happened," Caroline explained. "I agree that Uncle Larry isn't nice, but I didn't spend time with him. I enjoyed your favorite sister and can see why you like her. I also visited Aunt Peggy's beautiful house and had an absolutely delightful time. Grandmother Howard would love for me to come back for another visit."

Her mother had walked into the room to interrupt the interrogation. "Caroline, why don't you go to your room and unpack? Then, you can get started on the thank you notes to your grandmother and aunts."

Caroline smiled gratefully at her mother, grabbed her suitcase, and headed to her room with Smokey.

"Bill, from what Caroline told me in the car, she had a very nice time, and nothing bad happened," Patsy said. "I don't think you have anything to be upset about."

"I don't trust my mother and those sisters. Already, I find out she went to Jo's house even knowing I wouldn't allow it," he shouted, storming around their small kitchen.

"Bill, it's late, and we have church in the morning," pleaded Patsy. "Let's just get a good night's sleep, and we can talk to her again tomorrow."

Bill stared at Patsy. "I won't be attending church tomorrow," he told her.

"Fine," she said and left the room.

Bill awoke with lingering concerns about the household's situation. The residence remained serene, as everyone had gone to church. He reached for a beer and settled into his chair at the table. The persistent defiance from Andrew weighed on him, and it appeared that Andrew's rebellious nature was intensifying daily. However, given Andrew's outstanding academic performance and his commitment to a part-time job to cover car and insurance expenses, Bill had limited options for addressing the situation. But the girl he was dating was another matter. Bill didn't know how Andrew had met a Catholic girl, but that was unacceptable. He was only to date nice Southern Baptist girls! Then, there was Edward. He, too, had gotten lippy. Bill had slapped the boy a few times to remind him who was in charge, but it hadn't had the effect he wanted. Edward was doing well in baseball. He was still quarterbacking the football team, but that probably wouldn't last, given his small stature. It didn't matter, as it was all about baseball. That boy was going to the show! Bill would have seats behind the batting box to watch the games. He continued drinking, daydreaming about talking with the pretty wives at the games, until he heard voices. Damn, now he would have to deal with everyone.

Patsy entered the kitchen, disapproval evident on her face. Bill was well aware that she would be upset about his drinking, but he felt he had the right to do as he pleased in his own home. With that thought, he moved to the family room and switched on the game. He yelled for Edward to watch with him but didn't get a response.

Patsy came in to try and quiet him down. "I'm fixing the kids some lunch, Bill. Do you want anything? I'm certain you're hungry."

"Nah, I don't want anything to eat. Tell Edward I want to watch the game with him when he's finished eating."

Bill spent the afternoon drinking and dozing in his big chair. As the day grew dark and dinnertime came, Bill finally rose and stumbled into the dining room to eat the Sunday meal. He stared at Caroline briefly and then asked menacingly, "Did my mother teach you any of her witches' tricks?"

Caroline looked up from her meal and slowly said, "I'm not sure what you're talking about, Daddy. Grandmother Howard focused on teaching me proper lady things like setting the table and folding napkins. I don't know about any 'witchy' tricks."

Her brothers snickered at her answer. "Wow sounds like lots of fun. I'm sorry I missed the napkin folding lesson," Edward sneered. Andrew laughed out loud.

Caroline grew angry at their teasing. "You're just jealous because you couldn't visit Grandmother Howard. She's a lovely woman who told me stories about the Pritchard family and growing up in Iowa. I can't wait to see her again!" Caroline jumped up from the table and headed toward her room.

"Just a minute, young lady," Bill called out. "I have a few more things to ask you."

Caroline sat back down.

"Did your grandmother talk about my father? Did she tell you what a great guy he was?" asked Bill.

"She talked about when he worked at the Kansas City Star and used to write funny items for the front page," replied Caroline. "Aunt Peggy showed me some of the papers. I thought that was very interesting."

"Did your grandmother talk to you about female things like sex?" inquired Bill.

Patsy interrupted/ "Really, Bill, this is inappropriate for the dinner table."

Bill stared at Patsy and said, "I'll decide what topics to discuss at my dinner table." He turned back to Caroline. "Well?" he said ominously.

"Oh, no, Dad. We didn't talk about anything like that," said Caroline, turning red from embarrassment.

"Did you go to the Catholic church with your aunt?" he asked.

"No. Grandmother does not attend church anymore. She said she has learned everything she needs to know about religion. I learned that Aunt Peggy is Catholic, which surprised me, but I did not go to church with her," Caroline finished.

A brief silence hung in the air before Bill instructed his daughter to retreat to her room. Without hesitation, the girl promptly hurried off.

That evening, Bill started drinking the hard liquor and put Elvis Presley's records on the stereo. Everyone knew this was a bad sign. It meant Bill was going on a bender. Caroline went into her closet, and the boys stayed in their bedroom.

Bill got up from his chair in the family room and called his mother. He liked to call his relatives and harass them when he was very drunk. Grandmother Howard, sounding drowsy, answered after several rings. "Hello?"

"Hi, Mom, it's your favorite son, William."

Grandmother Howard knew immediately that Bill was drunk and that he was gearing up for a fight. "Bill why are you calling so late on a Sunday night?" she asked. "Shouldn't you be in bed?"

"Well, Mom, I wanted to see if you enjoyed my daughter's visit," he said.

"I did very much," she replied.

"Caroline said you didn't show her your witch tricks, but I don't believe her. Unlike you, she's not a good liar."

"Bill, I would prefer that you didn't spoil the memories of my good time with Caroline. She is a gifted, intelligent girl whom you are lucky to have. I hope you treat her well," she said.

"Oh, Mother, I will be treating her very special." He concluded the conversation with a chuckle before disconnecting the call.

The following day, after school, Bill waited for his daughter, who arrived as he had anticipated. He knew a phone call would come, and eventually, it did. On her way to the phone, Caroline attempted to rush past him, but he was prepared. Bill quickly seized her with both hands, drawing her close and restraining her with his left arm. Using his right hand, he plunged down her skirt under her panties to her private parts and began probing with his fingers. Caroline cried out for him to stop. He used his tongue to lick her ear and stuck it inside, quickly going back and forth. Caroline kept screaming while he thought about what his mother would have to say. *See, Mother, she's mine to do with as I please.* After a time, he'd had enough and threw the girl to the floor. "Go to your room and stay there till your mother gets home," he ordered.

Patsy arrived home late and promptly began preparing dinner. Once the meal was ready, she set Bill's plate in front of him and called for Edward and Caroline to join them. Andrew was out for the evening. He was difficult to keep track of. Edward came down and started eating with Bill, but Caroline didn't come. Patsy went to her room and tried to open the door but couldn't budge it. Something seemed to be blocking the door. "Caroline," she said, "open this door!"

She didn't hear anything in the room, and she kept trying to push the door open.

"Caroline! What is against the door?" Still nothing from inside the room.

Exasperated, Patsy returned to the kitchen to eat her dinner before it got cold. "Where's Caroline?" Bill asked.

"She seems to have barred her door somehow," Patsy replied. "Do you know why she might have done this?"

"Nope," was all he said.

After dinner, Patsy made another attempt to open the door to Caroline's room, but it remained blocked, and her calls for the girl went unanswered. She returned to the kitchen to complete her cleaning tasks. Later, when bedtime approached, Patsy tried one last time to open the door, but it was still sealed shut, and her calls yielded no response. Disheartened, she retired to her own bedroom and readied herself for sleep. She called out softly to Bill, but he was already fast asleep.

Bill got up early the next morning and tried to open Caroline's door. It wouldn't budge. He laughed. She would have to come out sometime. He could wait.

# Seeking Help

THE SNOW HAD BUILT up high outside her cave over the winter. Serena wrapped her legs in animal skins to keep them warm. This made it harder to walk to her traps. She felt fortunate that the Creator continued to provide her with small animals to eat throughout the cold, dark months. Serena could reduce the amount of food she required and conserve her strength. Like the animals, she slept more but needed to keep the fire going for warmth. Her magical skills were most helpful during this time: slowing the wood burning or making it burn hotter, depending on her needs. She could tell from where the sun rose each day that spring was coming. While the storms continued to rage, the snow took on a denser consistency, lacking the light and fluffy quality of deep winter. It was more prone to melting yet more challenging to navigate, causing her legs to get cold quickly. Nevertheless, these were all integral aspects of life in the mountains.

Early one morning, a lynx came to the mouth of her cave. Serena was quite surprised, as they rarely came near her. It was a young female lynx, and she stood at the cave's opening for quite some time, staring at Serena. The nymph remained still, listening closely to what the lynx wanted to convey before she moved off. Serena then entered a meditation and, after returning to consciousness, remained motionless. The lynx had told her someone would be reaching out with a secret message of great importance. Serena continued to wait by the fire, and as the afternoon came along, she heard whispering in the wind. The shadow spirit soon sat in front of her, crying. The image flickered, as her strength was unstable. "Caroline," Serena called out. "Stop crying and gather your strength. You need to be calm for us to converse."

Serena waited while Caroline blew her nose and breathed deeply to contain herself. Soon, the image was clear.

"Caroline, what do you need to tell me?" Serena asked.

"Serena, I did just as you said. I went to Kansas City and met my Grandmother Howard. She told me about our Celtic background and taught me how to read tarot cards! I learned some things about the darkness between my grandfather and dad. Then, I came home, and my dad did . . ." She trailed off. She couldn't finish and started to cry again. But Serena had seen the image of Caroline's father touching the girl.

"Caroline! It would help if you stopped crying so we could talk. Did you shield yourself as I taught you?"

"Yes, Serena, I shield every morning. I have been barring the door to my room until I hurry out to go to school. Then, when I come home, I bar it again. I'm starving because I miss meals, but I don't want to go to the kitchen because he's there! Serena, I don't know how to make him stop this."

Serena sat quietly, thinking. The problem shared was a human issue. She recognized that resolving the issue required the assistance of other people. Serena was aware of dark magic that could restrain the man, but she pondered its practicality. She couldn't keep him bound forever. It would be up to Caroline to stop her father. "Caroline, have you told your mother what your father does?"

Caroline shook her head.

"Did you tell your grandmother?"

Again, Caroline shook her head.

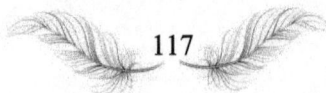

Serena said, "To stop your father will require a woman's power. You have not bled yet?"

Caroline shook her head.

"You have not yet come fully into your power. You will need a strong adult female to stop your father. You must tell your mother. It is her job to protect you. Once you have spoken to her, come back and see me."

Caroline nodded, her expression devoid of happiness. Serena could tell she was afraid.

"Caroline, you must learn to be strong. This difficulty is part of your path. I told you that yours was not an easy life. You will find peace, but first, you must prepare to do battle. Strengthen your shield, and don't show fear!" The young girl seemed to expand with these words. Her aura grew more substantial and darker blue. And then she was gone.

Serena stood to stretch her legs. She didn't understand humans. Why did they hurt their own so badly? Didn't they know how deep these wounds could go and how long it could take to heal? Many of them were not kind. She had seen how they killed the deer and elk, stalking in packs and shooting more times than necessary. And they never blessed the animals they killed or thanked the Creator for making the beautiful creatures. She found herself getting so angry that she wanted to hurt something! But this was not her way. She drew deep breaths through her nose and shook out her long limbs. The sky had turned dark. Serena went to the mouth of the cave to look at the clear night sky and the stars beginning to emerge. She prayed to the Creator, Caroline's ancestors, Anne, and the chief, seeking their guidance and protection for the young girl. Afterward, she returned to the cave, moving slowly.

Caroline sat in her closet with her power animals by her side, along with her cat Smokey. The cat sensed the spirit animals but wasn't afraid of them. Caroline felt safer when they were all with her in the closet together. Thinking about what Serena had said, Caroline wished she could avoid talking to her mother, but how else could she get her father to stop? Caroline lacked the strength to defend herself against him and had no command of any witchcraft abilities. Additionally, harming her father would only lead to more significant trouble.

She waited for her mother to call her to dinner. When she did, Caroline carefully removed the chair and table that she was using to block the door and slowly looked out. She saw her mother standing there. "So, you've decided to come out," her mother said.

"Yes, I'm hungry," replied Caroline.

"Well, come to the table. Everyone is waiting."

Caroline followed her mother and passed her father as she walked into the kitchen. He sat there with a smirk on his face. As she passed, he reached out and patted her bottom. Caroline yelled out, "Stop! Leave me alone." Her mother whipped around and looked at Caroline and then at her father. Caroline hurriedly got into her seat and looked down at her plate. Everyone sat down while her mother said grace. Then, they quietly ate.

Suddenly, her father said, "Caroline, you must be a virgin when you're married."

Her brothers groaned, and Andrew responded, "Can we have a meal without discussing Caroline having sex? What a topic to talk about while trying to enjoy Mom's roast beef and gravy."

"Besides," piped in Edward. "Who would want to have sex with Caroline?"

Caroline looked up and stared at her mother. Serena had said that a strong woman must help her with this problem. "Bill, I have said before that I don't feel this is an appropriate conversation for the dinner table," Patsy said. "I know you are in charge, but I don't think you need to harp on this topic constantly. I believe Caroline knows what you expect of her." She looked at Caroline, who nodded.

Her father didn't say anything else.

When dinner was over, Caroline hastily retreated to her bedroom and securely blocked the door once again. She diligently completed her homework and heard the phone ring multiple times before she decided to immerse herself in a book. Caroline had no desire to seek out her mother; instead, she patiently waited, hoping her mother would come and check on her.

Caroline was in bed reading herself to sleep when her mother knocked. Caroline got up and unbarred the door. Her mother came in and looked around. Caroline's bedroom was neat as usual, but a chair and table were out of place near the door. Her mother looked at it and walked over to Caroline, who had already climbed back into bed. The girl looked at her mother, waiting for her to begin.

"Caroline, why have you started barring your door?" she asked.

Caroline had decided to be straightforward with her mother, with little embellishment. "Mom, I'm barring the door to keep Dad out."

"Why would you do that?"

"Because I don't want him coming into my room and bothering me."

"Has he been saying things you don't like?"

"It's more about what he's doing," Caroline said.

Her mother hesitated, not knowing if she wanted to hear more. She started toward the door.

"Mom, I need to talk to you about this. You need to make him stop," Caroline pleaded.

"Stop what?" her mother asked.

"Stop grabbing me when I go to the kitchen, holding me down, and touching my private parts!"

"Caroline, what are you talking about?"

"Mom, I'm talking about my father touching parts he shouldn't."

"Caroline, your father wouldn't do anything like that."

"But he does, Mom. He grabs me whenever I go to the kitchen to answer the phone or get something to eat. He does it when nobody else is home."

"Caroline, it isn't right for you to make up these kinds of accusations about your father."

"What's not right is what he's doing to me! I need you to make him stop."

"Caroline, I don't appreciate hearing you making up these tales."

"Mom, why would I make something like this up? It's so disgusting! I can't stop it. You need to help me."

"Caroline, I want you to think about what you are saying and how this could affect the family," her mother said. Then, she walked from the room.

Caroline rose and secured the door once more, releasing her frustration by pounding her pillow. She felt exasperated because following Serena's guidance led her mother to accuse her of deceit. The challenge lay in finding a way to make her mother comprehend the truth.

Caroline knew that her father wouldn't dare lay a hand on her in her mother's presence; he was far too cunning for that. The next day, Caroline went to her friend Sarah and asked if they could meet after school. Sarah invited Caroline over to her house. Wet snow fell as they walked to Sarah's house. The girls were in the kitchen getting snacks when Caroline asked if they could go to Sarah's room. Sarah thought they were planning to practice gymnastics in the family room. She shrugged and led Caroline upstairs. Once they were in the bedroom, Caroline closed the door. She asked Sarah if the door could be locked. "Yes, just press the little knob on the handle," Sarah responded.

"My door doesn't have a lock," said Caroline. Then she sat on the floor and looked up at Sarah. "I have a big secret to tell you. You must promise to tell no one, particularly anybody at school. What I'm about to tell you must stay in this room."

"OK," said Sarah.

"I mean it," said Caroline. 'Swear. Swear on the Bible. Do you have a Bible?"

"Yeah, somewhere in the bookcase," replied Sarah.

"Get it," said Caroline.

"Geez, OK. You're making a big deal out of this," said Sarah.

"That's because it is a big deal," replied Caroline.

Sarah found the Bible, and Caroline made her put her right hand on it and swear that she wouldn't tell anyone about what Caroline would tell her; if she did, she would go to hell. Sarah protested about the hell portion of the pledge, but Caroline insisted, so Sarah swore. Then, Caroline told her about what was happening at home with her father.

Sarah's eyes grew huge, and eventually, tears appeared. She clasped Caroline's shaking hands and told her how sorry she was. Sarah said she felt sick to her stomach, and Caroline told her she always felt that way. Sarah asked how long it had been going on. "For a while," Caroline replied. "I don't know how to get him to stop. I told my mother, but she doesn't believe me."

"That's awful," replied Sarah.

"Thanks. That's why I'm telling you. I don't know what I'll do, but I needed someone to know."

"Do you want me to tell my parents?" Sarah asked.

"No," said Caroline. "I think the only adults who should know are people who can do something. I assume your parents would want to talk to my parents, which would make things worse at home. I need to find an adult who is willing to help me. I can't think of who."

"Do you want to talk to a teacher or the principal?" asked Sarah.

"I thought about that," said Caroline. "But that might get the police involved, and I'd rather not do that. I'm afraid even worse things might happen."

"Well, you should come home from school to my house as often as you can," said Sarah. "Then you won't be alone with your dad."

Caroline looked at her friend with a profound sense of gratitude. Her offer would be a big help to Caroline.

The girls finished their snacks and headed downstairs to practice gymnastics. Sarah was trying to help Caroline learn a back walkover, which wasn't easy. Around dinnertime, Caroline's mother arrived. She honked the horn, and Caroline headed for the car. She turned toward her friend, offering a warm embrace and expressing her gratitude. Afterward, she settled into the car, patiently awaiting her mother's words. But her mother said nothing.

Caroline continued to go to Sarah's house whenever possible. She let her mother know to pick her up there. On days when Sarah had something else to do, Caroline had to face a gauntlet if she needed to go to the kitchen, which she tried never to do. But sometimes, she needed to make a phone call about homework or get something to eat because her mother had to work late. Then, her father had his way.

The end of the school year was approaching when Caroline asked her mother if they were going fishing. "Caroline, I didn't think you liked the fishing trips," her mother said.

"Oh, I don't like to fish, but I love hiking in the mountains. Do you think we can go as soon as school is out?" Caroline asked.

"I don't know," her mother responded. "I must talk to your father and look at your brothers' game schedules."

"Well, I'd like to go as soon as we can," said Caroline. Then, she went back to her room, barring the door as always.

Caroline dreaded the coming of summer. How was she to stay away from her father all day long? It wasn't possible to stay in her hot room all day. She wanted to play with friends outside or invite girls to play with Barbies. She needed to figure out some way to escape from the house. She went to her mother to talk about going to camp. Caroline had never been, but she thought it might be a way to escape the house. Her mother mentioned Vacation Bible School.

Caroline didn't want to attend, as it was tedious. However, it took up the entire day, so she told her mother to sign her up. But that was only a week. Caroline asked when they were going to the farm. Her mother said again that she would have to look at her brothers' baseball schedules. Caroline hated that the summer revolved around her brothers. She felt as if she didn't matter.

Caroline asked if she could stay at the farm without the family, and she promised to help her grandparents. Her mother seemed surprised by this request and told her she would need to think about it. Then, Caroline asked again about going up to the mountains. Her mother said they would probably go but expected it wouldn't be until August. August! That was four months away. What would Caroline do? She ran to her room crying.

After a while, Caroline's mother knocked on the door. Caroline unbarred it, and her mother walked in. She sat on Caroline's bed. 'Caroline, I cannot believe anything inappropriate is happening with your father. But you seem rather upset about the summer, and I don't like you being home alone all day. I'll try to think of something for you to do. You're too young to have a babysitting job, but you might serve as a mother's helper. I'll put up a notice at church and see if anything comes of it."

Caroline had no idea what a mother's helper was, but if it got her away from her father, she was all for it. She thanked her mother. Her mother seemed to want to say something else, but she left, and Caroline re-barred the door.

A week later, Caroline's mother entered her bedroom for a conversation. She informed Caroline that a mother had responded to her advertisement. Caroline's mother had spoken to the woman and found out she had three children and wanted a young girl to come by every afternoon to help watch the kids while she did chores around the house. Caroline agreed immediately. Her mother told Caroline she would receive one dollar and fifty cents per hour for her work. Her mother suggested they open a savings account and put the money there. Again, Caroline agreed. Her mother said she would contact the woman and set everything up. She reminded Caroline that her father would have to take her to the woman's house, and she would pick Caroline up after work. Caroline hesitated about getting into the car with her father and asked if she could walk to the woman's house instead. Her mother dismissed the idea, deeming it too far. Caroline let out a sigh but said nothing further. Her mother left the room.

After Caroline re-barred the door, she lay on her bed and thought about what she would do with the money. She concentrated hard to see if she could reach Serena. Surprisingly, Anne's face appeared in her mind. She asked Anne what she thought she should do with her money. Anne said she should use the money to see her Grandmother Howard. *That's a great idea! She can tell me what to do about my dad.* Anne warned her not to tell her mother of her plans, as she might disagree. Instead, Caroline should write to her grandmother and ask if she could come. They could have everything arranged when she spoke with her mother.

Caroline thanked Anne for her help. Anne reminded her that she was always available and that Caroline should practice using her third eye to reach her guides.

*What's a third eye?*

"The third eye is invisible to other people," Anne explained. "It is located on the forehead and provides perception beyond ordinary sight. When you are at school, research 'chakras,' as this will help you understand."

*Thanks again, Anne.*

"Goodbye, Caroline."

The next day at school, during recess, Caroline shared her plans with Sarah as they practiced their gymnastics in the field. Sarah thought Caroline was lucky to have her own money and wished she could do the same. Caroline looked at her friend wistfully, wishing summer could be full of fun, swimming at the private swim club that Sarah's family belonged to. But Caroline realized she was on a different path from other girls.

Summer eventually made its appearance, marking the start of Caroline's job as a mother's assistant. Mrs. McGraff, a seemingly weary woman, was her employer. Her children, on the other hand, were unruly, creating chaos throughout the house. They engaged in wild behavior, quarreling among themselves and relentlessly tormenting the family cat, Whiskers—a situation Caroline found intolerable. She began each afternoon by telling the children they must be nice to Whiskers and showing them how petting the cat and giving it special treats made Whiskers happy and playful. Then, the cat wouldn't scratch them. Caroline wasn't wholly successful, and she often had to go to Whiskers' hiding place in the linen closet to coax the animal back down and show the cat some kindness.

Throughout the remainder of her time at Mrs. McGraff's, Caroline assisted the children with activities like coloring and playing board games. Each day, she diligently guided them in tidying up their toys. By the time Caroline returned home, she was thoroughly drained. However, she remained determined to accomplish her goal of completing every book on her summer reading list. With the upcoming transition to junior high next year, she was focused on her studies and literary pursuits.

She needed to talk to her mother about her clothing. She couldn't go to West Woods wearing clothes her mother made. She had to go to the local J.C. Penney or Sears for cooler clothing. She hoped her mother wouldn't make her use the money she made from her summer job to pay for the clothes because she needed the money to buy a bus ticket to Kansas City. She would love to go shopping with her Aunt Peggy, but she doubted her mother would give her money to do that.

Her father wasn't as bad that summer. He didn't start drinking until after Caroline had left for her job, and her mother was home on the weekends, so Caroline's time alone with her father was relatively safe. So far, he had caught her only a few times. She tried to see Sarah on Saturdays or before she went to Mrs. McGraff's. Sarah often did family activities on the weekends and was busy, but she didn't forget her friend's difficulty and tried to invite Caroline along when she could.

Caroline's mother scheduled a two-week visit to the farm in July, coinciding with the McGraff family vacation. Her father couldn't join due to work commitments. Caroline was elated at the prospect of spending time with her grandparents and relishing the tranquility of the farm. Each day, she visited the cats at the barn, helped weed the garden, and worked on a new quilt with her mother and grandmother. Her mother would draw the quilt patterns on pieces of cloth and allow Caroline to use the special scissors to cut out the pattern pieces. The women would talk about which colors and fabrics looked best together. Then, Grandma Andersen would sew the different parts while Caroline's mother would iron the seams. They worked every afternoon to finish the quilt top. Grandpa Andersen pulled out the extended wooden quilting frames to tie off the quilt. Grandma Andersen then ran the big stitches through the thick quilt top piece they had created, with the batting in between and the warm flannel fabric underneath. Caroline's mother cut the long stitches, and Caroline got to tie the knots. They had completed the quilt by the time the family's visit was over. Caroline was proud she had helped, and Grandma Andersen complimented her work. Grandpa gave her a dollar bill and a strong hug when her family left. Caroline hated leaving the farm, and for the first time, she cried as the car pulled away. Her brother Edward just stared at her and told her to stop being such a baby.

When Caroline got home, she counted the money she had made and how much she expected to have by the end of the summer. She wrote her Grandmother Howard a letter explaining her desire to come for a visit before she went back to school. Caroline's grandmother responded with enthusiasm, expressing her excitement for Caroline's visit. She suggested that the last week of August would work perfectly. In a friendly reminder, she cautioned Caroline about the sweltering Kansas City weather during that time and advised her to pack accordingly. With this encouraging response in hand, Caroline felt it was the right moment to approach her mother about the trip.

After dinner, Caroline asked her mother to come into her room. Caroline sat on the bed while her mother sat on the chair by the door. Caroline told her mother that she wanted to use the money she had earned on a bus ticket to Kansas City and that she had received permission from her grandmother to visit. Her mother was somewhat surprised at everything that Caroline had organized. The problem, her mother pointed out, was that her father had decided they would go on their trip to the mountains the last week in August. "Oh, no," Caroline said. "I have to go to the mountains to see . . ." Caroline stopped, as she couldn't tell her mother about Serena. ". . . the birds and wildflowers," she lamely completed.

Her mother said she would have to make a choice.

Caroline decided to approach her mother about the subject of clothing. "Mom, I appreciate how hard you work making my school clothes yearly," she began. "But I'm starting junior high in the fall, and I can't go wearing homemade clothing. I must get my clothes from a department store like my brothers."

Her mother looked angry. "Well, I hadn't budgeted for buying your clothing from a store. The best I can do is give you the amount I would have spent on fabric. I suggest that you plan to use your own money if you want any additional clothing."

*Shoot, I knew she would say this.*

"Can we plan to go shopping before we go up to the mountains? I want to be certain I have a great outfit for the first day of school," Caroline said.

"Alright," said her mother as she left her room.

Caroline realized she would have to write to her grandmother and explain that she couldn't come. She felt sad. She wished she could see her grandmother before she headed to the mountains, but she had already committed to Mrs. McGraff.

Caroline went school shopping with her mother before they left for the mountains.

She was disappointed at what she had been able to buy. Her mother's budget allowed her to buy only one pair of pants and two shirts. With her savings, Caroline added another pair of Levi's jeans with the red tag on the pocket and a cute peasant blouse. She would still have to wear some of her homemade clothing to school, but at least she'd have a nice outfit on the first day, along with her Dr. Scholls sandals.

Caroline packed her hiking jeans and older clothes in her duffel bag for the mountain trip. She went into the closet and concentrated on reaching Serena with her third eye to tell her she was coming. Following Anne's advice, Caroline dutifully visited her local library to delve into the fascinating realm of chakras. The librarian, taken aback by this uncommon request, nevertheless assisted her in locating a book on Eastern philosophy. Although Caroline found the material intriguing, she grappled with a lack of comprehension. She resolved to seek guidance from Serena, hoping for a deeper understanding of the subject.

The family drove up I-70, and Caroline tried to enjoy the green aspens and lodgepole pine trees from her middle seat in the back of the car. She couldn't look for the bighorn sheep she loved because they wouldn't come down near the highway until spring.

Once they were at the cabin near the Blue River, Caroline quickly unpacked, finished her chores, and asked her mother if she could hike. As it was getting late, her mother insisted that she could be gone for only an hour and that she had to stay on the path nearest their location. Caroline hurried out and went quickly up to her usual rock. She sat on it, closing her eyes and picturing Serena standing before her. While waiting, Caroline listened to the birds in the trees and felt the wind blowing through them. She smelled the pine scent that floated down. The soothing scents and gentle sounds of the surroundings had a calming effect on her, causing her shoulders to gradually relax.

Just as she started to unwind, a familiar voice reached her ears. Glancing around, she spotted Serena emerging from the forest, adorned in her distinctive animal skin dress. Caroline ran to Serena and hugged the nymph tightly. Serena seemed taken aback, surprised by the physical contact. Still, she realized the girl had experienced significant trauma, and she patted her back as Caroline began to cry.

Serena suggested they walk to their regular spot in the grove of aspen trees. A few leaves were beginning their annual change to a beautiful golden color. Caroline sat on the ground, which had been warmed by the sun, crossing her legs and waiting for Serena to speak. The nymph walked in the direction of the medicine wheel three times and then stood in front of Caroline. "I know of your difficulties with your father," Serena began.

Caroline interrupted. "Oh, Serena, it has been awful. I try so hard to avoid him, but there are still times when he has been drinking, and I must go to the phone to ask a friend a question about my homework, and he grabs me. I hate what he does. I've started carrying my hairbrush and beating him with it to get him to let me go, but it hasn't worked. He laughs in his cackling voice. I've tried talking to my mother, but she won't believe me and keeps saying my father would never do anything to hurt me. I don't know what to do to get him to stop. Help me, Serena."

Serena stood very still. Then, she said, "Caroline, I understand you are in pain with nowhere to turn. Have you talked to your Grandmother Howard about this?"

"Oh, no," replied Caroline. "I would never want to tell her about what's happening!"

Serena thought momentarily and said, "Caroline, your Grandmother Howard is the best person to help you. When do you go revisit her?"

Caroline's head hung down as she replied. "I had the option of seeing her or coming to the mountains. I choose to visit with you and to understand the things I've read and heard that don't make sense."

"Caroline, you must try to visit your grandmother as soon as possible and explain what is happening at home. In the meantime, I will answer the questions you have."

At this, Caroline perked up a bit. She began by asking Serena about chakras.

"Ah, these are an ancient system of the body's inner workings. Your first chakra is at your root to support the body." Serena pointed to the place between her legs. "This is your connection to Gaia or Mother Earth, and it is associated with the color red. It is also the part of a woman where new life begins." Serena then pointed to her mid-section just below the belly button. "This is your second chakra. The color of this chakra is orange, and it is associated with water. Your third chakra is here at your solar plexus. It is your yellow power chakra where the soul enters and departs. Your fourth chakra is your heart. It is green and tied to the air.

"Your fifth chakra is your throat, and it connects with the blue sky. The sixth chakra is indigo, where your third eye resides, and your seventh chakra is your violet crown, which you open to reach out to the spirit world."

"What is so special about the sixth chakra, the third eye?" asked Caroline. "This is the one I don't understand."

"The third eye is critical," Serena said. "You use this eye to see beyond the Earth world and into the universe. When it is open, you can easily see the spirit world and the ancient ways. But you always want your shield on when using your third eye so you don't invite unwanted entities into your body."

"Do I open this eye when I speak to you or my guides from my closet?" asked Caroline.

"Yes. You have been using this without being aware of it. Know that as you grow in awareness of this chakra, we can begin practicing its uses," said Serena.

"It won't stop my father, will it?" Caroline asked softly.

"Not directly," Serena replied. "But it will help you reach out into the universe and tell your grandmother and other people who use their third eye that you need help. These messages will alert the universe to send people to you who can stop your father. Does that make sense?"

"A bit. I still find it somewhat confusing. I guess it' something we learn at school," said Caroline.

"No, you will be told only about Western ideas in your school. You won't be taught Eastern philosophy or the learnings before Christianity took over the world."

"You don't seem to like Christians," said Caroline.

"I don't," replied Serena. "When this religious cult emerged, its followers began to chop down the sacred groves and kill women who practiced the ancient healing arts. Their beliefs are exceedingly inflexible, and they exhibit little tolerance for other longstanding beliefs. They don't believe in reincarnation and are obsessed with this person called 'the Devil' and hell, where he lives. No such person or place exists."

Caroline was taken aback. What Serena said went against the teachings at church. It made her think about her loving grandparents at the farm. How could they be wrong? "Serena, I know good people, like my grandparents, who believe in God and in Jesus Christ, who died for our sins. How could they be wrong when they are good people?" Caroline asked.

Serena responded, "Your grandparents would be good no matter what religion they practiced. They are older souls who understand that people need to practice love and forgiveness. They were born knowing of the spiritual world. Still, they were brainwashed so early that they forgot their original wisdom and became good Christians. In any religion, there are good teachings such as taking care of family, loving your neighbors, and treating others with respect, but too much in Christianity is used to scare you into specific modes of behavior like keeping a baby no matter how you got pregnant. Christianity's hierarchical structure places women in a subordinate

trouble answering this question. Finally, she said, "Then a wife should speak with her minister."

Now Caroline had her answer. When she got home, she would talk to their minister about what her father was doing.

Caroline picked up a book and started reading. She found that books were the best way to block out what was happening around her. She could disappear into the story.

As the family squeezed into the cramped cabin, Caroline found it challenging to secure any personal space. To her surprise, her mother tagged along when she embarked on her hike the following day. She was trying to talk more to Caroline about the Bible when Caroline interrupted and asked what she knew about Eastern philosophy. Her mother became flustered and mumbled, "Nothing." Caroline asked why the Baptist church they attended didn't celebrate females. Her mother quickly responded that their church honored Mary as a virgin and the mother of Jesus. Caroline asked if their church ever honored Mary as just a woman who lived a difficult life.

"Caroline, where are you getting all these crazy ideas?" her mother asked.

"I don't think they're crazy. I've been reading about different religions and their teachings in the library. Before Christianity, women were honored for their medical skills and were mathematicians. And in the Native American communities, women were often shamans."

Caroline's mother didn't respond to these comments. She just continued walking. Caroline realized her mother didn't want to discuss anything she didn't deem "pleasant," but Caroline wouldn't give up.

"Mom, since I didn't see Grandmother Howard this week, I was wondering if I could go over Christmas break," she said.

Her mother didn't answer for a few paces. Then, she said, "I'll think about it."

Upon returning home from their hike, Caroline, growing increasingly frustrated with her mother, decided to escape into the world of a book. Her mother seemed uninterested in discussing any of Caroline's interests, was unhelpful with the ongoing issues concerning her dad, and even hinted at the possibility of interfering with Caroline's planned visit to her grandmother despite Caroline's hard-earned money from her summer job. Determined to address her concerns, Caroline made up her mind to venture out on her own the next day and have a candid conversation with Serena.

After her dad and brothers got up to go fishing early in the morning, Caroline quickly got dressed and ran out the door, yelling to her mother that she would be back soon. Once she was sitting on top of the rock, she closed her eyes but tried to open her third eye, visualize Serena, and send her a message. Then, Caroline waited patiently.

After a while, she heard a voice saying, "You came early today. I was breaking my fast when your message came through. Is everything alright?"

"Serena, I tried so hard to talk to my mother about things I've learned from you about my dad, and I asked her about seeing my grandmother. She either doesn't respond or says, 'We'll see.' How can I improve things if she won't help?"

"Caroline, I don't see your mother as being the person who will help you with your problems," said Serena. "I don't think she can face what is happening in her home and pretends everything is fine. We must look in a different direction to solve your problem. We decided you would go to see your grandmother during the winter solstice. Is the place where you get a ride to her house within walking distance?"

Caroline stared at Serena for a moment. "What's 'winter solstice'?" she asked.

Serena replied, "It's the shortest day of the year. It is when the Earth reaches its maximum tilt away from the sun. But that is not the subject of today's conversation. Where is the place that takes you to your grandmother?"

"It's called a bus," said Caroline. "But the station is downtown. I can't reach it from my house." She started thinking and then added, "If I take the train, there's a station in downtown Arvada. Maybe I can ask Andrew to drop me off as a favor to Mom and Dad."

"Good," said Serena. "Spirit is speaking to you. You are solving your problems. Remember to continue to ask Spirit for help when you are having trouble finding answers."

Caroline's stomach began grumbling. "I'd better get back. I left before breakfast, and Mom will be wondering why."

Serena smiled and began walking toward her cave as Caroline ran down the path to the cabin.

Caroline looked at her outfit in the mirror. She wanted to look perfect on this first day of junior high. She was excited but a bit frightened, too. What if people thought she was a dork? She wanted to be a cool girl so badly. She checked her hair once again. She'd decided to wear a headband and let her long hair flow down her back. She had on her new bell bottoms with a peasant top. She checked her watch. With just five minutes to spare, she had to hurry; it was her first time taking the bus to school.

She reached the stop at the top of her street just as the bus pulled up. Caroline lined up behind the other kids and walked up the steps, saying hello to the bus driver. As she looked down the row of seats, it was obvious that the older kids owned the back of the bus. She didn't want to sit in the front with the uncool people. She needed to get as far back as she could. She slowly walked forward, looking for a friendly face. Sarah didn't ride this bus, and Caroline hadn't known who would be on it. Suddenly, a pretty blonde-haired girl said, "Hi." Caroline plopped down next to her. The girl introduced herself as Mindy. She had gone to Vanderhoof. Caroline introduced herself.

"What classes do you have?" Caroline asked.

Mindy pulled out her schedule, and Caroline did the same. They compared schedules and discovered they were in the same English class. They smiled at each other and began chatting about the things each one was nervous about. Mindy was embarrassed because she had gotten a pimple the night before. Caroline sympathized, as she, too, was starting to have breakouts. Her father pointed out anytime she had a spot, which made it worse. Fortunately, her mother had given her some cover-up, and Caroline carefully washed her face every night.

Before they knew it, the bus had pulled up to West Woods. Almost everyone knew the code: They waited until the older kids in the back of the bus got off, and then Caroline and Mindy took their turn. Next, they hunted for their lockers and found them by last name. Caroline was in the middle, but Mindy, whose last name was Thompson, was farther down. As they parted, Caroline said, "I'll see you in English class!"

Caroline scoured the halls for her social studies class and managed to find it just as the bell was about to ring. She looked around for a friendly face. There were a few boys from Vanderhoof, and she saw two girls chatting with each other. They weren't friends with Caroline. She felt her first bout of loneliness. When she saw an empty seat in the middle, she decided to sit there.

As the students waited for the teacher to arrive, Caroline thought about Serena and her guides, quietly asking them to help her through this challenging day. She suddenly felt a bit lighter and breathed long and deep. Then, the teacher arrived, and class started.

She saw Mindy as soon as she walked into English, and she sat beside her. "How's it going so far?" Caroline asked.

"Math was awful," Mindy replied. "The class seemed full of all the awful boys from Vanderhoof. They were disruptive, making understanding what the teacher was saying more difficult. I can already tell this will be my hardest class. What about you?"

"Nothing terrible so far," Caroline said. "I liked my social studies class, though I had only boys from my school. I'm looking forward to my math class this afternoon, as my best friend Sarah is in it. If we study the same things, we can help you." Mindy gave Caroline a big smile. Then, the teacher called the class to order.

After class, it was lunchtime, and the two girls walked into the lunchroom. They had never seen such chaos at school. Kids were talking, laughing, and shouting at other students across the room. Caroline and Mindy went through the lunch line. As they exited, they both looked for someone they knew to sit with. Suddenly, Caroline saw a hand waving. It was

Sarah. "Come this way," Caroline said to Mindy.

They sat with Sarah, who was sitting with another new girl named Tina. After introductions, the four girls began chatting about classes, what everyone had worn, and how nervous they were about school. The time passed quickly, and the girls said goodbye as the next period was about to start. Caroline and Sarah headed to math class. Math was becoming more challenging for Caroline, and she was glad to have her best friend in the class. Sarah wasn't as bright as Gwynn, but she was better at math than Caroline was.

Her first day of junior high came to an end. Caroline had survived and even met some nice girls. Mindy was standing in line to get on the bus, and she waved as Caroline came running up. "Oh, good, I wondered if you'd be riding home on the bus," said Mindy. "I was so afraid I'd be alone."

Caroline smiled at her new friend. "I'll usually be on the bus going home."

"Oh, you don't have any after-school activities? I have dance class on Thursdays," said Mindy.

"Oh, that sounds like fun," said Caroline. "I have piano lessons on Tuesday. I wish I could quit, as I'm not very good. The music is getting harder, and reaching all the chords and getting the fingering right with my small hands is difficult. I much prefer singing or playing my clarinet."

"Oh, will you be in the choir?" asked Mindy.

"No, I'll be in the band. I believe I have that class tomorrow. It'll be fun. Plus, I have gym, which I love."

"I'm not too good at sports," Mindy said.

"I'm certain you're better than you think," said Caroline. "And I'll help you if I can."

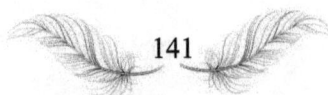

141

The two girls sat together and spent the rest of the ride chatting. The bus arrived at Mindy's stop first. Mindy waved goodbye to Caroline, who watched out the window as Mindy walked down the street. The bus pulled away before Mindy got to her home. The houses looked very nice there. As the bus reached Caroline's stop, her stomach began to hurt. It had been such a great day, and now she had to face her father.

When Caroline walked in the door, her father called out. "Caroline, why don't you come and tell your daddy all about your first day of junior high? Were there lots of girls with bigger boobs than yours? Or less pimples on their face?" Caroline hated this man. Why did he have to be so mean?

She turned and headed straight to her room. She knew she wouldn't get any phone calls. She had told Sarah not to bother calling because she couldn't come to the phone unless her mother was home. After dinner, the phone was usually tied up with Andrew talking to his girlfriend. Caroline had hoped her father would be at Edward's football practice. She lay down on her bed, her stomach growling. It would be hours before dinner, but it wasn't worth being grabbed to get something to eat. She pulled out her books and got busy with homework. Smokey came in and jumped on the bed with Caroline. She petted the cat as she read her social studies book. Smokey's purring always made her feel better.

The next day was tryouts for positions in the band. While Caroline had been first chair in her elementary school, there were now kids from other schools she'd be up against. She was nervous and kept fingering the notes on her clarinet. Her group went through tryouts first, as clarinet players ranked high, along with trumpet players. The teacher called names alphabetically, so Caroline was one of the earlier players. She performed better than anyone else thus far, earning a smile from the teacher. But there were still many students who had to perform. The boy she had always battled with over first chair didn't play his best. Caroline guessed he hadn't practiced much over the summer. But a boy she had never met before played, and he was terrific. When the assignments came out, he won first chair. Caroline was next to him. They shared a music stand, but the boy said nothing to her. He was rather cute with long brown hair. Caroline focused on her teacher and the music. But occasionally, she looked out of the side of her eye at the boy next to her.

During lunch, Caroline reunited with her newly formed group of friends. They discussed their classes, and then Caroline introduced the topic of the boy she sat next to in band class. This sparked an in-depth conversation about the attractive boys they had encountered in their classes or spotted while navigating the school corridors. None of the girls had ever had a boyfriend, but all were anxious to have their first one. They had no idea how to go about it. Caroline said they would have to watch the pretty, popular girls and pointed to a table a few feet away. "Watch those girls, said Caroline. "They'll have boyfriends before the month is out. We'll have to see how they do it." The other girls agreed.

Caroline was happy her mother was picking her up after school. She had tried again to change her lessons from piano to singing and had gotten her mother's typical "We'll see." Caroline mentioned that her friend Mindy was taking dance classes. Could she do that instead? Her mother responded with a flat, "No." Caroline was so frustrated. Her mother never listened to her! She did say that the church choir was after school on Wednesday. Caroline was moving up from the children's choir, which she was excited about. Her mother would pick her up after school for that. Caroline remembered to ask her mother if she could bring her a snack.

Caroline loved choir. The director had selected modern Christian music for the annual Christmas performance. Auditions for a solo were on the horizon, with the director assigning specific songs for the girls and boys to prepare. Caroline was the final person to receive a copy of the sheet music. The director looked at her and asked, "So, you're planning to go up against the older girls for a solo?"

"Yes, sir," Caroline replied.

"It won't be easy," he said. "We have several experienced female soloists."

"I know," said Caroline. "But I still want to try."

She then walked from the auditorium toward the minister's office. Dr. Randolph was an educated minister whom her parents greatly respected. The church secretary was at her desk. Caroline explained that she wanted to meet with the minister. The secretary asked why. "It's private," said Caroline.

"He has someone with him right now," said the secretary.

"Can I make an appointment with him next week?" Caroline asked.

The secretary looked at the calendar. "Yes, he's available."

"Then can you write down that it's an appointment with Caroline Howard?"

"Will your parents be joining you?" the secretary asked.

"No," Caroline replied, leaving the room and heading outside to wait for her mother.

The next day at school, Caroline pulled Sarah aside to tell her that she had made an appointment with her minister to discuss the issues with her father. Sarah was surprised and wondered whether the minister would speak to her parents.

"That's the point," said Caroline. "If he believes me and speaks to my parents, they must listen and do what he says. They can't go against the minister."

"Really?" asked Sarah. "Is he like a priest or something?"

Caroline thought about this for a moment. "I don't know anything about priests, but a Baptist minister is mighty powerful. I don't mean that he has special powers. It's just that what he says, you have to do. He can always find some Bible verse to back up his instructions."

"Is there a verse about not hurting your children?" asked Sarah, whose parents went to church only at Christmas and Easter.

"I don't know, but I intend to find out," Caroline said. With that, the girls rushed off to class.

The week went by quickly, and it was time for her meeting with the minister. Caroline needed to let her mother know she would finish later than usual. She was tired of constantly coming up with lies, but she couldn't tell her mother what she was doing. Caroline told her mother there was an extra practice for people trying out for solos and to come an hour later. Her mother smiled at her daughter and nodded.

When choir practice was over, Caroline walked down to the minister's office. She was very nervous and kept rubbing her sweaty palms against her jeans. The secretary recognized her and asked that she be seated, as the minister was still meeting with someone else. Caroline worriedly looked up at the clock, knowing her time was limited. Five minutes. Ten minutes. Suddenly, the minister's door opened. He shook hands with the couple who was leaving. Then, he looked over at Caroline and invited her in.

Caroline entered the minister's office. It was her first time there. She noticed a picture of Jesus, numerous bookcases, and diplomas on the wall. Her mother, a leader in church committees, had visited often.

Pastor Randolph asked Caroline to sit in the chair before his desk. Then, he sat in his oversized brown leather chair and asked, "How can I help you, Caroline?"

"Dr. Randolph, I have been struggling with a problem at home, and a good friend suggested that I come and talk with you and that you might give me some advice."

The minister smiled and said, "Go on."

Caroline looked down at her hands. How could she tell this man about the awful things her father did? She sent a mental message to Anne and Serena. *Please help me.* "Dr. Randolph, I don't know if you know, but my father drinks a lot. And when I come home from school, if no one else is at home, he grabs me, and he puts his hands . . ." She couldn't finish. It was just too awful to say.

Dr. Randolph coughed and then said. "I see. You don't have to go into graphic detail, Caroline. I can tell you are very troubled about what is happening with your father, and I am saddened to hear about this. Have you spoken to your mother?"

"I've tried, Dr. Randolph," Caroline responded. "But she doesn't want to hear what I have to say."

"That's not unusual, Caroline. No one wants to hear that their husband is misbehaving," said Dr. Randolph.

"But how am I supposed to get him to stop if my mother won't make him?" Tears welled up in Caroline's eyes as she remembered the words *Howards don't cry.* "I don't know what to do," she said in a shaking voice.

"That's why I've come to you. Can you make him stop?"

Dr. Randolph clasped his hands as if to pray and looked Caroline in the eye. "I will speak to your father about appropriate behavior with a daughter. I'm afraid that's the best I can do."

Caroline suddenly remembered what she had said to Sarah. "Isn't there a scripture in the Bible that says, 'Thy father shall not touch his daughter's private parts?'"

After some silence, Dr Randolph coughed again and said, "No, Caroline. There is not a verse in the Bible that speaks of this. But God tells us that children are a gift, and we must protect and care for gifts from God."

Caroline asked quietly, "Do you think that's enough to get my father to stop?"

The minister looked down at his hands. "I wish I could promise you, Caroline, but I can't. Your parents must choose to be good and loving to their children. I can't force them. I can only advise."

At that, Caroline began to cry. She felt trapped in a cage like a dog that anyone could abuse.

Dr. Randolph pushed a box of tissues in front of Caroline. "Let's pray, shall we?" he said. "Our dearest heavenly Father, please help your child Caroline, who is asking for your assistance in solving a big problem at home. She is a good girl who comes to church, sings in the choir, and honors her father and mother. Help her father to understand how fortunate he is to have a precious daughter like Caroline. Protect her from evil and bring only goodness into her life. Amen."

Caroline attempted to stifle her tears and made eye contact with the minister. She recognized that he had put forth his utmost effort, but she remained uncertain as to whether it was sufficient. Glancing at the wall clock, she noted the time. *Oh, no, Mom will be here.* She jumped up and said, "I have to go!"

"Caroline," said Dr. Randolph. "I will ask your parents to come in and meet with me. Is that alright with you?"

Caroline realized she had opened a door, and on the other side was either more pain or freedom. She couldn't control the outcome. Like the minister, she could only pray. "OK," she said in a small voice and then walked out the office door.

After Caroline got home, finished homework, and practiced her solo at the piano in the living room, she sat on her bed thinking about the prayer the minister had said. Would it work? Would the evil leave her life? She could only wait—and pray.

About a week later, as Caroline sat in her room eagerly awaiting dinner, she heard the door slam open. Then, in a loud and angry tone she rarely used, Caroline's mother called her name. Caroline headed out her door. Her parents were sitting in the living room, her father in the blue chair and her mother on the plaid sofa. "Caroline, we have just returned from a meeting with Dr. Randolph. What are these stories you told him about your father?"

Caroline began to shake and looked at her father. Was she too old to be whipped with the belt? He had the look in his eyes that she feared. She turned to her mother and said, "I've told you I don't like my father touching me. You've ignored me, and he continues to do it. I prayed and heard God say I should speak to Dr. Randolph."

"I am certain God never told you to tell Dr. Randolph such lies, Caroline," said her mother.

"They aren't lies!" she exclaimed.

"You are never to repeat what you said outside this house. Do you understand, Caroline?" asked her mother.

With tears in her eyes, Caroline nodded, not looking at her father. Then, she left the living room, re-barred her door, and went into the closet, where she cried. Her mother called her for dinner, but Caroline didn't leave the closet until the house was quiet. She knew danger would increase, and she had no idea how to make life safe.

# Korea Calling

HE HATED THE FREEZING nights in Korea. The 3rd Battalion, 1st Marines were assigned to X Corps and landed on Blue Beach at Inchon on September 15, 1950, breaking through the smoke and seawalls that guarded the area. Bill was glad he wasn't a foot soldier. Instead, this time, he was inside the new M-26 Pershing tank. He had trained on the gunnery during dry runs onboard the ship heading to Korea. He had practiced setting up firing missions, elevating and lowering the gun barrel, and rotating the turret, working as a team with his loader and best friend, Dick Martin. The Marine Corps wanted each unit to understand this new weapon fully.

As he lay on the cold hull, Bill tried getting comfortable. He followed the "layer up" order and wore all his clothing under the pile-lined parka. But nothing could make the tank softer for sleeping or make him feel safer. As required, all the tanks were organized in a circle to protect them from an assault by a stealth squad of North Korean People's Army, or NPKA, soldiers aided by the Chinese.

As the tank resounded with a chorus of snoring and intermittent artillery fire, Bill's mind wandered back to the past. The Howard family had relocated to Kansas City during Bill's high school years. He had enrolled at Paseo High School but had prioritized using his handsome appearance to pursue romantic interests and engage in sports, neglecting his studies. He remained irritating to his father, Spec, who now worked for the Kansas City Star. World

War II was part of daily life, and a photo of his oldest brother, Pete, hung in the living room. Pete was the family hero, as his naval unit had served at Pearl Harbor, D-Day, and the North Africa invasion. Bill wanted to fight and, at 17, had begged his mother to sign the papers allowing him to enlist. It was 1945, and Bill wanted to join the Navy like Pete, but the only military branch taking recruits was the Marine Corps. He signed up. Bill met Dick during basic training at Camp Pendleton.

While basic was hard, they loved nights away from the base, drinking and seeking gals ready for fun. When World War II ended, Bill returned to Missouri to find a job. He earned a GED during his service and wanted to attend college. However, the admissions officer made it clear that Bill lacked the essential educational qualifications for success in college, especially considering the numerous other veterans with superior credentials. Bill felt like he was competing against every war veteran as he relentlessly sought employment. Unfortunately, living at home provided no solace, as his father seized every opportunity to belittle him.

His diligent search led to a position selling insurance at an office in North Kansas City. He began attending a local Southern Baptist church. Growing up, Bill had participated in the Methodist church, but he liked the Baptist minister and what he preached each Sunday morning. At church, Bill met Patsy, a sweet farm girl from eastern Colorado. She had moved to Kansas City and found a good job working for a diamond importer. Bill chased easier girls on Saturday nights and sat next to Patsy at Sunday church.

Then, the North Koreans overran the South, and Bill still belonged to the Marines. The generals called in the 1st Marine Division under Colonel Thomas Ridge in August 1950. Bill sent a letter to Dick suggesting they ask for a transfer to the tank division, thinking it would be safer. They had heard horror stories about people burning alive inside the tank and often wondered if it was the right choice. Good luck assigned them to the same tank, which the unit called Ol' Thunder.

After the chilly night, Bill's unit held a rear point coming out of Hagarui-ri, moving south to Koto-ri. They drove through Hell Fire Valley, where bodies and broken vehicles abounded. As they bounced along, Bill tried not to think about what was underneath the tank.

While he appreciated the technical aspects of the gunner's job, sighting in was not easy. Plus, the mountainous terrain of Korea made landing a good shot difficult. The cold affected equipment, and he couldn't guarantee the gun would release properly when called for. He grew anxious about his shots hitting American troops.

During the thick of battle, Bill thought of nothing but the job. He never allowed death—either his or those of other Marines—to enter his mind. But when they came to a halt and ate the lousy chow, Bill would smoke cigarettes and wonder what Patsy was doing back home.

He never thought much about what kind of life he desired. He wanted a good job, a modest house, perhaps a family, and time for drinks with friends—not much more.

But then his head would start to hurt. It was always in the spot where the board had connected with his skull. Nothing could make it feel better. No booze to dull the pain. He would get angry, which Dick never understood. And Bill couldn't explain it. He never wanted to seem weak. Bill hated weakness. He'd laugh at ol' Spec whenever the man tried to tame him. At times, Bill found himself admiring the enemy. They tenaciously entrenched themselves on the hillside, incessantly firing upon the American forces until death silenced their trigger fingers.

He would be glad to go home. Bill didn't want to defend trucks full of injured soldiers from enemy attacks anymore. He never wanted to smell shit or death again. He would make an easy life full of everything he enjoyed. Everyone would march to his orders. And he would always be warm.

# Showdown

*T*HE HOUSE WAS OPPRESSIVE, filled with rage. Caroline hated coming home after school. Nothing had changed in her father's treatment; in fact, it had grown worse. He delighted in adding new degradations, such as pulling on her nipples. Caroline stayed in her room. She begged her mother for a phone in her bedroom. All she received was an angry stare.

Caroline knew she had to put an end to the abuse. She retreated to her closet and attempted to connect with her spirit guides. She sought assistance from the chief and Anne, struggling to employ her third eye as she had been taught. Her anxiety made it challenging to attain the serene state required to access the spirit realm. She would breathe deeply, counting *one, two, three*, up to ten.

Suddenly, one afternoon, Anne appeared. She wore her typical attire from the Victorian era. Caroline practically cried to see her as she knelt in the closet in front of the woman. "Anne, you came," whispered Caroline.

"I am always here," said her guide. "But reaching into the spirit realm takes practice, as you have found."

"Anne, what do I do to stop my father and change my mother's feelings toward me?" begged Caroline.

"You will not succeed without the help of an adult whom your parents respect or fear. I know you tried the pastor at your church, which was wise and should have worked. I'm sorry it did not. But you have the answer. All you must do is reach out to this person," Anne said.

Caroline thought about this. Whom did her parents fear and respect? She thought of names. Her parents didn't have many close friends. Her mother's were all from church, and her father's were from work. These were not people who would help. She didn't feel comfortable talking to her friends' parents like Sarah suggested, and approaching her parents would increase their anger. Caroline hesitated, aware that her mother would never forgive her if she discussed this with Grandma Andersen. Then, a sudden realization struck her like an electric shock: Grandmother Howard!

Anne smiled at Caroline. "I knew you would think of an answer," she said.

Caroline replied, "How do I let her know?"

"Can you not use that device, a telephone, I believe it's called, or perhaps write a letter?" asked Anne.

"I think a letter. But I need her to do more than call my parents. They would hang up the phone and turn around and punish me," said Caroline.

"No, I agree. You need the strength of action. Would your grandmother come to your home?" asked Anne.

"It has been a long time since she came here," said Caroline, wistfully remembering the happy visits from her grandmother before she went to school. Together, they had watched her grandmother's favorite soap operas and old black-and-white musicals as her grandmother told her stories about the great actors. "I'll write to her and ask her to come," said Caroline. Anne smiled and began to fade away.

Caroline climbed out from the closet, sat at her tiny desk, and took out a piece of lined school paper and a ballpoint pen. Slowly, using her best cursive handwriting, she began her letter:

*Dearest Grandmother Howard,*

*I am sorry to write you this letter, as I am afraid you will be ashamed of me. I have nowhere to turn. My father is doing the wrong things. I am scared to write exactly what he does to me, but I know they are things that fathers aren't supposed to do to daughters. I went to the pastor of our church, and he spoke with my parents, but that just made them angry. Now, Daddy is worse, and Mother barely speaks to me.*

*Grandmother, please come here and make my father stop hurting me and my mother not be mad at me. Will you do this for me?*

*Sincerely, your granddaughter,*

*Caroline Howard*

Caroline went to the mailbox outside of school during lunch the next day. Sarah went with her. Under school rules, they weren't to leave the grounds, but this was just outside the perimeter. Caroline and Sarah safely reached the mailbox and returned to the schoolyard before the bell rang.

Caroline went to Sarah's house after school. While savoring peanut butter cookies, the girls contemplated various scenarios regarding Caroline's grandmother's actions and how her parents would respond. Later that night, as Caroline lay in bed, she thought about running away if Grandmother Howard didn't arrive. She recalled mentioning this to Sarah, who tightly held Caroline's hand. "No, I don't want you to leave," she said.

"I feel it might be my best choice," said Caroline.

"But where would you go?" asked Sarah.

"I believe going to the farm would be the best choice. I know my grandparents would protect me."

"But how would you get there?"

"I assume I can take a bus. It won't be just one, but I'm sure the people at the station will tell me how to reach the farm," answered Caroline.

"But how would you get to the bus station?" Sarah asked.

"That's the biggest problem. I could get Andrew to drive me. He pays so little attention to what happens at home that he might think Mom arranged the trip."

"Maybe we could think of a place close to the station and have him drop us off there," suggested Sarah.

"But what about my suitcase?" asked Caroline.

"You would probably have to take only items that fit in two backpacks. We would each carry a backpack, and then you would take them both to your grandparents," said Sara.

"But how would you get back home?" Caroline asked.

"I'd call my parents," Sarah said quietly, lowering her eyes and staring at her hands.

"You'd get in big trouble," said Caroline, reaching for her friend's shoulder.

"It would be worth it," Sarah said with a smile. The girls embraced to seal their pact. Caroline left Sarah's house with the assurance that there was a sanctuary waiting for her.

While waiting for a response from Grandmother Howard, Caroline tried to fill her days with pleasant activities. She practiced her singing and clarinet in preparation for the concerts at school and church. She carefully avoided her father, which meant staying late at school whenever possible, waiting for her mother to pick her up, taking the regular bus home, rushing to her room, and blocking the door. She was often amazed at how her brothers could go on with their lives without seemingly noticing anything about Caroline's torture. Sadly, they had never been close. She was envious of their lives: Edward was off playing sports and hanging with the popular kids, while Andrew was working, dating, and spending time with buddies. Andrew had disappointed their father by dropping out of sports and taking up smoking. Caroline often wondered if he did things to make their father mad.

Then, Caroline would remember what she was doing. She was on a more dangerous path. But it had been over a month with no word from Grandmother Howard.

Caroline and Sarah brainstormed while baking brownies in Sarah's spacious kitchen. Caroline admired the kitchen; it featured green appliances, wallpaper adorned with green and red apples, and delightful cream lace curtains adorning the windows. The lace reminded Caroline of Anne. While Caroline didn't want to leave home, she knew there was no other option. In her mind, she began to say goodbye to people and things she loved, like Smokey. Caroline couldn't bring the cat to the farm, as there were already a lot of cats there. She hoped Andrew would take care of him. She knew the anger her mother would harbor because of her actions, but Caroline was determined to stop her father no matter the cost.

Caroline worked to raise the money she would need for a bus ticket. She snuck in a phone call one Sunday while her mother sewed and her father slept. The woman on the phone at the bus depot told Caroline that she could reach a small town near the farm. It would require riding a local bus from Denver and making many stops, but Caroline didn't care. The price was 55 dollars. Caroline asked her mother if she was old enough to babysit, and her mother consented. She designed flyers, dropped them off at neighbors with small children, and placed one on the church bulletin board. The approach worked! She received two calls and started her babysitting business. She babysat children almost every Friday and Saturday night. While she missed sleepovers with her friends and dancing to the latest 45s, survival was more important.

Hidden in her closet was a metal Danish cookie box containing her babysitting money. Edward was known to steal money for the batting cage or other activities with his friends, as he couldn't be bothered to work. Caroline checked the amount weekly and knew she was getting close.

She went to Sarah's after school one day and consulted the calendar as to the date she should leave. The girls had decided to go to the pinball arcade within two blocks of the bus station. Sarah would say she was going with Caroline and Andrew—the same lie Caroline would tell her mother. She was certain Andrew would go along with her lie as long as he only dropped them off. Caroline thought she should have a bit extra to pay for gas.

In November, the girls chose the first Saturday in December for Caroline's escape plan. Caroline connected with Anne, shared her plan, and received encouragement. Anne assured her that help was on the way, and Caroline nodded in response. As Anne faded away, Caroline lay on a blanket in her closet, contemplating Serena's cave as a potential sanctuary. She knew reaching it alone would be challenging but worth it. She decided to keep it as a backup plan in case her grandparents sent her back. Smokey, the cat that knew her hiding spot well, joined Caroline in the closet. They shared a comforting moment before Caroline drifted off to sleep.

# Retribution

NOW WAS FALLING IN Arvada as Thanksgiving approached. Caroline looked out her bedroom window and wondered if the weather would affect her plans. She was reluctant to venture into the

mountains, and locating Serena in the current season seemed daunting. Nevertheless, her determination to halt her father's humiliating actions remained unwavering.

Caroline was getting dressed for school when the phone rang. She didn't bother trying to reach it. Her friends knew not to bother calling. It was probably for one of her brothers.

She added a green sweater to her outfit as the DJ on the radio station said it would be in the 40s today. Suddenly, her mother was standing in her room. "Did you call Grandmother Howard?" her mother asked loudly.

While her mother had caught Caroline off guard, she could answer truthfully. "No, Mother. I know that I'm not to make long-distance calls without permission."

"Well, your grandmother, driven by Aunt Peggy, is on her way to the house. Do you know anything about this?" asked her mother.

Caroline responded, "No, I had no idea. But isn't it wonderful that they're coming to visit?"

"It is not," said her mother. "They will have to sleep in your room, and your aunt will have to sleep on the cot, which she will hate. I don't know what I will do with you."

"Don't worry, Mom. I can sleep in my sleeping bag and make everyone cozy in my room. Will they be here when I get home from school?"

"Probably," her mother responded as she walked from the room. "Strip the sheets from your bed," she yelled.

*Gladly,* thought Caroline. She couldn't help but smile. Help was on the way, just as Anne had said.

Caroline finished her chores and ran to the bus stop. When she reached school, she found Sarah and excitedly told her what was happening at home. The best friends hugged warmly and laughed about the "cavalry showing up." Sarah made Caroline promise to call and tell her everything that happened. Caroline smiled, saying, "This might be the one time I will happily run to the phone."

As Caroline impatiently awaited the final school bell, the day seemed to stretch endlessly. She squirmed with anticipation, contemplating whether she should prepare a suitcase as a precaution in case Grandmother Howard and Aunt Peggy decided on a sudden departure. Given her parents' reactions, she felt it wise to be prepared to join them.

When the bus reached Caroline's stop, she broke the rules by jumping up and running to the door before the vehicle came to a halt. She apologized to the driver but explained that her grandmother had just arrived. Caroline started down the steps, praying to God to help her stay strong and to keep her family from punishing her. *Maybe they'll finally understand that I did what I had to do.*

She ran down the steps and headed home as quickly as the snowy streets allowed. She sent a message to Serena as she opened the front door: *Please, please, help my grandmother to help me.* Caroline pushed the door open slowly and lightly walked into the living room. She removed her boots, listening for voices. From the dining room came the sound of adults, and she could tell it wasn't a pleasant conversation. As she walked toward the room, her father said, "Here comes the troublemaker."

*Shit, he's going to lie, and I have to call him out. How I hate that man.* Caroline entered the room, searching for her grandmother's face. She saw it and walked to where her grandmother sat, a glass of iced tea in front of her. She looked at her Aunt Peggy, who had an animated expression. Across the table was her mother; the anger on her face made Caroline gag. Her father had the nasty smile he wore whenever he abused her.

"Grandmother, I'm so happy to see you," Caroline said as she leaned down to kiss the lightly wrinkled cheek.

"Caroline, it's good to see you, too. Why don't you pull up a chair next to me and join the conversation?" said Grandmother Howard firmly.

Caroline grabbed an extra chair, moved it close to her grandmother, and sat down. She turned to her aunt. "It's so nice to see you too, Aunt Peggy."

"Well, Caroline, after receiving your letter, Mother and I felt it was best to come here. It's quite a long drive, but your grandmother was determined to come, "said Aunt Peggy.

"It seems, Caroline, that you have once again dreamed up some ridiculous story to tell your grandmother," said her father slickly. "You are getting too old for this kind of behavior. We need to toughen the rules to get you in line."

"William," said his mother, "Caroline didn't tell us any story, as I've already explained to you. My understanding is that you have been hurting the child, and no one would make you stop." She looked straight at Patsy. "I have come to ensure this home is safe for all my grandchildren. By the way, where are Andrew and Edward?"

Patsy replied, "Edward is at football practice, and Andrew is at work. Edward will be home by dinnertime. Andrew will be here sometime later this evening."

"Perhaps Peggy and I should settle in and rest until dinnertime. We can take up this conversation after we eat," announced Grandmother Howard. She and Aunt Peggy got up from the table. Caroline jumped up with them and began to lead them into her room. Grandmother Howard asked her son, "Why don't you get our bags?" Then, she followed Caroline into her room.

Caroline could tell that her mother had been in the room, cleaning it up. Fortunately, she'd hidden all her precious items, like the money, in the closet.

Grandmother Howard sat down on Caroline's twin bed. Aunt Peggy walked in and looked around. "Where am I sleeping?" she asked tiredly.

"I'm sorry, Aunt Peggy. I only have a twin bed in my room," said Caroline. "I was hoping Mother would give you the boys' room, as there are two twin beds up there, but it's a big mess, and the bathroom is gross. I believe Mother is bringing in a cot for you."

Her aunt stared at Caroline.

"I'm so sorry, Aunt Peggy," Caroline added.

Her grandmother said, "Peggy is a Howard. She can tough it out for a night or two." She turned to her daughter. "We will stay at a hotel with a nice room on the way home so you can get a good night's sleep."

At that moment, her father walked in with the women's luggage. "How long are you planning to stay?" he asked rudely.

His mother looked him in the eye. "As long as it takes to ensure my granddaughter is safe, William."

Her father turned and walked out the door without saying anything else.

As her aunt began to unpack, Grandmother Howard turned to Caroline and said, "Why don't you sit down next to me and tell me what you didn't say in your letter?"

Caroline looked at her grandmother's lovely face, and tears began to pool in her eyes. "Oh, Grandmother, it's so embarrassing to say," she said.

Her aunt responded, "Has he touched you in your privates?"

Caroline drew up her legs and held them tightly. She had begged them to come, but how could she tell them what her father had done?

Her grandmother reached over and drew the girl's head into her lap. "Caroline, nothing your father has done is your fault. Did you tell your mother what he was doing?" she asked quietly.

"Yes, Grandmother," Caroline said softly.

"And she did nothing?" her grandmother asked.

"Yes," she whispered. "And then I went to the pastor of the church."

"A Southern Baptist church," her aunt snorted.

"Peggy, it won't help to disparage her parents' religion," said Grandmother Howard. She looked down at Caroline. "Your church believes a father can do as he wants to a daughter or a wife. I don't like this religion because I don't feel it's safe for women. But for now, let's focus on what happened to you. Have you told anyone everything your father has done?"

"No," said Caroline. "I've told my mother, my pastor, and my best friend Sarah some of what my dad does. But not everything. It's so gross."

"I'm sure it is, Caroline. But to stop it, I must know what your father has done."

While Aunt Peggy unpacked both ladies' things, Caroline told her grandmother the entire story. When finished, Caroline cried as she never had before while her grandmother stroked her back. Patsy knocked on the door to tell them dinner would be ready in ten minutes. Grandmother Howard and Aunt Peggy just looked at Patsy with eyes full of anger.

Grandmother Howard said, "Let's clean ourselves up. It's always good to look your best before going into battle."

Caroline went to the bathroom and washed her face, while the woman changed their clothes and freshened their makeup. Caroline stood waiting as they readied themselves. With a nod from Grandmother Howard, they walked into the dining room. Edward had arrived home and was quite surprised to see his grandmother and aunt at the table. Grandmother Howard walked over and gave Edward a big hug. She then sat and waited to see if Bill would say a prayer. Bill turned to Edward and asked him to give the blessing. Edward was surprised and stumbled through a few words. Patsy then began to pass the food.

After they filled their plates and started eating, Grandmother Howard turned to Edward and asked him all about school and sports. Edward always shone when the light was on him. Throughout the meal, he regaled his grandmother with stories of his prowess. At one point, Grandmother turned to Bill and said, "What has happened to your table manners, William? You eat like a pig."

Bill just looked at his mother and smiled with food in his teeth. His mother shook her head and turned back to Edward.

After the meal, Edward stood, embraced his grandmother, and expressed his gratitude for her visit. His grandmother briefly held his hand and conveyed her love and pride, saying, "Remember, Edward, to not only be a strong man but to also be kind." The boy nodded in acknowledgment and then retreated to his room.

Patsy began to clear the table, and Aunt Peggy got up and said, "I'll take care of the dishes, Patsy. I believe Mother would like to talk to you and Bill." Patsy sat back down at the table, Bill went to get his cigarettes, and Caroline looked at her grandmother.

"Caroline, normally, I prefer to speak to your parents privately," said Grandmother Howard. "But I believe you should be here as we talk. Then, there won't be any confusion as to what is said."

She continued: "William, Patsy, I am very disturbed by what Caroline has told me."

Patsy interrupted. "Kathryn, Caroline has a tendency . . ."

"I am not finished. I do not doubt that what Caroline has told me is true. I know this because I know you, William. Sadly, everything she has told me, I know you are capable of doing. I am sickened to think my son would abuse his beautiful daughter in such a way. I am here to ensure no one hurts Caroline again. She must know that if you touch her inappropriately, she can call me. If you cannot raise a beautiful, talented girl like Caroline in love and safety, I will bring her to live with me. Is this clear?"

Bill began his horrible cackling. Caroline shivered. "You think you can come into my home after my daughter has made up a bunch of ridiculous shit and tell me what to do, Mother? It's not as if you were a great mother. You let Dad do whatever he wanted to me. And now you'll ride some high horse and give me orders? Go home, Mother."

"William, I don't deny that I made mistakes when you were growing up. I should have stopped your father from ever hurting you. I can't change the past. I was weak. But I'm not the same person I was then. And I won't watch another child in my family be hurt by a parent."

Bill continued to cackle as he walked to the garage and grabbed a cold beer. He walked back through the kitchen, where his sister washed dishes, and flicked his beer tab at her. He sat back down and took a big swig from the can. "You are a silly old woman, Mother. You think you're still in charge of this family, but you're not in charge of me. I do what I want in my home." Bill looked Patsy in the eye as he spoke, daring her to say something.

Grandmother Howard watched the interaction and responded. "From what you are saying, William, you intend to continue treating Caroline however you like. If that is the case, I will leave here tomorrow. And I will take Caroline with me."

At that, Patsy cried out, "No! No one is taking my daughter out of my house. I'm sorry that Caroline has made up these stories and upset everyone. I'm certain she has learned the ramifications of her actions." Patsy stared at Caroline.

Grandmother Howard fixed her deep brown eyes—the same ones Caroline had inherited—on Patsy. "I am very disappointed, Patsy, to learn that my granddaughter came to you for help, and you continue claiming she is lying rather than believing her and stopping your husband from hurting your daughter. You expect me to leave this vulnerable young girl here, where she's not safe? Patsy, I'm not that type of grandmother, and I'm certain your mother would share the same sentiment."

Patsy audibly caught her breath.

"I'm tired of this conversation," said Bill. "Caroline, go to your room. We'll discuss your punishment later. Mother, I think you and Peggy should leave tomorrow. I need another beer." He began to get up.

His mother stood and cried out, "Sit down, William!" As she did, the light shadow behind her began to darken and grow. Caroline watched in amazement as her grandmother rose in size, and her voice deepened. "William Howard, I accuse you of harming your children!" Her voice filled the house, drawing Edward from his bedroom to peek in, his eyes wide. The room continued to darken as Grandmother's shadow and voice grew deeper and louder. "The universe demands that you cease your unmanly behavior and respect the women of your home!"

Bill stared at his mother and began to shake. "No, Mother," he whispered.

"I condemn your behavior and the choices you have made. These are stains on the record of your life, and to remove the negative karma, you must ask your daughter's forgiveness and amend your ways. Otherwise, you will return once more to a life full of pain and hardship!"

Patsy's mouth hung open as she thought, *Is Bill's mother a witch?* Caroline stared at her grandmother and wondered who this woman was. Edward ran back upstairs and hid under the covers in his bed. Aunt Peggy stood in the doorway for a few minutes and then returned to the kitchen to finish up.

Bill nodded at his mother, who started to diminish in size. The room's lighting returned to normal. Grandmother then faced Patsy and explained, "I'm not a witch, but a goddess trained in understanding God, angels, and luminous beings. I don't adhere to earthly religions but follow spiritual teachings predating figures like Muhammad and Jesus. Your daughter shares my gifts and communicates with the spirit world. She will remain under my protection. I cannot make this a happy home for the children who live here, but I can make it a safe one. And I can ensure that Caroline continues to nurture her gifts. I shall call her regularly and expect her to answer all my questions truthfully. If I must travel here again, it will be to take her home with me for good.

"Now, I shall retire to bed. Peggy and I will leave tomorrow so long as I am satisfied there will be no more problems. And I wish to see Andrew before I go. Make certain that happens, Patsy." Grandmother turned and headed toward Caroline's room. Caroline hurried after her with Aunt Peggy strolling behind.

Her grandmother lay on her bed. Caroline sat beside her, her smaller hand in her grandmother's larger, softer, wrinklier one. Smokey, the cat, came walking in and jumped up on the bed, curling up next to Grandmother Howard and purring loudly.

"Grandmother," said Caroline, "were you ever planning to tell me about your special powers?"

Her grandmother breathed deeply, her lovely white curly hair spreading on the pillow. "I don't know, Caroline. It truly depended on what happened. As we drove here, I prayed to God to help me do whatever was needed to improve your life. If showing my powers was called for, I would do it. But it drains me quite a lot." She closed her eyes.

Caroline wondered aloud, "Did my father always know about your gifts?"

"He has seen them a few times, though not quite to this degree. His older brothers might have told him something, as they saw my abilities when I dealt with their father. That was when I had to grow my knowledge and seek greater power. He was dangerous, and I had to free the boys from him."

"Did he try to hurt you?" Caroline asked.

"Yes, he had a gun and threatened to kill me if I tried to leave him. Men were like that then."

Aunt Peggy coughed loudly.

"And still are today. That is why you need to stand in your power, Caroline. And to know that there are good men in the world. They are just harder to find. Now, let me sleep."

Caroline and Smokey remained with Grandmother Howard throughout the night. Caroline felt anxious about what the house would be like once her grandmother left. When she woke up the next day, Caroline discovered that her grandmother and aunt were no longer in the bedroom. She hurried out and found them seated in the dining room with Andrew. He was laughing, as was Grandmother. Caroline slipped into a chair and listened to them talk about Andrew's girlfriend. Grandmother Howard said she was sorry she wouldn't get a chance to meet her. From the kitchen, Caroline's father yelled, "She's a damn Catholic!"

Aunt Peggy cried back, "So am I. Keep quiet unless you have something positive to say."

Caroline's mother came to the doorway and saw Caroline, who stiffened as her mother brought out a bowl of oatmeal to eat. Caroline finished breakfast and then went to her room to prepare for school. She had missed the bus, but she thought her aunt would take her as they left town. Caroline still wondered if she should ask to go with them.

Her grandmother entered the room as Caroline finished fixing her Farrah Fawcett hairdo. "You have such beautiful hair, Caroline. Just like your father."

Caroline turned to her grandmother with a smile. "You are always so kind to me. Don't you think it would be better if I went and lived with you?"

Her grandmother closed her eyes and, when she opened them, replied, "No, Caroline. Your place is still here. I know you are worried, but I believe your relationship with your parents will improve. And you have other things to accomplish here. But I have told your father that you must come and see me for a week every year. And I love your letters, so please write to me, and I will reply." Tears welled in their eyes as they held each other's hands, feeling the universe's strength pass between them. "We will finish packing and then drop you off at school. Please don't worry, Caroline. It's not good for your health. Remember what Serena and I have taught you. Use those skills. Listen to the universe." Her grandmother pulled the girl into her arms and hugged her as if she would never let go.

# A Secret Exposed

*T*O CAROLINE'S SURPRISE, LIFE at home did change. Her father never apologized for what he had done, but he never touched her again.

Caroline remembered her grandmother saying that his actions were his karma. Her father drank less and still spent time at Edward's practices and games. Andrew graduated from high school and, much to her parents' dismay, decided he didn't want to attend college.

Instead, he secured a job selling auto parts to local automotive shops, and it quickly became a job he loved. Eventually, he made the move to Chicago to work for a larger company with a more extensive sales team. Caroline's mother was devastated by his departure, and Caroline sympathized with her. In an effort to console her mother, Caroline tried to be more considerate and noticed a positive response in their relationship.

Summer came, and Caroline begged her parents to go to the mountains. Edward had a break from baseball season, so the remaining family headed up to their regular cabin by the Blue River. Colorado had received more than the average snowfall during winter, and the runoff kept the river running high. Fishing was more challenging, but Caroline's dad and brother still went out daily. Caroline's mother had started cross-stitching and was working on a cover for the piano bench. Caroline asked to go for a walk, and her mother nodded. Caroline ran to her rock and began to sing a new song she often heard on the radio.

Some say, "Love. It is a river
That drowns the tender reed"
Some say, "Love. It is a razor
That leaves your soul to bleed"


Some say, "Love. It is a hunger
An endless aching need"
I say, "Love. It is a flower
And you its only seed"


"It seems a long time since you were here singing one of your pretty songs," said a voice instantly recognizable to Caroline.

"Serena! You're here," she cried out. Caroline ran over as if to hug the beautiful nymph but stopped herself. Serena reached her hand out and grasped Caroline's shoulder. Serena's hand was large and cold but soft like Caroline's grandmother's.

"It is good to see you," Serena said. "I believe you have much to tell me. Why don't we walk to my cave?"

Caroline was excited to see the place where Serena lived. It was a long climb up the mountain. They were just about to the tree line when Caroline thought she could see an opening. The trees were old at this altitude, but their shadows spread like a curtain to camouflage it.

"Come inside," said Serena.

Caroline's eyes grew round as she looked at the multi-colored skins hanging on wooden racks and a large piece of furniture that perhaps was a loom. Amidst the cave's dimly lit interior, a treasure trove of antique books adorned the surroundings, their weathered pages echoing with the whispers of history. Amidst this literary labyrinth, a massive wooden bedstead loomed in the distance, resembling something out of a forgotten legend.

Guiding Caroline through the cavern's shadows, Serena ushered her toward a forlorn hearth. Uttering unfamiliar incantations, she conjured forth a dancing flame from the ancient logs. Wooden benches, draped with the hides of creatures long gone, offered a semblance of comfort, and Serena gestured toward a more modest one. Serena sat on a larger bench as befitted her height. She asked Caroline to tell her everything that had happened.

As Caroline looked down, rubbing her hand across the soft pelts, she explained everything that had happened. The nymph sat still, listening, and rose only to pour cold, fresh water into red pottery cups. When Caroline finished, Serena told her she had done well. "God gave you a difficult challenge. You found a solution that few your age could have. Your actions tell me it's time to train you on more advanced skills. How long will you be here?"

"Just for a week," Caroline said.

"That gives us little time. Our first task is for you to learn how to find the cave and hunt for food."

Caroline was surprised. "Why do you want me to hunt?" she asked.

"Because you must know how to survive here in case you come and I am not around."

"Are you going somewhere?" Caroline asked in a panicked voice.

"I have no plans to leave this place, but the universe constantly changes, and you never know what might happen. It is best to plan."

Caroline returned to the cave each day for the week. Serena guided her along diverse paths to their hidden spot, educating her about edible plants and showcasing her traps, even demonstrating the art of animal skinning— a task Caroline didn't relish but endured without complaint. Serena began to teach Caroline some simple magic, such as starting fires. Also, she showed Caroline a book full of different animals and the types of messages they brought.

"Your spirit guides may speak to you directly when you sleep or enter a trance. But they also may send you a message through the animals," explained Serena. "You must be aware of the different ways the spirit world communicates with the living world. When you leave here, you must practice listening by finding different places that are easy for you to hear."

Caroline knew she could go into her closet, but she didn't have a place outside to listen. In their backyard was a large elm tree. She thought that might be an excellent place to hear messages and gave herself that task upon returning home.

The week flew by. Caroline was surprised at how long her mother allowed her to be alone, away from the cabin, but she never said a word. Caroline had breakfast, went to Serena's, and was home by mid-afternoon. She tried to help her mother with dinner, but she could only set the table and fill the glasses with iced tea. Edward and her father talked about the problems fishing with the river running so high, so they didn't have the usual trout dinners, which Caroline didn't mind. When the week was up, Caroline didn't want to leave the beautiful mountains. How wonderful it would be to live here all year, watching the seasons change, warming herself at a fire wrapped in the soft skins, hunting for food when needed, and working to receive messages from the birds and mammals. Caroline wasn't afraid of missing

Serena, as she knew how to speak to her spirit-to-spirit. She was excited to write to her Grandmother Howard, sharing all she had learned. And maybe next year, she would meet a cute boy to like.

Caroline sat in the back seat as they drove back to Arvada. While she looked out the window, she saw a small group of bighorn sheep. When the largest male looked up, she could hear the message he sent: "You're ready for new challenges. Charge ahead."

As the heat of the summer began to dissipate, Caroline went into eighth grade, while Edward started his senior year. Caroline joined her parents at Edward's sporting events. She knew her father expected Edward to get a sports scholarship, and they were confident he would attend college.

Andrew called his mother regularly from Chicago and surprised Caroline by asking to speak with her. They talked about school and music. Caroline was now first chair in the band, and while she couldn't take vocal classes as well, she could sing at church. Caroline had no desire to continue attending their Southern Baptist church. Given all she had learned from Serena and her grandmother, she didn't see any purpose in attending a Christian church. But her mother still insisted, and as long as Caroline could sing in the choir, she put up with the service. Now, however, she sat at the back of the hall and never spoke to Pastor Randolph, even when he reached out his hand to her after service.

Sarah sang in the school choir and met a boy named John, who transferred from Drake Middle School. At first, Caroline liked John. He was a cute, funny boy who made friends quickly. Before she knew it, Caroline and Sarah were sitting at the cool kids' table during lunch. Caroline had to get up earlier to look good for the other cool kids. They came from wealthier families than Caroline's, so she continued babysitting to earn money to buy the right jeans and tops at the mall.

Sarah was going out to parties on Saturday night. Caroline longed to go with her, but she was usually babysitting. Caroline would spend the night at Sarah's when she had a free evening. They faked sleeping, then escaped from the house around midnight and walked to Wolff Park to meet up with John and the other kids. Caroline started smoking cigarettes and was regularly offered pot, but she wasn't ready to try it. Caroline noticed that Sarah was changing. She was obsessed with John, and he always came first. If they went to the movies, Sarah would meet up with John and make out in the back row while Caroline sat alone.

Sarah constantly talked about how John touched her, which made Caroline uncomfortable. While she could understand Sarah's feelings, Caroline didn't want any boy touching her. Sarah told her boys would expect certain things if they dated her, which scared Caroline. She thought kissing and holding hands would be fun, but she definitely didn't want a boy touching her breasts. Anytime she thought about it, she remembered what her father had done and said.

John had a close friend, Steve, who was not dating anyone. Sarah nudged Caroline to try her hand at flirting with him, which she did. At Sarah's initiative, a bowling night for the quartet was arranged.

In Steve's company, Caroline found herself smitten, daydreaming about a romance with him even when she should have been focusing on her studies. When the four of them went to see *Star Wars*, Steve put his hand on Caroline's leg, slowly inching up her skirt. Caroline sat perfectly still, hoping he would stop himself so she didn't have to do or say anything. Steve moved his hand around her shoulders and reached down toward her breast. Caroline froze with fear. Steve began blowing in her ear, and Caroline couldn't stand it any longer. She jumped up and ran to the ladies room. She sat there until the movie ended and then walked out to meet Sarah. Steve ignored her, while Sarah and John looked at her angrily. Sarah's parents picked them up, and Sarah didn't speak to Caroline until they were alone in her room. Then, Sarah lit into Caroline, telling her she wouldn't get a boy like Steve if she behaved like a frigid little mouse.

"Sarah, I'm not comfortable having boys touch me," Caroline said without going into details.

Sarah responded angrily, "Look, Caroline, I know your dad did some bad stuff, but you need to get over it to have normal relationships with guys. I can't set you up with John's friends if you don't know how to act cool and enjoy kissing and all the other things guys like."

Caroline refused to cry in front of Sarah, feeling it would make her friend angrier. It seemed best to say nothing other than, "I'll work on it."

"Good! Now, let's call it a night."

Abruptly, the phone rang, and Sarah hurriedly answered it in a hushed tone. Caroline realized it was John on the other end. She had no inclination to eavesdrop on their conversation, especially if it involved critiquing her performance that night. She used her pillow to cover her ears and worked on falling asleep.

When Caroline got home the next day, she pulled a lawn chair out of the garage and sat under the big elm tree in the backyard. She listened as the turning leaves rustled in the light breeze. Using her third eye, Caroline called out to Serena, the chief, and Anne, asking for advice about handling relationships with boys and the best way to remove the overwhelming fear of being touched. She focused her third eye on images that made her happy, such as her grandparents and the farm. As she was deep in concentration, Smokey leaped onto Caroline's lap, curling into a snug ball. Caroline gently caressed the cat's velvety fur. After a while, Caroline noticed no sign of a response to her query. With that, she made the decision to retire to her room and change into the school's colors for Edward's football game.

That night, Caroline had a dream that Anne came to visit her. She talked about the difficulty young women have today because there were no rules on how a man should treat a woman as in earlier times. Anne told Caroline that she might want to speak with her doctor about her fears, and he might find a way to help.

As Caroline readied for church the next morning, she thought about her dream. Caroline wouldn't see the pediatrician anymore, and her mother didn't force appointments. She knew some girls went to a special women's doctor, so perhaps Caroline could talk to one of those. After church, during the quiet afternoon before she headed back for choir practice, Caroline approached her mother. It was not an easy conversation, as her mother immediately asked if this had anything to do with boys. Caroline didn't want to tell her it did because her mother would jump into a conversation about sex (or not having sex), which Caroline couldn't comprehend at this point in her life. She discussed her painful periods and tampon difficulties, both awkward topics, but they appeared to help. Her mother agreed it was time for Caroline to see a gynecologist. She would make the appointment.

At school next week, when she could find alone time with Sarah, Caroline told her about visiting the gynecologist. Sarah seemed relieved and told Caroline she thought this was a good idea. "Maybe the doctor can give you some pills to make you less weird around boys. You might also try drinking or smoking pot, as that might help relax you," Sarah suggested. Caroline agreed even though she didn't want to lose control with a boy, as he might take advantage of her. But she knew saying something like this to Sarah wouldn't help.

Sarah seemed much happier around her friend, talking, as always, about school gossip, homework, and Caroline's upcoming audition for the church musical. She also talked continuously about John. While Caroline was bored hearing about him, she kept her enthusiasm high to make her friend happy.

Caroline now went home after school. Her father might be there or out watching Edward's practices. Caroline's fear of him was lessening, and she no longer barred her door. But her senses told her to stay alert. She found the time spent under the elm tree peaceful.

She listened to the birds and tried to imitate their songs, as she loved to do. She looked for messages from the animals but only noticed that Smokey came to her almost every time she sat under the tree.

Caroline's mother kept her promise and informed Caroline about her upcoming gynecologist appointment. Caroline harbored mixed emotions about the meeting but held onto the hope that it would provide solutions to her issues. When the day came, Caroline's mother picked her up after school. Caroline sat in the waiting room reading *Glamour* until a nurse called her into the exam room. There, she was given a hospital gown and told by the nurse to change into it. Caroline didn't understand. The nurse explained that the doctor would examine her female areas to ensure everything was healthy. Then, the nurse pulled a tray over to a table full of odd items and lifted up devices she called "stirrups" that she told Caroline to put her feet into. She instructed Caroline to move as far down the table as possible, gave her a cloth to place over her lower regions, and left the room. Now Caroline was truly scared. She closed her eyes and begged for Anne to come and help her. She was thinking about running out of the room and telling her mother she didn't want to see this doctor when the exam room door opened.

Dr. Tate walked in, and Caroline's fear increased. She didn't expect a man to examine her! She assumed it would be a woman, though, as she thought about it, she had never met a female doctor. Dr. Tate told Caroline he would insert his finger to check her vaginal area. As the doctor's finger went inside her, Caroline thought she would throw up. The doctor moved his finger around, then sat up and asked Caroline if she was a virgin. Tears began to flow down her face. Why had she thought this was a good idea? "No sir," she answered in a quavering voice.

"How many boys have you been with?" he asked.

Caroline tried to stammer out a reply. "I haven't been with any boys. My father . . ." Caroline could not continue. She was too ashamed.

The doctor stopped the exam and asked Caroline what her father had done. Caroline tried to explain. The doctor asked if she had told her mother. After Caroline said yes, the doctor asked if her father was still touching her. Caroline explained that her grandmother had come, and she had made her father stop. Dr. Tate then helped Caroline remove her legs from the stirrups and asked why she had come to see him. Caroline told him about her fears of having boys touch her and how she was embarrassing herself among her friends. Dr. Tate told Caroline not to do anything she was uncomfortable with and that if she decided to have sex, she needed to see him to understand how to prevent pregnancy. Caroline shook her head and explained that she didn't want to have sex ever.

Dr. Tate quietly but firmly suggested that Caroline might want to talk to a professional like a psychiatrist to discuss what had happened to her and to help her develop healthier feelings about men. He went to a pad and wrote out a name and number. Then, Dr. Tate told Caroline to get dressed. Before he left, Caroline asked if he would tell her mother.

Dr. Tate responded, "If your father touches you again, I want you to come to me and, with your permission, I will speak to your mother. You are now my patient, and I will keep in confidence anything you tell me, so I will not say anything to your mother today. I want you to know, Caroline, that I am very sorry about what happened to you. I strongly urge you to speak with this psychiatrist to help you gain more normal feelings about men and sex." He left the room, and Caroline dressed.

As they drove home, Caroline shared with her mother the doctor's words. Without hesitation, her mother veered the car onto a quiet side street and switched off the engine. Gazing intently at Caroline, she spoke sternly: "You must never divulge what you believe happened to you to anyone—not to your friends, grandparents, doctors, and certainly not to any boys. You must put aside any memories involving your father and your grandmother's visit. Do you understand me?" Her mother gave her a stern look that Caroline had never seen before. The girl nodded her head.

After she got home, Caroline went to her closet. She called to Anne, and the spirit quickly came to her. Caroline cried and, through her tears, told the spirit what had happened. Anne sympathetically told Caroline that her mother was wrong but that she understood Caroline's situation. "You may have to keep this secret until you leave home. I don't know much about how men are today, but you must find an understanding man to help you overcome your fear. I'm not sure if boys your age are capable of that. Talk to your grandmother and aunt. They might have some recommendations for you. I would not engage Serena, as this is not something she can help you with. But I will be here whenever you need me." The spirit dissolved away.

Caroline laid her head on a blanket and wondered why God had given her this life. It was such a hard one. Why couldn't she be like Sarah, with a lovely father and a boyfriend she was crazy about? Sarah's life seemed so nice and easy. Caroline grew angry at the universe. All she could think about was fairness and balance. This subject the girl could discuss with Serena. But not today, as she was too angry and sad.

The next day, Caroline prepared for school with a heavy heart, lacking enthusiasm. Throughout the school day, she went through the motions, listening to her friend's chatter about her boyfriend. Sarah eventually recalled Caroline's doctor's visit and inquired about it. Caroline replied with a curt "fine."

When her friend proposed trying again and arranged a setup with one of John's friends, Caroline politely declined, stating she wasn't ready for a boyfriend at the moment. Sarah gave her an odd look, shrugged, and turned her attention to another girl at the table.

Caroline concentrated on her music. She worked hard on the number for the next band concert and the song she was preparing for the church musical tryout. But Caroline began noticing there wasn't any improvement. She was perturbed about her solo. Her voice didn't sound as good as usual.

On Sunday, Caroline dressed with care. Tryouts took place right after church. The choir director called up each of the soloists by key. First was the bass, of which there was only one, then the tenors and altos. Finally, it was time for the sopranos. This group was the largest and most competitive. Caroline always believed she was the best, but her heart was pounding today. She tried to take deep breaths to keep her fear at bay. When she was called up, her hands were sweating. As she began singing, her voice was shaky, which wasn't normal. She finished the song knowing she hadn't sung her best. The other sopranos smiled, patted her hand, and said such drivel—that the director knew she was a good signer and wouldn't hold this performance against her. Caroline smiled but didn't respond. The director told the soloists he would post the list on his office door before choir next week. Caroline went to look for her mother, whom she noticed was sitting in the back of the church sanctuary. "I heard your tryout, Caroline. Was there a reason you were so nervous?" she asked.

"I just haven't been feeling my best this week," Caroline replied.

"I'm certain it won't affect you winning a solo," her mother responded.

*Winning,* Caroline thought, *that's all this family cares about! What if I'm not a winner?*

As if to prove her point, Edward came home the next day angrier than Caroline had ever seen him. Her father kept yelling, "Didn't you explain to the coach that you have a better passing record?"

"Yeah, Dad," Edward replied, "but it doesn't matter. I'm still short, and he wants to train the junior quarterback so he's stronger next season. That means the bench for me!"

*The bench,* Caroline thought. *Edward has never sat on the bench. He's always first-string.*

Her father went straight to the garage for a beer. Caroline could tell it

185

would get nasty in the house and headed for her chair under the tree. She tried to block the yelling. She felt terrible for Edward. The athletic scholarship was critical. She asked her spirit guides to speak with Edward and help him through this challenging time. She knew her father would never accept Edward being anything but a winner. No one cared about Caroline's situation except her mother, and she cared only about how their home life appeared to the women at church—a place Caroline didn't want to go. It seemed as if a dark cloud hovered over their entire house. Was that why Andrew had left? To get away from the darkness that surrounded this family. Caroline looked toward the mountains, sending a message to Serena: *Please remove the darkness that surrounds me. Fill my life with brightness.*

On Sunday, Caroline approached the choir director's door, patiently waiting as the other kids scoured the list for their names. Emotions played across the faces of her peers. Kevin, a boy she had always admired, approached her and offered his congratulations. "You'll sing that part beautifully," he assured her.

With a surge of hope, Caroline made her way to the door. While she hadn't secured the lead solo, the second solo was a favorable role for someone not yet in high school. She had confidence in her ability to perform the assigned song with excellence. At choir practice that afternoon, Caroline received her music. The director told her to always sing confidently. Caroline held onto his words. She called Sarah to share the news when she got home from practice. "I'm glad for you, Caroline," she said. "By the way, are there any cute boys in your choir?"

"Oh, Sarah, do you ever think of anything but boys?" a frustrated Caroline replied.

"What else is more fun?" asked Sarah.

"Being with your girlfriends, for one," replied Caroline. "You need to stop being so boy-crazy, Sarah. You don't want it to affect your grades or your friendships. They will last longer than a boyfriend."

"Caroline, only you would say that because you fear boys. One day, I hope you understand how different life can be when there is someone special in your life," explained Sarah.

"Aren't your friends special?" asked Caroline.

"Certainly, but they don't make you feel like a boy does," Sarah said with a laugh.

Caroline didn't want to listen to the boy talk any longer. "I'll let you go," she said. "I'm sure John will be calling soon."

"I hope so," said Sarah dreamily.

Caroline turned her focus to the church musical. As this was the only way she could sing and perform until high school, Caroline made it a priority. She continued babysitting on the weekends, as she didn't see the point in going to the park when she didn't want to participate in the drinking, smoking, and foreplay that predominated the gatherings.

As the snow began falling, Caroline continued preparing for the holiday concert at school. As first chair in the band, she had a small solo part and a duet with the lead flutist. Sarah seemed more distant, but Caroline assumed it was due to John. As Caroline didn't want to talk about him, she left Sarah to gossip with the other girls in the cool group who had boyfriends.

The Christmas concert was just around the corner. Icy streets and snow blanketed the town. Although riding the school bus in the cold allowed her to have conversations with Mindy, their friendship couldn't compare to the companionship Caroline shared with Sarah. She longed for the warmth of their relationship.

As Caroline walked into band practice, she heard snickering from up in the trumpet section. She sat in her chair, put her clarinet together, moistened the reed, and warmed up, paying no attention to what was happening around her. Suddenly, a boy from the back of the class yelled, "Hey, Caroline Howard. I heard your old man raped you!"

The room went deathly still as everyone looked at Caroline. She tried to see who would have said such a horrible thing. She knew it was one of the boys from the trumpet section. She homed in on one who was good friends with John. He was grinning at her.

*Oh, God, what do I do? I have to say something.* "Your information is wrong," was all she could come up with.

Fortunately, the teacher walked in, and the band gave him their complete attention. He inquired about everyone's readiness, announced the piece they were about to perform, raised his baton-bearing right hand, and initiated the beat. However, Caroline found herself unable to play. Her instrument remained silent as if she were paralyzed. The band teacher fixed his gaze on her, but she couldn't muster the breath required to produce a sound through the reed. In distress, she clung to her clarinet, seized her case, and exited the room.

She headed to the nurse's office and threw up all the horror in her body. Everyone would know what the trumpet player had said by the end of the day. Her mother had told her not to say anything. There was only one person she had ever told: Sarah. Could she have told John? No, she wouldn't. She was Caroline's best friend. She knew to keep Caroline's secrets.

asked Caroline how she was feeling. "Sick. I'm feeling very dizzy. My head is spinning."

Nurses always took special care with her. "I believe you should go home," said the school nurse. "We don't want you catching anything, and many germs are floating around." Caroline lay on the bed, trying not to think until the nurse told her that her mother was at the front desk. Caroline went to her locker and grabbed all her books. Silently, she walked with her mother toward the car, already feeling the weight of the stares.

Upon arriving home, Caroline barred her door and went straight to her closet. She didn't even know who to ask for help. How would spirit guides understand facing an entire school that knew her deepest, darkest secret? She began to cry but stopped herself. Tears wouldn't help. She went from the closet to the phone and dialed her grandmother. As she joined the line, Caroline blurted out the incident as if it had been violently expelled from the depths of her stomach.

Her grandmother listened and said, "You have two choices, Caroline. You can try to change schools, but that means telling your parents the words uttered, or you will need to be stronger than ever and face the people who judge you wrongly."

"Grandmother, why is my life so hard and why are other kids' lives so easy?" Caroline asked plaintively.

"Oh, Caroline, I often wondered that myself," Grandmother Howard said. "Try to remember that you chose to take on something significant. People who are special are often tested harshly, like warriors. This rumor is your testing, so you must be strong. Stand your ground, and don't let anyone take anything from you. Don't give away your intelligence or talent. Grab hold of those things and turn them into your shield against those who are jealous of you."

"Why would anyone be jealous of me?" Caroline asked.

"Only jealous people hurt others as you were hurt," said Grandmother Howard. "That's why you can never let them take you down. And only allow people near you who are kind. Learn to read people as you read the signs from the animals and birds. Then, surround yourself with goodness."

Caroline thanked her grandmother and said she'd better get off the phone.

"Write to me, Caroline, and let me know how you are. I will send you as much strength as I can."

Caroline moved to her room at a sluggish pace, settled on her bed, and braced herself for the impending phone call. Shortly before dinner, her mother appeared in her room, mentioning that Sarah was on the line. Caroline took a deep breath, rose from her bed, and approached the phone. In a subdued tone, she greeted Sarah with a simple "hello."

"Oh, Caroline, I can't believe what that boy said. How horrible for you!"

"Yes. How horrible for me," said Caroline tonelessly. She continued, "I wonder how that boy, whom I don't know, could spill one of the darkest secrets that I've told to only one person who goes to my school."

There was a long, painful pause on the other end of the phone. "Uh, Caroline, well, uh, John kept asking me why you didn't like boys considering how cute you are, and lots of guys would date you, but, uh, then you were so weird with Steve and, uh, he asked me if you were some religious freak and, uh, well, I tried to explain without telling him everything about your dad being, well, uh, kinda a drunk and that he did bad things, but, uh, I never told him

190

*exactly* what your dad did, but I told him it was a secret and, well . . ." Sarah finally ran out of steam. Caroline didn't say anything, and at last, Sarah said, "Are you still there, Caroline?"

"Yes, I'm trying to decide what to say to you," Caroline answered. "I could ask you if you went to John to find out if he did this, but I know he'll lie to you, and you'll believe him. So, now everyone in school will think I'm some freak because I live in a house with a man who hurt me. Perhaps, Sarah, I should ask you what you think I should do."

Caroline waited as Sarah sputtered on the other end of the line. Finally, her former best friend said, "I'd hate to see you switch schools."

"Well, Sarah, I would have to go to a school that isn't in Arvada. That's the only way I can escape the rampant rumor throughout the district. But that would mean I'd have to tell my parents what happened. Do you think I want to do that, Sarah? Don't bother answering the question. I think this conversation is over. I'm glad to learn that John and his need to know about my sexual feelings are more important than being my best friend. Enjoy your new cool group. I hope they treat you as well as you treat others." With that, Caroline hung up the phone.

She was proud of how she'd handled the call. She told her mother she wasn't hungry and returned to her closet. She centered herself and peered into the spirit world, asking for the chief. Before long, she felt herself sitting on the plains, with the smell of horses and alfalfa grass on the wind. She saw the teepees and thought of the safety they represented. "Caroline, little singing bird, why have you called to me?" asked the chief.

She tried to tell him what had happened.

"Should a man have done that to a female child, he would have been banned from the tribe, if not killed," said the chief.

"I wish it were that simple in this place and time," Caroline explained. "But to get my father to leave would require my mother's help, and that won't happen. My choices are to leave and live with another tribe, with my grandmother's tribe, and start all over, or stay and live with the shame."

"Why should you be ashamed?" asked the chief. "You have done no wrong. But I understand your dilemma. You are still young and haven't finished your training. That is of the greatest importance. You must become what you agreed to in this life. You will face challenges as you walk the shaman's path. It is a difficult but important role for a tribe. Your gifts will make a difference in your world, in your time. I will strengthen your shield for the battles you must fight."

"How do you strengthen my shield?" asked Caroline. "We don't use those in this time."

"We have shields in every time," said the chief. "Your shield in this life is carried inside you. It is the strength you carry, and it shows in your gifts. Do you understand your gifts?" he asked.

"Not really," she replied. "I know I have spiritual gifts to speak to you and Serena, but I thought everyone had that gift. The difference is whether they feel it and use it. I want to think I have the gift of music, but I'm not sure how I am to use that."

"Some tribes have legendary teachers and healers who show the tribe how to reach the Great Father and the great spirits of the other world. Rarely is that person also given the gift of music, which helps the tribe celebrate a successful hunt or honor one who has passed on. Train in your gifts, as they are unique to you. Understand that a message will show the right time to unveil your gifts to help others. You will find this brings you great joy and satisfaction. Worry less about the now and concentrate on what is to come. Look above the trees and see the universe that needs your help." Then, the chief laid his hands on Caroline's head so she could feel his strength surging through her. Slowly, the picture of the plains faded away along with the chief. Sarah slept briefly, got up, unbarred her door, and went to the kitchen to fix herself a sandwich. She opened her books and worked on her homework. With determination, she practiced her clarinet, steeling herself for the challenges awaiting her on the following day.

# Loving Yourself

ERCHED AT THE ENTRANCE of her cave, Serena let the breeze gently caress her face and ruffle her hair, which cascaded down her graceful neck.

The wind was her messenger, carrying voices, each with its own tale. Today, a special message rode the crisp, invigorating air, lighting up Serena's eyes with a radiant smile: Caroline was on her way. The girl had been through many challenges and carried too much pain. Serena knew she had to teach Caroline how to release the pain, as the lightness would help her find happiness in the dark world below. Serena often wished she could make more remarkable changes in the girl's life, but that time had not yet come. The training must continue.

This time, Serena would embark on the formidable task of instructing Caroline in the art of deciphering the Akashic Record, also known as the Book of Life in some circles. Mastering this skill was no easy feat, for the Akashic Masters were the authors and gatekeepers of these books, meticulously selective in granting access. Caroline's journey would demand unwavering dedication as she strove to prove her worthiness in unlocking the narratives of countless lives within these sacred tomes, transcending her own. But, as tradition dictated, they would commence at the very beginning. The robins and blue jays in the trees that prevented humans from seeing the cave were singing madly. A voice was attempting to sing and whistle along with them, and as she reached the front of the cave, she sang out, "Serreena."

"I believe your voice is getting better. You reach the high notes with less difficulty," Serena said as she looked down at the human girl. Caroline had reached her full height, but she was a tiny woman like those who lived in the rocky islands beyond this continent. Serena had sisters who lived in the trees that remained in the upper part of that island, but many had to leave, as humans had cut down so many forests. They could never understand how many creatures used the trees as their homes. However, Serena entrusted the resolution of this issue to the Great Mother, who brimmed with wrath, poised to chastise these humans for their reckless exploitation of her generous gifts. Thankfully, Serena resided in a sanctuary shielded from human encroachment, a haven preserved by the blessings of the Earth Goddess. She remained steadfast in her devotion, constantly paying homage to the Goddess of Earth, and she deemed it essential to convey this veneration to Caroline as well.

"Caroline, how long do I have you this time?" asked Serena.

"Only a week. I hope that if and when I go to college, I can come up here to work in the summers. Then, I can see you more often," she answered.

"That would be good, as a week every summer is not enough time to teach you everything you must know."

"What must I learn now?" asked Caroline.

"It is time to teach you about the Akashic Record," Serena began. "This is the record of everything that occurs in the life of every soul."

"Everything?" Caroline asked.

"Everything of significance," replied Serena. "Accessing the records requires specialized skills, some of which you already know but most of which you don't. It's a most difficult exercise but one you are to learn."

"Serena, you often use phrases such as 'you are to learn,'" Caroline said carefully. "How do you know what I am to learn?"

"Caroline, do you not think the Akashic Masters, angels, and spirit guides have spoken to me of your potential and future? They said to train you in everything I can, and that is what I do," Serena said simply.

"But what am I supposed to do with this knowledge?" Caroline asked, trying to get a more precise answer.

"The future is not written, Caroline. You have encountered forks in the road before and have chosen a direction. You will continue to make decisions based on the challenges you encounter. But your unique knowledge will aid you in making decisions just as it has in the past."

"But if I am to 'teach,' who am I to teach? I can't imagine teaching kids the knowledge you gave me in grade school," Caroline said with growing frustration in her voice.

"Caroline, you speak of going to college. Can you not imagine a college professor explaining the knowledge you gained to help people better understand the universe and the gifts God has bestowed that humans don't even use?"

"But how do I explain that I learned all this from a wood nymph, Anne, and the chief, my spirit guides?" Caroline asked with increasing volume. "People will think I am nuts!"

"Caroline, calm yourself," Serena said soothingly. "You will find the way if you trust yourself. Listen to the universe just as I've taught you. It will guide you. Now, please sit down and let us begin our work. The day grows short."

Serena elucidated to Caroline that the Akashic Masters sought readers who could nurture self-love—a concept that Caroline found challenging to fully comprehend.

"You don't think about loving yourself," Serena said. "You have a hard enough time loving your family. But self-love is essential to all we do in every life. Loving yourself involves acceptance of who we are and the belief in self-actualization. That means understanding that throughout every life, we must evolve, and we must love ourselves throughout the evolution as our soul works to reach purity. "Caroline, do you love yourself?"

Caroline thought about this. The truth was, she didn't. She was disgusted with herself. She was the awful girl whom the kids at school whispered about. Who could possibly love that girl? Not only did she lack self-love, but she also held the belief that no man would ever love her. As these thoughts swirled in her head, tears began to slowly drip down her face and onto the grey flannel shirt she wore in the cold cave. The wood nymph got up, sat beside Caroline, and embraced her. Caroline began to feel a tingling warmth move through her body. It was a different kind of warmth. It was like lying in bathwater at the perfect temperature with flower petals floating around and the slightest hint of gardenia perfuming the water. "What is this feeling, Serena?" she asked in her smallest voice.

"This, sweet girl, is universal love. This love comes from everyone who knows you, watches over you, and believes in you for the girl you are now and the woman you will become," Serena responded in her unique voice.

"Why do I never feel this way at home?" Caroline wondered aloud.

"The family we are born into plays a purpose in our lives. While I know your home lacks the love you seek, do not assume it is without love. It's just that your emotions are alert to danger, like a rabbit crossing an open field where a hawk might soar down. Relax and understand that the family of origin is not the family you create."

"You mean, there is a boy out there who will like me?" Caroline asked as the tears began to dry.

The wood nymph laughed, a sound Caroline rarely heard. "Yes, Caroline, you will find love, a great love. Your challenge will be to allow it into your life. That does not mean you shouldn't be cautious, as you will still encounter unkind people who have lost their way. You must seek to learn how to detect people, particularly men, who have the sincerity to love all that is unique to you."

The two sat quietly for a time. After Serena felt Caroline had collected herself, she said, "Your most important exercise for today is to practice loving Caroline. Focus only on the good parts, and leave the bad, along with the dark energy it carries, to the side. Lay it down, and do not carry it with you. Practice that for the rest of the day. Tomorrow, I will teach you how to open and read the records."

Caroline left the cave, her thoughts brimming with Serena's words. Along her hike to the cabin, she reached a tranquil spot by a mountain stream that flowed into the Blue River. Gazing into the still water amid floating twigs and leaves, she studied her reflection. Although her appearance mirrored what she saw in her bedroom mirror at home, her expression gradually shifted. She smiled, laughed, and frowned, observing how her face changed. She thought about what face people saw these days and realized she always looked down, hoping people wouldn't notice her. And if they caught her eyes, they would see anger because she never wanted anyone to glimpse the pain. Sitting beside herself, she heard a blue jay begin to sing. Music brought solace, allowing the genuine Caroline to surface. She found comfort in the upcoming musical and choir trip, anticipating a time when she could begin to embrace and love the Caroline of the present. Deep in thought, she returned to the cabin.

Throughout the next week, Caroline practiced opening the doors to the Akashic Record. This work was secret and never written down. She memorized the opening prayers and looked for the signs she was inside the records. Caroline could read only her own records, as someone had to permit her to read their life story. Caroline returned to the lives when the chief and Anne were with her. These lives were interesting but almost always ended with a harsh death. "Why did my life end by a shot from a military officer or an overturned carriage? Why does it seem I died so rarely as an old person calmly crossing the Rainbow Bridge as I slept?"

"We can ask for an easy life, but we often don't learn as much during those lives and thus must return more often. You have always asked for the hardest tasks. That is unique to your soul. So, your lives are full of difficulty. But you gather greater skills that you bring forward into your next life. Look at Caroline Howard. She trains in the most difficult metaphysical skills and speaks to the spirit world. Her destiny is to make big changes in her world. God doesn't grant an important life to a weak, untrained soul. Because that person, should they choose the wrong path, could do great damage to the Earth. You understand the responsibility of your gifts."

Too quickly, the week was up, and it was time for Caroline to leave Serena again. Her heart was heavy because the wood nymph had shown her real love during this visit. She could physically recall how it felt. She wanted to find someone in Arvada who could make her feel that way again. As Caroline walked from the cave, Serena said, "Remember, Caroline, we cannot find love until we love ourselves. That is the most important lesson from this week."

Caroline waved goodbye and began her descent, the crunching sound of the forest emanating from each step she took as she moved back to the world of humans.

# Musical High

AROLINE LOOKED FORWARD TO high school. Several middle schools fed into Arvada West. Caroline hoped this would help dissipate the gossip that had enveloped her at West Woods. She had

sat under the elm tree and prayed to the Great Spirit to help her find a new group of friends who hadn't heard the gossip or, perhaps, wouldn't believe it or wouldn't care.

She stopped playing the clarinet, much to the dismay of her mother and the high school band teacher. He implored Caroline to continue, but she explained that her goal was to sing, and the school wouldn't allow her to do both. So, the clarinet went in the closet, and Caroline auditioned for the highest-level music class, the acapella choir. To her relief (as she still struggled with nerves), she was selected as one of the few 10th-graders to join the group. She practiced almost daily at home because she never knew when she might be called to the front of the room to sing a new song section with the other selected alto, bass, and tenor. It was an honor that gave her great satisfaction.

Loneliness settled in, as Sarah had become a cheerleader, while Caroline opted to steer clear of the spotlight at school despite all that Sarah had imparted. Sarah remained close to John and their group, and Caroline made attempts to connect with classmates she met in her classes. However, by high school, cliques had solidified, making it challenging to break into any social circle. Her mother gradually realized the phone no longer rang for Caroline, and the once sociable girl started coming home directly from school every day, enduring the unpopular bus ride that most high schoolers sought to avoid. She also watched Caroline sitting under the elm every day after school.

"Caroline, is there some reason you like sitting under that old tree?" her mother asked.

"Oh, I like to listen to the birds that nest there and practice my singing," she replied.

Her mother said, "Have you met any nice girls at high school?"

"Yes, but no one special." Then, Caroline left and headed to her room.

One day, while entering the lunchroom, Caroline was drawn to a boisterous laugh. It came from a boy she recognized from Oberon but whom she had never interacted with. He was seated among a cluster of choir and drama club students. Caroline had always been apprehensive about labels and knew that associating with the drama kids might brand her in a certain way. However, she pondered whether it could be any worse than the isolation she currently endured. What if this group, too, rejected her? Loneliness weighed heavily on her, leading her to rationalize that perhaps these kids wouldn't find her peculiar. Making a courageous decision, Caroline took the plunge and approached them. "May I sit here?" she asked.

The freckled boy, who'd laughed loudly, stood up and gave her a grand bow. "Why yes, my dear," he replied. Caroline hesitated, as she was always afraid of being made fun of. The boy noticed and changed his tune. "Don't mind me, I was just being dramatic. Drama nerd and all that."

Caroline laughed and replied, "Well, I'm a music geek, so that doesn't bother me."

"Then, have a seat. I'm Scott." He introduced the rest of the people at the table. Caroline recognized one girl, Leslie, from the choir. They greeted each other and began chatting about the new piece they were working on. For the first time in a long while, Caroline began to relax. Everyone was friendly, and for once, she wasn't alone.

A few weeks later, the kids were discussing the spring musical. "Anything Goes" was selected, and everyone was aflutter to sing and act in a Cole Porter musical. Caroline wasn't familiar with it. During study hall, she went to the library to look it up. She read about Ethel Merman, the woman for whom Cole Porter had written Reno. Caroline called her mother and asked her if she would drive her to the main library in downtown Arvada. While her mother perused books by Christian authors, Caroline listened to the album from the musical; there was only one copy of the album, and because many students were trying to check it out, the head librarian had decided each student could have it for only an hour.

Caroline immersed herself in Ethel Merman's resounding vocals and the songs performed by the other actors. It dawned on her that her previous training in church musicals hadn't adequately prepared her for this distinct style of singing. Yet, the singer within her reveled in it. She sensed that her voice harmonized best with the numbers of Hope Harcourt, and she decided to audition for that role. However, the question remained: how to prepare?

Contemplating her options, Caroline thought about discussing it with Scott. She had grown fond of his outgoing personality and knew they wouldn't be directly competing for a role. To her surprise, Scott readily offered his assistance and extended an invitation for Caroline to visit his house, where they could explore different audition songs together.

Caroline was amazed by Scott's home. His family was wealthy. The

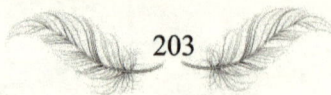

walls in the living room, which contained a black grand piano, were in the loveliest pale shade of green. They coordinated beautifully with the blue and white Chinese pieces. Sunlight poured through the windows, covered by a floral fabric in a unique green shade. Caroline looked closely at the material and saw it had flowers and birds. Scott's mother, dressed perfectly, came in to see what she wanted to drink. Caroline was used to two choices at her home: water or iced tea. They weren't even allowed soda. Scott asked for a Coke, so Caroline did as well. Then, Scott went to the bookshelf full of sheet music. "What type of singer are you?" he asked while flipping through different music books.

"I'm a soprano."

"What's your range?" Scott asked.

"I've never been asked that," she replied, thinking aloud.

"Well, let's find out!" Scott sat down at the piano to warm up his fingers, playing chords up and down the keyboard. He was so good!

"Can you accompany yourself?" Caroline asked.

"Yes. I've been playing since I was young."

"I would love to do that, but I was never that good a pianist."

"Let me see your hands," Scott said. They compared right hands. "My God, your hands are so tiny. Come to think of it, you're rather tiny all over. Now, here's a song you might know. It's from 'The Sound of Music.'" Scott began to play the familiar chords of "My Favorite Things." Caroline started to sing, twirling about. She didn't know all the words, so she just hummed when she came to a phrase she didn't know. Scott began moving the song up into different chords. He eventually stopped and stared at Caroline. "You have a beautiful voice and a wonderful range."

"Thank you," Caroline responded with a big smile.

"What part are you trying out for?" he asked.

"Hope Harcourt," she replied, her voice growing quieter. She was afraid of how he might respond.

Scott whistled and then said, "You know that will be tough. Second lead for a sophomore. But you certainly have the voice for it, and it's the right role for you. OK, let's find you the perfect song for your tryout."

Scott and Caroline spent the rest of the afternoon trying out different songs. By the time her mother arrived, they had decided on "Before I Gaze at You Again" from "Camelot." Scott loaned Caroline the music, and she ran to the car after giving him a big hug. Her mother noticed a lightness in Caroline that she hadn't seen for a long time.

When Caroline arrived home, it was dark and cold outside. But she still picked up Smokey and headed to her chair under the elm tree. As she brushed away the snow from the aftermath of the latest storm, Caroline expressed her gratitude to the universe for introducing Scott into her life. She believed he was the kind of friend she had longed for. She also asked her spirit guides to warn her if she was wrong in trusting Scott. She felt she heard a response through the wind: *Trust your intuition.* Her gut said Scott was a faithful friend. She picked up Smokey, who had fallen asleep in a ball on her lap, and carried the kitty inside.

Caroline practiced "Before I Gaze at You Again" every day. Scott had told her to think about the character of Hope, so when she performed the song, she sang it as Hope would. Caroline had never approached singing this way before, but she realized inhabiting a different person was all part of acting. Though inexperienced, as she'd always sung as herself, Caroline understood this was necessary to win the role. She talked to Scott about becoming Hope and how to do it. She went to Scott's after school and, working from a copy of the script, read lines with him while he explained the basics of acting. She knew it didn't come to her naturally, but, as Scott instructed, she tried not to "show the work."

The tryout was merely a week off, and Caroline had caught wind of the rumors circulating about which girls were vying for various roles. The fact that the best singer, a senior, aimed for the lead role brought her immense relief. However, her anxiety peaked over the competition for the part of Hope, particularly concerning a girl named Karen Alexander, who possessed formidable vocal talents. She was a sophomore with a wide vocal range. Karen sang alto in the acapella choir but was known also to sing soprano. She was noticeably strong in harmonizing, a technique that Caroline was still learning. In some ways, Caroline was behind the other singers, having spent so much time in the band—and the skillsets weren't necessarily transferable.

The big day finally arrived. Caroline was nervous and worried that the performance anxiety that had appeared during the church choir musical tour would return. Scott was there to audition for a small role and give moral support. When the director called Caroline's name, she focused on getting into character as Scott had taught her. Initially, her voice was soft while she found her footing. This was the first time she had soloed in the big school auditorium. She breathed to strengthen her voice and fill the immense room with sound.

When done, she heard applause—something she wasn't used to, as clapping in church was discouraged. She stumbled a bit, unused to the attention, as she descended the stairs to her seat. Scott greeted her with a big smile and a high five. She listened to the rest of the auditions. She felt some girls were better but thought her chances were good.

Once again, she waited for the selection posting on the drama teacher's door. As she walked to the door, she saw Scott. His face was expressionless, and she knew he was immediately trying not to show her his reaction. She read the list. It took a minute to find her name, as it was far down next to the list of Bonnie's girls. Not only did she not get the role of Hope, but she also didn't get any part with a solo. She couldn't remember this happening before. Caroline looked at the list again and saw that Karen had won the role of Hope. Caroline couldn't believe it. She felt Karen was wrong for the part, but it wasn't her decision.

Walking over to Scott, Caroline asked if he had gotten a part. She hadn't checked. He nodded and started back down the hall with Caroline. As they got to the school entrance, she finally blurted out, "I don't understand! I thought I had a good audition, better than Karen. Plus, the part fits my voice better than hers. What's going on?"

Scott told her to sit, and though the steps were cold and wet, they plopped onto the concrete. He took a few minutes to compose his thoughts. Then he replied. "Do you understand school politics?"

"Not really," said Caroline.

"This is a classic example of school politics. Karen has been building alliances within the musical hierarchy. Both male leads like her, and she doesn't have any, um, well, baggage."

"Are you talking about the rumors surrounding me?" asked Caroline softly.

"Yeah," said Scott. "I don't care about that, and you wouldn't think drama geeks, of all people, would pay any attention. But even the drama kids have an anointed order. You should be at the top, given the quality of your voice, but the male singers make the decisions, and the top two tenors choose the three female leads. I heard that the student director disagreed and fought for you, but they beat him down figuratively."

"I wonder if I should have continued playing the clarinet. I was first chair, and no one seemed to care, and that was the class where all this started."

"Caroline, you're swirling. I don't know how good you were at the clarinet, and perhaps you should have been a marching band geek, but you have a natural talent for singing. Things should change. Just work on being a great team player in the musical this year, and I bet you'll see a difference next year."

Caroline came to understand that Scott's message was straightforward: embrace the role assigned to her, endure for now, and set her sights on moving up the ranks the following year. It was the game they were playing.

She showed up on the first day of rehearsal with a smile and a helpful attitude. The director asked her to be the understudy for the Hope role. It felt like a knife in her gut, but she agreed. Throughout the spring, she helped paint sets and even asked her mom to help sew costumes. On opening day, her father approached her and said he was sorry she hadn't won one of the leads. Caroline was shocked by his statement. Her father had been working hard to stay sober, which made her mother happy.

Caroline hadn't realized how difficult this day would be. She did everything according to direction and played her part with as much conviction as possible. Watching Karen perform Hope's solos from the wings, she thought the girl did fine but struggled with some of the high notes. Caroline stayed for a bit of the cast party but eventually couldn't hide the fact that she wasn't having fun. Scott hugged her and whispered how proud he was of her. She gave him a wan smile and headed to the car where her mother was waiting.

Caroline concluded her school year with the acapella choir concert on a warm spring evening amidst blooming red tulips and purple irises. Proud to be part of the group, she relished the show. As she lay in bed, her thoughts turned to the upcoming summer. Edward would return from college, Andrew would join the family for the mountain fishing trip, and a week with Grandmother Howard was planned, as were farm visits. Although she had made friends in the vocal and drama clubs, Caroline felt somewhat adrift, and she sought guidance from Serena to make sense of it all.

In the afternoon's quiet, Caroline sat at the mouth of Serena's cave. It was a warm day, and she loved feeling the sun against her skin. A cooling breeze came through, keeping her enveloped in bathwater temperature.

Today, Serena was explaining how to read an aura. After Caroline explained the fiasco with the school musical, Serena felt this would help Caroline read people and situations better. Caroline appreciated how Serena could supply the correct teaching to help with life's difficulties.

As Caroline listened to her beloved birds, Serena sat beside her. She never had to ask what Caroline was thinking. Instead, she tried to direct Caroline toward the bigger picture.

"I love the view from here," said Caroline softly, not wanting to disturb the birds' singing.

"Yes, you can just see the valley from here, though it's easier in the winter without all the leaves," said Serena.

"I'm hoping that next year I can work up here. I must find housing that satisfies my parents and doesn't use up my entire paycheck."

"You will find the mountain summer glorious," replied Serena.

"My, you don't usually use such effusive words," observed Caroline.

"Well, it is my favorite time of year. Perhaps it is because the season is so short up here. You must enjoy it fully."

"Serena, something has been troubling me. My friend Scott often says I was born at the wrong time. When practicing singing, I tend to choose pieces from the Thirties and Forties, particularly big band numbers. They resonate with me. I've looked at my most recent past lives, and it seems the last one is the most difficult to read."

"That may be due to the subject. If you permit me, I can look at that life and help you understand it."

"Of course!" exclaimed Caroline. "You have permission to look at my records at any time."

Serena left the girl to sun herself while she went to her study table farther inside the cave. After a while, she returned to speak with Caroline. "I can see why that life might have been difficult for you to read. That is why the record may seem dense and the information not easily forthcoming. The harder the life, the harder the task to read the record," explained Serena. "Much of this life took place during a big war. Did you see that?"

"Yes, the last life was during World War II. I'm uncomfortable with it because I was on the enemy's side. I was part of a group whose name I don't want to utter. It was so bad. I wouldn't want anyone but you to know about it."

"I cannot speak to the perception of this war among your kind," said Serena. "But there are important learnings for you. Yes, music was an essential part of this life. As you may know, you made a living as a professional singer. You saw the political changes coming to your country and disagreed with them. You worked secretly to get people to change their support for the war. And then, sadly, you were killed when a bomb dropped on the place you were hiding."

"That's something I don't understand about the lives we pick," said Caroline angrily. "Why would I choose to be on the enemy's side and then die in a bombing? It's like the only purpose of this life was to be cannon fodder."

"Again, you are evaluating the life from below the trees, not above them. You knew this would be a difficult life, but you had lived in this part of the world many times previously and had been happy. You wanted the German people to love their country but not for war. Regrettably, your species struggles to grasp the profound advantages of peace. Instead, there's a tendency to create weaponry and explosives for the purpose of eliminating communities, akin to what happened with the Native Americans who coexisted peacefully here. It appears that your species fixates on wealth and territory, often resorting to aggression against other groups to acquire them. This life was important in helping you understand this basic fact. You brought that knowledge into this life. Now, you see the importance of peace and the need to work together to benefit the planet harmed due to all the greed. You will be a better advocate for the Great Mother."

"Ugh. Sometimes I would like a life that has me winning the lead in the school musical and having dates to the school dances, not 'advocating for the Great Mother,'" groused Caroline.

"But that does not make you a special person, nor would that give you the knowledge and experience to do exceptional work. We have discussed before that your tasks are for a reason. However, why don't we sit here in the setting sun before you have to go and manifest you having a date to the next dance?"

Caroline laughed. "Now, I like that idea!"

A hummingbird passed by the two women, and Caroline asked that it take her message to the Great Spirit. It left Caroline hopeful that the next school year would be better than the last one.

Caroline sat in the noisy school lunchroom, looking around at the different groups of teenagers and how they assembled themselves according to their desires. Jocks wanted to achieve the "big man on campus" title, and girls tried to be sexier to draw in a cute guy and get him as a boyfriend. She wondered if these people prayed to God, asking for their desires, and how God chose which one's dream would come true. Her eyes momentarily fastened on Sarah, sitting in her cheerleading outfit with the cool kids. She was still dating that awful John. Sarah looked as if she received everything she wanted. Why was that? What contract had she signed that allowed her to be cute and popular and to live with a lovely family? Perhaps her dark cloud had to do with John. Had she allowed darkness into her life that would bring trouble? He certainly had brought trouble to Caroline. But Sarah stayed with John rather than protecting her friend. Was that her learning at this point in her life?

"What has your head in the clouds?" asked Scott.

"Oh, hi. I'm just looking over the tribes in the cafeteria."

"'Tribe' is a good word for it," Scott replied as he scanned the room. "I just hope there aren't any wars and people are left alone to be themselves."

"I couldn't agree more," responded Caroline.

"Now, what are you focused on?" he asked.

"I was thinking about getting more involved in homecoming. You know, school spirit and all that rah-rah. I'm not a cheerleader or pom-pom girl, but maybe I could do something with the Wildcats Club."

"That's a good idea. I've decided to run as a school government representative. I'll dress in perfect politician attire, and you can be my first lady."

Caroline laughed. Scott was so sweet and cute. He could go with any number of gals as his girlfriend. But dating didn't seem to be his thing, which gave Caroline more of his time. She would do her part to help with his campaign. Perhaps all this activity would be looked upon favorably by the choir crowd. Caroline tried to be friendly with everyone, but some kids wouldn't be happy when the teacher chose the soloists for the Christmas concert. She hoped this would work in her favor, as there wouldn't be a tryout. She asked her spirit guides daily to help her do whatever was necessary to win a solo. She felt this would help her audition for the next school musical.

Caroline darted down the hall, her pace nearly airborne, in search of Scott. She finally located him in the library. "Guess what?" she nearly shouted before lowering her voice to a whisper. "I got one of the solos! Karen got one as well, as did our phenomenal tenor. But I was selected for a difficult piece that shows off my upper range."

"Caroline, that's awesome. You can't worry about Karen. You are completely different singers. Focus on your attributes and make your solo the best. And before you ask, I'll find time to work with you." They had been busy on his campaign posters, and Caroline had helped draft his speech. Scott had complimented her writing skills, which wasn't something Caroline dwelled upon. Writing had always flowed naturally for her. Conversely, math remained a perpetual challenge. It perplexed her how she could navigate the paths of stars yet encounter difficulties with advanced algebra.

All the important people in the drama club attended the acapella concert. Karen had once again filled the auditorium with her voice during her solo. She didn't expect to hear anything from the choir director. His style was direct criticism, not to shower anyone with praise.

Her mother had said some kind words during their annual trip to the ice cream shop in downtown Arvada. "Have you considered whether you want to attend college?" she asked Caroline.

"Yes, I believe so."

"Have you thought about where you would like to go?"

"It would be nicer to go farther away than Boulder, but I'm not sure I'd like the other schools any better. CU has the best programs."

"Have you looked at costs yet?" her mother asked.

"No, I haven't."

"Perhaps you should speak with the school guidance counselor. She was helpful with both Andrew and Edward." Andrew, who could have received a scholarship anywhere in the state, had skipped college. Edward was another story. He had received a small baseball scholarship, and their father had blamed him for not campaigning harder with the coach. His first school hadn't worked out, and Edward seemed to change schools every semester, trying to find one that would play him. But time was running short for him to gain the eye of a professional baseball recruiter. Edward seemed so angry all the time that Caroline never went near him. She felt awful for him, but anytime she tried to help or make a suggestion, it was met with a cold, dark stare, so she stayed out of his way.

As they savored their ice cream, Caroline's mother reminded her to register for the ACT and SAT in the spring. She emphasized the importance of obtaining initial test scores by year-end to allow for retakes if necessary, all in pursuit of securing admission to a better school and, hopefully, a scholarship. Caroline acknowledged that her best chance for a scholarship was in the field of vocal performance, which was highly competitive.

Nevertheless, she assured her mother that she would initiate the process once the new semester commenced.

Of more importance to Caroline was the announcement of the school musical. She tried participating in the conversations during lunchtime when the elected director threw out different ideas. The group discussed "The Sound of Music," which Caroline loved, but many thought high schools used it too often. Another Julie Andrews musical was "The Boy Friend." Caroline realized there was so much about musical theater that she didn't know. All she could do was support the different ideas and then run to the library and research the musical to see if there was a soprano lead. "Cinderella" came up for discussion, but the group sought a musical that offered two strong tenor and soprano roles. That gave Caroline insight into what was going on.

She talked to Scott about the situation one afternoon. "Yeah, Jason is a senior this year and wants a big solo. But everyone knows Alan is the most talented. Even though he's a junior, he'll be auditioning for the lead," said Scott. "While Ellen isn't as good of a singer as you, she's a senior, and Jason will push to sing with her. That leaves one lead open. Not the best situation. Have you thought about an audition song?"

"I have," said Caroline. "I'm thinking of doing a song from 'Cinderella.' It may seem cheesy, but I love Rodgers and Hammerstein."

"You can't go wrong with one of their musicals. What song are you thinking of? 'Ten Minutes Ago' or 'In My Own Little Corner'?"

"'In My Own Little Corner,'" Caroline replied confidently. "I feel it best represents me."

Scott looked at her for a minute. "I agree. Let's see if I have that music." Scott found it in his library, and they practiced the song all afternoon. Scott suggested she add some footwork to show how she could move.

The drama teacher soon announced the musical "Guys and Dolls," leaving both Caroline and Scott less than enthused. The casting prospects weren't promising, given the limited singing roles. The spotlight was primarily on the four main leads, and the female parts required a soprano and an alto. Scott, a baritone, was taken aback by the requirements for the male leads. He wondered if they were planning to alter the keys for the males. "Jason is exceptionally good at composition. He may have ideas about altering the parts he feeds the director."

"Do you still think 'Cinderella' is a good audition song?" asked Caroline.

"Let me think about it. I still have to decide what I'm going to sing," Scott said.

"I think you have a better chance, as your voice has a deeper range," said Caroline encouragingly.

"That's sweet, hon, but don't forget the politics. It's the world of dramatic arts. You can't find a group of more competitive, vicious, and back-stabbing people."

"I don't like to think that's who I am or who you are," said Caroline.

"Why do you want to do this?" asked Scott. "You have to be truthful about yourself at some point. My skills are in the arts. I have to play the game and play it successfully, or I might as well not bother. What else is a guy like me going to do?"

"Oh, Scott, don't be silly," Caroline cried. "You're good at lots of things. You won the race for student council representative. Perhaps you can enter government service or the law."

"Hon, you're a riot. I'm on student council because it's a path to a higher profile. That will help with college applications. I focused on where I could be successful. Sometimes, Caroline, I think you're too sweet and naïve."

"Oh, I'm tougher than you think, but I'm not political enough for the drama club."

"You might as well learn to play the game. It's in almost every field."

Scott's mind was on audition music, so Caroline strolled to one of the beautiful picture windows to look out. Serena never mentioned being political. She would have to ask her guides how this fit into her path.

"Here's a thought," Scott said. "Perhaps we can audition together and perform 'Till There Was You' from 'The Music Man'!"

"That would be lovely," Caroline said thoughtfully. "Do you think it will be alright?"

"Yeah, I think it will make us stand out in a good way. After all, this is still high school. There usually aren't any set rules for auditioning other than having a vocal number. How you perform it is pretty open."

"Let's do it," said Caroline. She and Scott worked on the number for the rest of the afternoon.

Eventually, tryouts arrived. Caroline felt more confident this time, being better prepared and eager to audition alongside Scott. As the students assembled in the auditorium, Caroline observed her surroundings. Then she whispered to Scott, "Karen isn't here!"

Scott glanced around the room and responded, "You're right! I wonder what's going on."

Students auditioned in alphabetical order, and Caroline came before Scott. They walked up together and told the director, "We've prepared a duet. Is that a problem?"

"Not at all," he replied. "Great idea."

Scott gave the accompanist their music, and after the opening notes, they began to sing. Caroline's voice was more substantial. Scott suggested that she modulate it on the parts they sang together but let her voice soar when she sang alone. When finished, they were pleased.

The week leading up to the list's release was nerve-wracking for Caroline. She and Smokey sought help every afternoon under the elm tree, regardless of the weather. Finally, the day arrived when the list was posted, and Caroline had achieved her goal—she secured the lead role! It was a day of immense joy, and she rushed home to share the news with her parents, who seemed genuinely pleased. As Caroline sat with Smokey on their chair, she expressed her gratitude to the universe, acknowledging even those trickier elements that might have played a role in Karen falling ill. Scott had won the third lead, so they worked through the book each afternoon for a week.

Official rehearsals hadn't started when the director sent a message to Caroline to meet with him after school in the auditorium. She couldn't believe the words she heard. There had been a protest because Karen couldn't audition. The drama teacher decided that both girls would need to audition again. Caroline felt this wasn't fair, and the director seemed to agree. "Unfortunately, I have no choice on this," he said. That meant the drama teacher had intervened along with the male leads.

The re-tryout was the day after tomorrow. Caroline couldn't audition again with Scott. She went to him in a panic.

Scott slammed his fists against a locker. "This is bullshit. You won that role fair and square. It's politics at its worst. I'd lodge a complaint, but it wouldn't do you any good."

"More importantly," said Caroline, "what will I sing? It's too short of a time to prepare anything new."

Scott thought for a minute. "OK, the role of Sarah Brown has already been given to Ellen. That was the perfect role for you. Adelaide is the contention, and she's a bombastic alto. Not exactly you. That's probably why they demanded Karen get a chance to audition. Do you know any tunes where you can lower your voice and belt out the song?"

Caroline leaned against the lockers, trying to think. A message came to her: *Cabaret*. "Scott, what about 'Cabaret'?" she asked.

"Ooh, that's perfect. Do you know it?"

"Not really, but I've heard it. Do you have the music?"

"I think so, said Scott. "Give me an hour to prep after school and expect a long night. Do you have props like a top hat or a boa?"

Caroline just stared at him.

"Right. I'll try to check the prop room. See you this afternoon."

Caroline tried to keep the panic at bay. "Guys and Dolls" wasn't the best musical for her, but she had won the lead even if her voice and style weren't perfect. Caroline knew Karen had an edge. Even so, she wasn't going to give away her role.

Scott and Caroline rehearsed, taking care not to strain her voice excessively. Caroline diligently followed her practice routine at home, putting in extra effort. When she finally retired for the night, she couldn't help but plead with the universe: "I don't understand why you've made this even more challenging. Can I catch a break, just this once?" Then, she drifted off to sleep.

Caroline slept poorly and didn't feel she looked her best. She wanted to look and feel confident before the second audition. Scott had decided to sit in the back so that he was there for moral support but wouldn't make it look as if Caroline needed help. The director said they would go alphabetically again. That meant Caroline went first. She walked to the accompanist and handed him her music. She walked to the center of the stage and said, "I've prepared a new piece for this audition. I apologize in advance if I forget a few of the words." She turned her back to the audience and signaled the pianist. He began to play, and Caroline went into character. She tried to lose herself in the performance. Upon completion, there was no applause, and she hadn't anticipated any. This performance was to show them that she deserved to retain the role.

Karen performed Ethel Merman's "I Got Rhythm." Caroline was surprised by the choice given last year's musical, but it showcased Karen's lower range. When Karen finished, she smiled and walked down. She hadn't added anything to the performance as Caroline had, but she probably felt it wasn't necessary.

The director came to the stage, thanked the girls for the audition, and noted that Caroline had prepared two different numbers to help them decide.

He closed by saying they would re-post the line-up in two days. Caroline felt the director was still on her side, but she wasn't sure that was enough.

Scott came down to get Caroline and drive her home. He didn't speak until they were alone. "You did great, and you know it. I believe you proved you can handle the part. Now, we have to wait. Try not to worry."

Caroline didn't say anything. She thanked him for the ride and all his help with the audition.

That night, lying on her bed, using her gifts, Caroline gazed into the universe to see her future. She saw nothing, but she knew the rules. "We are blind to our fate," Serena often said.

It was time for the re-posting of the cast list to appear on the drama teacher's door. Caroline waited. She listened to her gut and knew she had lost. Karen arrived with the other leads to read her name. Caroline only had to decide how to respond. She never looked at the list. Why bother? She congratulated Karen and walked away. Jason came running up to her, telling her how great she had done in the audition and asking her to remain in the show. He said they needed an understudy for one of the leads.

She looked at him intently and said, "I must not have given a great audition since I didn't retain the role I already won and started to work on." She told him she wouldn't continue with the show. She wasn't excited about "Guys and Dolls" and wasn't interested in serving as an understudy yet again.

Singing was now painful. Once again, she wondered if she should have remained in the band. Or perhaps music had played its role in her life, and it was time to move on. Her heart was heavy, and she just wanted to go home and cry alone so that no one could see her hurt.

The following day, Caroline found herself disinterested in attending school. It wasn't a matter of dreading social interactions; she had mastered that skill. Rather, it was the sense that the toil of school had lost its significance. She yearned for the farm and the comforting presence of her grandparents. As for the second tryout, her mother never brought it up. There wasn't any need. What she hated most was Caroline dropping out of the church choir. But Caroline disagreed with the principles of that church, and without choir, there was no reason to continue. For once, her mother didn't fight her.

When Caroline asked to go to the farm for spring break, her mother agreed. Caroline would have a chance to rest and perhaps find her love of music again. But rather than talking to her mother about singing, Caroline spoke about getting a job in the mountains that summer. Her mother was surprised and a bit concerned. However, Caroline was 17, and her mother didn't feel she could hold on to her too tightly. Changes were coming to the family, and Caroline would need to make decisions about her life's direction.

When Caroline got back home, Scott came to see her. He was worried about his friend. He asked her if there was anything he could do for her. "Maybe you could find me a date to the junior prom. It would be nice to go to one dance," she said.

Scott laughed. "If you promise to get all dolled up in a killer dress, I'll take you to the prom," he said.

Caroline looked at him with surprise. "I'm certain my mother will make me a dress," she said.

"Let's go shopping together, and I'll help you pick out the pattern and the fabric. You might choose something too conservative," he said.

"You'll go to the fabric store?" she asked.

"Sure," Scott replied. "I've gone with my mom many times."

Caroline's mother was thrilled Caroline was going to the prom, and she gave her the cash to buy everything necessary to make the dress. Caroline was surprised at the amount. She and Scott had a blast picking everything out. Scott selected a slinky sapphire blue fabric. Though her mother was concerned about how much skin Caroline would show in the dress, she made it just as Caroline requested.

The day of the prom, Scott took her down to The Denver department store, where he now worked, and had one of his friends at the Estee Lauder counter apply her makeup. She went home and curled her hair in long tendrils. When Scott picked her up, he stood good-naturedly smiling for photos. He gave her a lovely corsage of Colorado blue columbines. On his navy suit, Caroline pinned a white rose boutonniere with a sapphire blue ribbon to match her dress.

Scott took her to the best Italian restaurant in downtown Arvada. It was full of other prom couples. For the first time, Caroline felt like any other high school junior. In the school gym, they danced to the latest songs from Donna Summer, Earth, Wind & Fire, and The Trammps. Scott suggested they leave early, as he had a surprise for her. They drove back downtown to the Brown Palace. Scott pulled his mother's mink stole out of the trunk and told Caroline to put it on. They went to the hotel disco. As they began to enter, Scott turned to Caroline and told her to act as if she were a rich bitch who went out clubbing all the time. "You know how to act now," he said. "Do it!"

Caroline flipped her hair back and sailed into the club full of attitude. They sat at the table, and when the waitress came by, Scott ordered two whiskey sours. When the drinks arrived, Scott gave Caroline a big grin and said, "Cheers!" That became their regular Saturday night activity.

Scott even convinced Caroline to stay in town over the summer. He assisted her in securing a flexible position at The Denver, where she worked in various departments as needed. Scott provided transportation whenever possible, while her mother—pleased with Caroline's newfound enthusiasm—shared her car. Caroline invested most of her summer earnings in stylish attire for her outings with Scott. Scott suggested they frequent hotels to avoid age-related issues, and they explored the city together.

When Caroline went to see Serena on her weekly trip, she told the nymph about what had happened with the musical and how she spent her time. Serena couldn't understand everything Caroline said, but she was pleased to see Caroline "exploring her universe." While Caroline hadn't come up to the mountains to work, which disappointed Serena, she promised to do so next year.

"It is time for you to begin thinking about the future," Serena said. "I want you to go to the lower level and sit by the pool. Ask your spirit guides to give you a glimpse of what might come."

Caroline did as instructed. She looked into the cold, clear water and saw herself sitting at a table with a typewriter. Caroline shared the vision with Serena, who smiled in response.

# A Fresh Beginning

AROLINE'S SENIOR YEAR DID not go as expected. Her first surprise was news from her parents: They were moving, leaving Colorado for a place called Branson, Missouri.

Caroline had never been there. "I plan to work in real estate there, and your dad and I will build spec homes," her mother explained. "Your dad has been offered a package by the Denver Post to retire early, which we feel he should take. Computers will soon do his job, and the money will help us start the new business. I also feel a new place might help your dad with his drinking."

Caroline's father was off the wagon and back on the booze. He no longer bothered her, but he was as mean as ever. He appeared to channel the bulk of his anger toward Edward—a situation that Caroline deemed unjust. Edward's future seemed uncertain after his baseball career faltered, and the thought of him brought Caroline pain. She longed to utilize her skills to assist him, yet he maintained a barrier between them.

Her college applications came up over dinner one night. Her father's words shocked her: "After all the trouble you caused, you think I'm gonna send you to college? That would be a waste of money. You should concentrate on finding a boyfriend who will date you and a job that can provide for you and any children you might have." He delivered a brutally unexpected blow that deeply wounded Caroline.

She sat in the room she had lived in since childhood. She no longer went into the closet. She could lay on her bed or gaze out from her seat under the elm tree to talk to whomever she wanted to on the other side. But today, she didn't look outward. She tried to think about a life in which this would no longer be her home. She didn't want to leave Colorado, at least not yet. She still wanted to spend the summer in the mountains with Serena. But the only way she could go to college was to pay for it. She wondered whether she needed to apply to a community college and where she would live.

She heard a faint knock on her door. "Come in," she said.

"Caroline, do you have a minute to talk?" asked her mom.

"Sure. What's up?" she asked.

"I wanted to talk to you about college," her mother said.

"Yeah, I was thinking about that, too. Perhaps I can get a loan . . ."

Her mother interrupted. "Caroline, it's unfair that your father would pay for your brother's college and not yours. I believe the drinking is beginning to affect his thinking."

Caroline laughed to herself. *Gee, Mom, haven't you noticed that he's never been fair to me? Or kind. I wish he would drink himself to death. Then, I would be done with him. Maybe I could get a scholarship for kids with only one parent still alive . . .*

"As I said, Caroline, I will pay your college fees. I suggest you apply to Boulder, Fort Collins, and maybe Greeley. Those are all good schools. I don't know if you can get a scholarship now that you aren't in a music program, but perhaps you can ask your school counselor. Anyway, I will pay for tuition, room, and board. Any extras, you must pay yourself. I would prefer that you didn't work during school and that you concentrate on your grades, but you need a job during the summer, and you must save as much as possible. You might have to curtail your nights out with Scott, assuming he's not always paying."

"Why would Scott pay for me?" Caroline asked.

"Well, because that's what boyfriends do," said her mother.

"First, it's not the Fifties where boys pay for everything. And Scott's not my boyfriend. He's my, my . . ." Caroline had never defined their relationship. Scott was a person she trusted, the most genuine friend she'd had since Gwynn. "He's just a good friend," she finished lamely.

"Oh, I didn't realize that," said her mother. "Perhaps you should spend less time with him so other boys would feel they can ask you out."

Caroline burst out laughing. "Boys ask *me* out? No, Mom, that will never happen at A-West. I'll forever be the weird girl."

"Why would people think that, Caroline?"

She didn't want to spend time trying to explain to her mother now what life at school had been like for her. She'd let her mother stick her head back in the sand.

"I'm certain there are nice boys from church who would be happy to take out a pretty girl like you," her mother continued.

No, Mom, I will never date a Southern Baptist boy. Thank you for paying for school. I appreciate that so much. I'll make certain all my paperwork is in."

"Alright, I'll let you be.' said her mother as she walked out.

*And I'll ensure I have a summer job in Summit Country.*

Caroline called the ski areas near Serena's cave. Keystone seemed like the best place, and they offered housing. They would send her a packet to fill out. Caroline gave them her name and number and told them she would take anything available but reminded them that she had retail experience. Caroline consulted her guidance counselor, collaborating to complete her college application paperwork. She knew she wouldn't fancy Greeley, so she chose not to apply there. Boulder remained her top choice, even though many classmates planned to attend. Its status as the largest school offered her the prospect of blending in and avoiding encounters with A-West students.

Graduation was coming fast, which made Caroline happy. She was so ready to move on from here, and with her parents leaving, she would never have to return to Arvada and the painful reminders. She was thrilled to leave her house and all its darkness. The only thing she would miss was the elm tree. And Smokey. Because Caroline would be living in dorms, Smokey was going to the farm. She hated to let go of her beloved cat. One evening, Caroline brushed Smokey repeatedly until the cat went into a trance. Caroline connected with Smokey, explaining why she was going to the farm. Smokey might not have been thrilled, but he grasped the situation. Caroline expressed her gratitude to the cat, as she had learned to do, for being a steadfast companion all these years. She intended to request her grandparents' permission for Smokey to reside indoors, though Grandpa Andersen might insist on Smokey joining the other cats in the barn.

It hadn't occurred to Caroline to try out for the musical that year. The drama teacher chose "Fiddler on the Roof" to showcase Jason's talents. Caroline laughed, as even Karen hadn't auditioned for the lead female role because it was so small.

Scott told her he was asking Lisa to be his date to the senior prom. He liked Lisa, and Caroline thought highly of her as well. While disappointed, she knew she couldn't expect Scott to take her as a friend two years in a row. To her surprise, however, a sweet boy named Paul, who played on the varsity soccer team, asked her to go. She didn't know him well, but he hung out with a fun group, and she agreed. Caroline picked out the dress and fabric this time. She decided on red. *Might as well go out with a bang*, she thought. She went to the dance with Paul and his friends and had an excellent time. She was happy to have a positive event to close out her life in Arvada.

The Monday after the dance, a letter arrived from Keystone. She had a summer job!

# Mountain Girl

*H*ER MOTHER DROVE CAROLINE up to the mountains to help her get settled. They had packed up her room, and her mother took a few favorites, reminding Caroline, "You'll always have a room

at home." All the items Caroline planned to take to her dorm room at CU went to Keystone. "If there isn't a room where you're staying, we'll rent a storage locker," her mom said.

Caroline's excitement knew no bounds as her long-awaited dream of spending the summer in the mountains—working, hiking, and training with Serena—had finally become a reality. Though her room at the Keystone housing had bunks for four girls, one had dropped out at the last minute. Her two roommates were best friends from East High, named Cindy and Meg. They told her to use the extra space for her belongings. To a kid from Arvada, rooming with girls from East was considered super cool, and Caroline was excited. Fortunately, Meg had a car with which to explore other parts of the county, like Breckenridge. The county offered a free bus system, so Caroline could go to the Silverthorne station and hike up to Serena's cave.

The first time she arrived, Serena had everything ready for her. "Now that I have you for the summer, we can accelerate your learning," she said. "Why do we need to accelerate it?" Caroline asked. "Now that I'm here, I thought we could move more leisurely and go deeper into certain subjects."

"Change is in the wind," answered Serena. "We must hasten to be ready." Caroline knew better than to question her.

That summer, they discussed angels and archangels, how to call them, and for what reason. "Archangel Michael uses his sword to open the Rainbow Bridge, and Jaguar helps to round up the lost souls and cross them into the light," Serena explained as she showed Caroline how to perform this work. Serena showed Caroline how to remove discarnates and other negative entities like poltergeists. Caroline talked to Serena about the dark creatures she had felt in her childhood room. Serena confirmed there had been a poltergeist. She had seen it attached to Caroline when she'd first met her. Serena surmised it had been on her father and transferred over to Caroline. She had removed it shortly after they met. "Nasty creatures that come from dark energy," said Serena. "Not easy to get rid of."

Caroline asked a question that had bugged her for a long time. "Do you remember when I fell out of the car?"

"Yes, that was the first time I saw you. Your wings made certain you didn't hurt yourself."

"So, I have wings?" asked Caroline.

"Yes," said Serena. "That is not uncommon, but most humans never apply them."

"Can we bring them out again?" asked Caroline.

"Of course. I'm surprised I didn't think of that. Let's go to the entrance to the cave."

Caroline panicked. "You're not going to push me out and expect me to fly to the ground below, are you?"

Serena released one of her rare laughs. "No. But the air and wind will help you feel them. Now, stand outside and move into a trance state. Feel your shoulder blades. Move them around to loosen the area. Feel yourself flying over the plains as you've done when visiting the chief. Look to the ground from the air as if hunting for animals. Feel your wings opening as you fly. Feel the weight on your back. Pull in your feet so they don't disrupt the flow of air. Can you feel your flight feathers? They are unique."

Caroline felt the wings unfold. The weight unbalanced her, but once she adjusted and held the wings at the right angle, she could feel the air lifting her.

"I want you to fold the wings back in," said Serena. "You aren't meant to use them all the time. They are a type of protection that allows you to move from danger. You can practice using them as I have shown you."

Caroline relished every moment they spent delving into animal communications. "Cats, naturally, are the most receptive to spirit world communication, given their comfort with it compared to dogs," Serena said. Caroline shared her experience of communicating with Smokey. "You approached it correctly with a cat," Serena said. "Learning to converse with various animals requires dedication. Keep in mind that they often convey messages through images. Practice with Smokey the next time you encounter her."

Another topic they spent quite a bit of time on was the death rites. "The shaman in a tribe is responsible for administering the death rites," Serena explained. She took Caroline through the rituals of many cultures so she would understand the similarities and differences. "Goddesses have supervised this work since the beginning of time. The most important work has to do with the burial rites. Parts of the soul can break off during a life. You want to gather the soul together to ascend as a single unit. Make certain the soul does not stay with the body. You also want to protect the body from use by any witches that practice the dark arts. Place four rocks in the corner of the body wrapping or casket. Chant the shielding rites over each rock." Caroline hoped that Serena wasn't spending so much time on this because she foresaw the coming of the death of someone Caroline loved, like her grandparents.

When possible, Caroline spent the night. That made it easier to work on astrology, as Serena could chart the different signs in the night sky. They researched Caroline's birth chart, allowing Serena to show how her birth foretold personality traits, marriages, and pregnancy. Serena said that, as time permitted, they would work more on astrology. "As you might know, Asian cultures often use a birth chart to select marriage partners or the date to start a new business," she said. "It's a significant topic, and we could spend the rest of our lives seeking to understand just that modality." Using the five sacred colors, they made mandalas in the sand or on the cured hides. They took walks, looking for herbs and rocks to feed Caroline's mesa.

Caroline's roommates frequently inquired about her whereabouts. At that point, she simply shook her head, offering no further explanation, leaving them to wonder if she had a hidden boyfriend somewhere. Caroline was discovering the advantages of cultivating an air of mystery. It made her more intriguing to others, and she could keep her secrets to herself. Nevertheless, Caroline did manage to socialize with the girls, albeit while cautiously managing her finances. Meg, who had plenty of money, was generous, whether it was buying cigarettes (a habit Caroline had picked up while out with Scott) or drinks. Underage drinking was commonplace at the ski resorts, although most people opted for Coors, which Caroline disliked. She ordered whiskey sours whenever possible. Her mother sent her a weekly letter telling her how they were settling in. She said she would return to Colorado to pick up Caroline at the end of the summer and help her move into the dorm. Caroline wrote back that her mother didn't need to bother, as Scott had offered to pick her up. She saw him often, as he visited the mountains to attend frat parties. The Boulder fraternities held recruiting parties in the mountains, allowing Caroline to meet boys from other schools and even other states. Boulder was a famous school for rich kids from out of state, particularly California. Cindy and Meg would also be going there in the fall. They were rooming together and told Caroline they wished they had met sooner, as they would have signed up for a suite.

Caroline was fine with the lottery but didn't want to live with anyone from A-West. She was glad to have made new friends with whom to begin fresh relationships. They asked Caroline if she was planning to rush a sorority. Caroline didn't know what that meant. They explained all the advantages of living in a sorority house.

"So, the only cost is housing?" Caroline asked.

"Well, there are other expenses," Meg explained, such as dues and gifts for big sisters and little sisters and dresses for rush week and the different parties. Caroline laughed and said she probably didn't have the extra funds for that. The girls were kind enough not to bring it up again. Caroline was glad she had learned about this before she made a fool of herself by going through rush. Scott said she could be a little sister at his fraternity. Caroline had no idea what that meant and couldn't fully understand it. However, she was glad to go with him to the frat parties. She met several cute boys and even got asked out a few times. It was nice to date in the mountains, as there were no expectations about what you wore. Jeans and a button-down shirt with a sweater were all one needed.

The summer solstice marked the most joyful day of the season for

Caroline. She joined Serena at the cave's entrance and offered prayers to the Moon Goddess under her various names. Caroline's magical abilities flourished as she honed her skills in igniting and extinguishing fires, as well as scrying using polished plates or the tranquil waters of a nearby pool.

The high mountain summer ended far too soon. As Caroline said goodbye to Serena, the nymph asked if she had decided what to study in school. Caroline's mind flashed to the image of a typewriter. "No," she replied. "I want to take different elective classes and see what I like."

"I take it you won't continue with your music," Serena said.

Caroline considered the students selected for the University of Denver's music program. She knew Karen was planning to study in Boulder. "No, I definitely won't be studying that or journalism." Her mother had made it clear that her father would not allow Caroline to get a journalism degree even though he wasn't paying for college, and she had promised not to work for a newspaper.

"Don't allow the gifts you have to go unused," Serena advised. "While the original plans might not have come to fruition, that doesn't mean something you love won't play a role in your life."

Caroline gave the nymph a long hug, which she now allowed. "I won't," she whispered into her ear.

# The Guitar Man

AROLINE STACKED BOOKS ON the top shelf of her desk in the dorm room while her mother made the bed. Grandmother Andersen had sewn Caroline a lovely twin-sized quilt in the tiniest blue and yellow squares for her high school graduation gift. Her mother had purchased yellow and blue sheets and matching towels. Caroline liked the room but was a bit anxious about meeting her roommate. Before this summer, she had never shared a room with anyone else. She appreciated the opportunity to practice with Meg and Cindy, who also resided in Baker Hall. Similar to them, her roommate had arrived early for rush week. Caroline harbored some anxiety that her roommate might have encountered girls from A-West and heard some unkind gossip about her. Nevertheless, Caroline persisted in her silent plea to the universe for a chance at a fresh start.

"Well, I guess that's it," said her mother, looking around anxiously. Caroline was ready to send her mother on her way but sensed something was bothering her. "Hey, Mom, I appreciate you coming back and helping me get set up," said Caroline. "I know it's a long drive for you."

"I didn't mind," said her mother. "It gave me a chance to check on your grandparents."

"Mom, do you like living in Branson?" asked Caroline.

"It's a nice community, and I like the church, but it's a big change."

"How's Dad?" Caroline ventured.

"I wish he were doing better. I've researched several treatment centers, but he won't go."

Caroline hated thinking of her mother doing this by herself. "Has Andrew come to visit?" she asked.

"Yes! He came down to help us unpack. It's nice to be closer to him. I hope Edward looks for a job in Kansas City or St. Louis when he graduates. However, the job market isn't strong in the rust belt states right now. I'm glad your dad took his package from the Post, but he needs to stay busy. I'd hoped the house-building business would keep him occupied. Don't get me wrong, it is helping, but he wants to be more of a supervisor, which wasn't what I expected."

Once again, her father had to be in charge while her mother worked. Caroline hated it. "Don't be afraid to put your foot down, Mom."

Her mother gave her a wan smile, then jumped up and said she needed to go. Caroline felt worried. All around her mother was a dark aura, with only a tiny amount of light colors coming through. "I'll be praying for you, Mom. Please keep writing. I enjoy your letters."

Her mother turned and gave Caroline the biggest smile of the trip. "I will, Caroline. Please be safe." And with that, she was gone.

Caroline sat on her bed. The sun coming through her windows brightened the colors in her quilt. She touched it and saw her grandmother sewing it during a warm spring afternoon at the farm. Caroline could smell the freshly turned earth, ready for planting. The image made her smile but also brought on loneliness. Everyone was so far away. While she was glad to be free of her parents' control, she wanted to feel in charge of her future, which was unclear whenever she tried to look at it. She knew better. "The future is uncertain." Serena always said, "You are writing it every day."

*Yes, that's true. But some direction wouldn't hurt,* Caroline thought.

"Hi," came a loud voice. Caroline looked toward the door and saw a bouncing blonde girl. She seemed to bounce everywhere. Caroline knew immediately that she was rooming with a popular girl—not what she had hoped for. "I'm Amanda. You must be Caroline."

"Yes, it's nice to meet you.

Have you been at rush parties?" Caroline asked.

"Yes," answered Amanda in an exhausted voice. "There are so many sororities, and it's hard to decide which is the best because the houses are so pretty and the girls so nice." She plopped onto her bed. "How come you didn't get through rush? You're attractive. I'm sure you would get in somewhere." Amanda's words were running together.

"It's not for me," replied Caroline. "I like smaller groups of friends."

"Oh, huh, well, I come from Pueblo, and that's already small," Amanda responded. "I'm so excited to meet all the new girls and boys. Oh, my, are there lots of cute boys."

"Yes," Caroline replied. "I have a good friend who just pledged the SAE house."

"Oh, that's a good one," Amanda said, interrupting Caroline. "Is he cute?"

Caroline laughed, "Yes, he's cute and very nice. I'm meeting him this evening now that I've settled in."

"I have another round of parties to attend." Amanda sighed. "But I hope I can meet him soon!"

"I'll let you know when they're having a party," said Caroline. The one person she didn't want to share was Scott. He was her only security at this school.

Caroline reviewed her class schedule and made some decisions. She opted to prioritize her required courses, with the exception of math, which she planned to tackle in a different semester. She also included a creative writing class, inspired by the persistent image of a typewriter in her mind. She couldn't help but wonder if this meant she should purchase one. Caroline hoped this wasn't a foreshadowing of flunking out of college and ending up as a secretary at a mundane downtown company. As she glanced at the clock, she realized she was running late and hurried out the door.

Scott was sitting in a booth at Round Table Pizza, a popular, inexpensive restaurant in Boulder. Caroline had ridden her bike. She'd had a ridiculous argument about bringing it to school, as her mother was worried it would get stolen. "Mom, I don't have a car, and Boulder is a big campus,"

Caroline had argued. "I paid for it, and I need it at school. Besides, why should you drag it to Missouri?"

Scott regaled Caroline with stories about the different SAEs. "One guy is a total surfer dude from Laguna Beach. His hair is so blond it's practically white. He talks in surfer language, and you can tell he's a total stoner, but he's found Christ and always goes to church."

"What a waste," responded Caroline.

"Agreed," said Scott. He went on to tell her about his roommates, who were from Kirkwood, Missouri, a suburb of St. Louis. "They came for the skiing. They seem nice enough. I think you would like them. By the way, how's your roommate?"

Caroline groaned and told Scott about her. She mentioned Amanda's desire to meet him.

"She'd probably like my roommates better. But she might not be a skier if she's from Pueblo."

Caroline was hoping to meet more kids from up in the mountains. She felt a kindred spirit in them, and the natural barrier might mean less knowledge of what went on in Arvada.

Scott interrupted her daydream. "Have you seen anyone from A-West?"

Caroline's skin grew cold. "Fortunately not. I expect someone will be in my dorm building, but no one on my floor." She thanked the universe for giving her this small but essential break.

"As you can imagine, they're all over Fraternity Row," Scott said. "There'll be plenty of parties with the end of rush. Do you want to go?"

Caroline didn't want to run into guys from high school, but the crowds should be large enough that if she saw one, she could slip away. She would shield and ask for extra protection from anyone from A-West. Serena had taught her a repellent charm to help her with unwanted men known to cruise Boulder at night. She might try it on an A-West football player. "OK. I'll probably have to ask you what to wear."

Scott laughed. "Don't worry. Pull out your preppiest outfit. Or you can always go as a mountain mama. My skier roommates would love that." He smirked. Their pizza arrived, and they dug in.

Caroline was so glad Scott had decided not to attend DU. Boulder's Greek life had been the deciding factor, and regardless of Caroline's growing negative feelings about it, she was happy that it had brought Scott to CU. She relished the pizza but knew there would be few nights out like this. It would drain her cash too quickly. Tonight was special, though, as classes were starting the next day.

When Caroline opened her dorm room, the lights were off. With a quick movement of her fingers, she lit the room with a soft glow that allowed her to enjoy the night lights of Boulder, which were visible through her window. She would need to find a place outside near her dorm where she could sit and listen to the messages from the universe.

When the morning came, Caroline put on her second favorite outfit: her worn Levi 501s and a pink button-down shirt. She had cute sandals that had gotten worn down over the summer, but they were comfortable for the long walks between classes. She brushed her hair until it was shiny and pulled it back with a tortoiseshell headband. Fortunately, Amanda had left early, so Caroline had quiet time to shield herself and prepare for the day. She decided to arrive just before classes began so that she could scan the room for potential friends before picking a seat. Interestingly, her creative writing class was the first.

Professor Porter had placed the desks in a circle, which Caroline found strange. It made her nervous—no way to hide here. After everyone was seated and Caroline noted that there was no one she knew, the teacher explained the purpose of the setup. They would be reading many of their compositions aloud. Input on writing was essential, and she wanted everyone to feel equal. She had people introduce themselves and mention something they would like to write about. When Caroline's turn came, she told everyone this was her first day of college and class at CU. This garnered her some sympathy, as many older kids were in the class.

She mentioned she had spent the summer working at Keystone and loved the mountains and nature. Professor Porter responded positively and said the outdoors allowed for themes and color in writing. She highlighted how they would explore writing across various genres—a revelation that caught Caroline off guard, as she had presumed the focus would be solely on fiction. The professor emphasized that mastering the art of writing for diverse audiences could enhance and fortify one's overall writing abilities. Caroline found herself growing fonder of this instructor and held out hope that her other professors would prove equally captivating.

She returned to her room, surprised by the mounds of homework she already had. She had to develop a study schedule to accomplish all the writing requirements. Her roommate suddenly bounded through the door, disturbing the quiet Caroline craved. "Are you ready to go to dinner?" she asked loudly. "I'm starving!"

Caroline appreciated the invitation and quickly got ready to head downstairs. After they had gone through the line, Amanda cried out, "Oh, there are some nice girls I met during rush." Caroline looked over and zeroed in on Karen from A-West. Fortunately, she saw Meg and Cindy at another table.

Caroline quickly said, "Why don't you join them? I'm going to catch up with my friends from Keystone." Then, she raced through the crowded room. She hoped Karen hadn't noticed her. Caroline sent her thoughts to Karen and saw the girl was about to ask Amanda about her roommate. She sent a different message to Karen, clearing *her roommate* from her thoughts. *It worked*, Caroline said to herself as relief flooded through her. Now, she was glad for all the hard work with Serena over the summer.

As Caroline, Meg, and Cindy left the cafeteria, Caroline saw a message board full of flyers. She decided to walk over and take a look. Meg and Cindy weren't interested, so they headed upstairs. Caroline read the different pamphlets but didn't see anything of interest until she came across one advertising an open mic night at a local coffeehouse called Penny Lane. It invited singers to come by. Serena's comment about music came to mind, and Caroline thought about the enjoyable afternoons she'd spent with Scott singing songs at the piano. There might be ways to enjoy music still. She made a mental note of the time and location and headed upstairs to start on her homework.

Caroline relished one of her conveniences: having a phone right in her room, with free campus-wide calling. When Scott called and mentioned a party scheduled for Saturday night, Caroline suggested the idea of first visiting the coffeehouse, Penny Lane. Scott responded with some disinterest, deeming it somewhat dull. Caroline made up her mind to swing by the coffeehouse before heading over to the fraternity. Scott's response was a simple "Perfect!" before he hung up the phone.

Penny Lane was an eclectic, bohemian coffeehouse, seemingly more of a place one might find in Greenwich Village than Boulder. The stage was small but looked like it had an upright piano in the corner. Caroline found an empty table in the back. She didn't recognize anyone and settled in to listen. An announcer introduced each act, and performers generally soloed using a guitar. One person chose the piano.

Near the end, a performer went onstage. For some reason, he stood out to Caroline. The man had curly dark blond hair and wore an old, wrinkled blue button-down shirt. She thought she caught a glimpse of a gold chain around his neck. Seated at the piano, he began with an opening melody before transitioning to the guitar. Combining two Beatles songs, both by the highly acclaimed John Lennon, who had gained immense popularity with his latest album release, he displayed a unique style that intrigued Caroline. These performers stood out from the crowd; they weren't vying for a role or a solo.

Instead, they sang for the sheer love of it, much like the birds in the trees outside Serena's cave.

Caroline left soon after the curly-haired boy finished playing. She had promised Amanda that she would be at the party to introduce her to Scott. Amanda had pledged to the Chi Omega sorority, and Caroline expected she would have no problem meeting guys. But Scott was expecting her as well.

The party was crazy. There were so many people! Caroline was still trying to figure out how she would find Scott. She went to the top of the steps by one of the columns, where she recognized some of his frat brothers. Suddenly, arms were wrapped around her in a big hug. She jumped and then realized her mistake. It was just a drunken Scott. "Where have you been?" he slurred.

"At Penny Lane. Don't you remember?" she asked.

"Oh, yeah, with the granola heads," he mumbled.

"They weren't like that at all. Several were quite talented. They didn't seem like people who were part of the music program. They just sang for the love of it. Like you and I used to." She punched him in the arm, and he burped.

"Let's get you a drink!" Scott said.

She hated this part of a frat party. The beer smelled like her dad, and the "punch" was toxic, blended to get girls drunk with one cup. She dreamed of the days of whiskey sours in the Brown Palace. But a CU frat party worked differently. She opted for beer.

Scott saw his roommates and yelled out. He eagerly ushered Caroline over to introduce her to the group. They were charming, humorous, and just as intoxicated as Scott. They quizzed her about her skiing experiences, but she hesitated to reveal her limited knowledge. Instead, she steered the conversation toward her summer hikes along the ski trails—a topic they appeared to find engaging. However, their attention quickly shifted, and they moved on.

Amanda came up with a loud "Hi!" Fortunately, Scott was within grabbing distance, and Caroline pulled him over to introduce her roommate. He gave her a bow like he'd done the first time Caroline had met him. Amanda was immediately smitten. Caroline left them to talk about nothing as she wandered around. She spotted a bench under a tree and gravitated toward it. Then, she sat down and gazed at the sky. Suddenly, someone caught her eye. It was the guy from Penny Lane! She hadn't expected to see him here. He was talking to a few older guys who were far less drunk than the other frat brothers. Caroline studied him. He seemed very relaxed, just like his shirt. He had piercing blue eyes and a wonderful smile. Caroline wondered if it was all for show. Underneath, would he be the tender, soulful guy she saw performing on stage? The party crowd was surging in her direction. It was time to move. As she got up, the guitar player looked her way. He smiled.

Was that for her? She smiled back but kept walking, looking for a less crowded spot. Scott found her and took her to meet more people. She smiled and talked. Someone passed a joint around, and Caroline took a hit. Sporadically, she gazed around to see if the guitar player would walk by. Scott was now stoned and drunk. Caroline decided it was time to head home. It had been an exciting night.

She locked up her bike and noticed a large oak tree with a stone bench underneath. *Aha,* she thought. *Let's see if this will do.* She sat on the hard stone, growing colder as the nighttime temperature dropped. Though there were sounds of drunken people, she blocked them out and opened her third eye to the universe. Some sad sounds were floating by. Caroline knew this meant a young person had died, lost in the space between the worlds. While Caroline could call for Archangel Michael to help the lost soul cross the Rainbow Bridge into the light, she wasn't comfortable performing this ritual where others might see her. She listened some more but didn't hear any messages specifically for her. She then turned to listening to the music of the universe. The movement of the stars created a unique melody. Caroline found it peaceful. As her eyes began to close, she realized it was time for bed.

The fall sped by. There were football games on Saturdays. On homecoming weekend, Caroline went as Scott's guest to the game and the alum dinner afterward. She thought it was sweet of him to include her. For the game, to show team spirit, Caroline wore a Buffs sweatshirt that her mother had purchased. For the dinner, she changed into one of the nicer outfits she had bought when working at The Denver. Scott complimented her, making her feel as if she wouldn't stand out in the wrong way. All the guys had sobered up from the game and cleaned up to impress the alums. Scott had brought some of his best jackets with him and was looking particularly cute. He seemed to gravitate to another boy, a ginger, but he didn't introduce her, which was unusual.

Scott came up to her and suggested they go dancing at The Coast. Caroline had heard of this place and thought the idea was fun. "Can we get in?" she asked.

Scott mentioned that a frat brother was working the door that night.

"Did you bring your mom's fur?" Caroline winked.

Scott had a big laugh and directed her out to the parking lot. She climbed into a car with several other SAEs and sped off. Caroline relished dancing at The Coast, with Scott treating her to a whiskey sour. Whenever her favorite songs played, she pulled Scott onto the dance floor. However, she eventually noticed he had left the table, leaving her with the other two guys they had arrived with. She danced with them briefly, but when one became overly forward, Caroline decided to explore the club. She spotted Scott engrossed in conversation with the red-haired guy, so she chose not to interrupt. Eventually, Caroline found a spot to put down the drink and watch the dance floor. She was starting to think it was time to find a way home.

Suddenly, the air around her began to tingle. Then, a voice came to her ear, saying, "Somehow, I thought you liked quieter places where troubadours played."

She turned her head toward the voice and saw the guitar man! Like Scott, he wore a navy jacket and a rep tie that might have had the SAE symbol on it. However, the tie was loose, and he seemed to exude the same air of comfort as he had at Penny Lane.

Caroline stumbled a bit as she found her voice. "I love all kinds of music, and I enjoy dancing. What brings a gentle guitar player to a place like this?"

He smiled at her question. "I enjoy dancing occasionally myself. It's homecoming and not a weekend for quiet guitar playing."

"I thought I saw you at an SAE party," she said.

"Yes, that's my fraternity," he said with a shrug. And, as it seemed the proper follow-up question, he asked, "Do you belong to a sorority?"

"No, not my thing," Caroline replied.

"A bit of a loner?" he inquired.

"I like to walk my own path," she replied.

Suddenly, Scott was beside her. "Hey, Daniel," he said, "Have you met my friend Caroline?"

The guitar player looked at her and said, "No, not properly introduced." He reached out his hand to Caroline. "Daniel Portnoy."

"Caroline Howard," she responded and shook his hand, which was definitely worn at the fingertips.

"We were discussing music," Daniel said to Scott.

"Caroline's the perfect person to talk to about that subject," Scott replied.

"Hmm, that's interesting," Daniel said warmly.

"Hey, Caroline, I've got another place to be, and this is probably the best time to get you home," said Scott in a rush.

"Ah well, can't let the coach turn into a pumpkin," she responded. As Caroline began to walk after Scott, she turned to say, "It was very nice to meet you, Daniel Portnoy."

"And you," he replied, saluting her with his drink. For just a moment, their eyes met, and it was as if she recognized him from long ago. Regrettably, the connection was severed when Scott tugged her toward the exit.

Caroline lay on her bed in the dorm. She was glad Amanda was at her new sorority house and wouldn't be in until late. It gave Caroline time to think about Daniel Portnoy and what was in his eyes. It was as if she could look in far enough to see his soul. Serena had spoken many times about the eye serving as the window to the soul containing the knowledge of the universe and all lives lived. She had heard girls around the dorm talk about meeting their soul mate. Caroline wasn't sure if that was just an explanation for lust. She would have to ask Serena about it when she went to the mountains over Christmas vacation.

It had been kind of Meg to invite her. Caroline had been planning to take the bus to her grandparents over break but was glad to add a trip to the mountains. Meg's family spent a week there, and she promised to take Caroline skiing. Caroline longed to learn to ski better, especially if she decided to live up there year-round. Meg also told her there were snowshoes, which Caroline planned to use to see Serena. She knew she wouldn't have long with her, as the trek would take time, and Meg might grow suspicious if she was gone too long. But it would allow her to ask questions. Also, she wanted to tell Serena about her writing class. Dr. Porter had encouraged her, saying she had a talent in this area. Caroline enjoyed writing stories and often wrote about the past lives she had seen on her journeys in the Akashic Record. Dr. Porter always commented on the realism in her fiction. She had suggested a class for Caroline to take next semester. It would be a lot of work to tackle math, freshman English, and the elective writing class. Caroline enjoyed college, but it was hard work. Fortunately, she had the time to study, as Amanda was gone often. She had found a good study spot in the library as well. She wanted to please her mother by getting good grades.

Midterms came, and the results helped Caroline understand where to spend more time studying. Amanda teased her about being a straight-A student. Caroline didn't believe she was that smart. She wasn't like Andrew, who had never needed to study. For Caroline, good grades required effort.

She went to Penny Lane a few more times. She didn't see Daniel Portnoy again, and when she saw Scott, she didn't want to go to his fraternity house. She didn't want Daniel to think she was stalking him or something like that. Besides, he probably had a steady girlfriend. No guy that cute was single.

The semester ended, and Caroline packed to go with Meg. She felt good about her efforts but remained anxious about her grades. Her mother received her mail from the school. Caroline knew she would look at them first, but she kept telling herself it wouldn't do her any good to worry.

Meg's family was amiable, and Meg let her borrow an old ski outfit and ski equipment. It was interesting to ski down the runs she hiked in the summer. Meg took her on the green runs on the mountain's front side and reviewed how to snowplow to stop and traverse to reach different runs. Caroline followed Meg down *School Marm* and *Last Chance*, working her knees to carve the turns as Meg did. When they took a break for lunch, Caroline was tired but exhilarated.

Meg asked if Caroline minded skiing alone in the afternoon while she went on the more challenging blue runs. While Caroline was still nervous about getting on and off the lifts, she wanted her friend to have as special a day as she was having. They set a time to meet at the bottom of the hill, and Meg was off.

Caroline worked up the courage to take  on the hill by herself. She found that other skiers were helpful, everyone understanding her concern about the lift and giving advice on improving her skills. Caroline found skiers, in general, were kind, and all loved the beauty of the mountains one saw while riding the lifts. Caroline didn't even mind the cold. She ate homemade soup with sandwiches when she got to Meg's family condo. The family played board games at night, but Caroline was tired. She fell asleep before her head hit the pillow.

The next day, she slept in, enjoyed some sun while reading for pleasure, assisted Meg's mother with dinner preparations, and gave her a thoughtful hostess gift. Caroline skied and took breaks for hot chocolate, ensuring she didn't overexert herself. Tomorrow, she planned to snowshoe up to Serena, having sent a message on the wind while savoring the rich chocolate. She hoped the snow wouldn't be too challenging and asked the universe for guidance in finding the easiest path to the cave. She got up early and ate a hearty breakfast with the skiers. Then, she accepted a ride to the hiking trail with Meg's mom, assuring her she wouldn't take any risks on the adventure and knew the area well.

Caroline took off on the snowshoes, with the poles helping her climb the mountain. The snow was light at the bottom, but it got deeper the higher she went. Caroline took some breaks and trudged along. As she approached the entrance, she saw Serena standing in a clearing. She waved her arms, and Serena gave the signal to halt, then came down to meet her. "You didn't have to climb up to the cave," Serena said as a greeting.

"I thought it would be warmer here," Caroline replied.

Serena nodded and walked ahead, breaking the snow down to make it easier for Caroline to walk. She had her warm cloak of skins draped around her and additional skins snugly wrapped around her long legs. Upon reaching the cave, Caroline saw that Serena had already kindled a substantial fire. Caroline collapsed onto the skins by the fire to rest.

Serena brought her a warm tea, which Caroline quickly swallowed. She worked to slow her breathing while Serena settled onto a bench. When Caroline finally sat up, Serena smiled and said, "I can see that shorter human legs make walking in the snow more difficult."

Caroline laughed and said, "I'll have to get in better shape if I plan to come up in the winter. But it is beautiful here." She looked at the trees, particularly the pines with snow on their branches, looking like individual

Christmas trees.

"Is there anything in particular you wanted to work on?" Serena asked.

Caroline found herself taken aback by the inquiry, as Serena usually had a meticulously structured agenda. She replied, "Yes, I do. I'm interested in delving into the concept of soul families. You've touched upon it before, and the girls at school often discuss meeting their soul mates. I'd like to gain a deeper understanding of this."

Serena nodded and commenced her explanation. "Souls organically form families. The teachers you are assigned and how quickly your soul grows in knowledge and understanding eventually form families that stay together for all time. As a soul contemplates living life again to improve its understanding of such difficult concepts as forgiveness, members of the family might choose to go back with the soul and play a particular role in helping the family member."

Caroline interrupted. "You mean my father could be a member of my soul family and chose to be the difficult person in my life?"

"Yes, that can happen," Serena replied. "But I don't think your father is a member of your soul family, though he could be from a nearby family known to you. If you speak of someone you love as a soul mate, then yes, there is usually one or two souls you are particularly close to who serve as a husband or wife in many lives. However, it's essential to understand that your journey, as decided in your soul contract, drives the people you meet and perhaps marry. These closer souls are not in every one of your lives. They also have training, and you might not be on the same planets at the same time."

"So, a person I fall in love with might not be my soul mate?" Caroline asked.

"No. He might be a soul who chose to work with you because you are working on similar skills. I suspect humans get too concerned about finding this soul mate rather than walking their path and self-actualizing. Have you finally met a male you have feelings for other than your friend Scott?"

"I briefly met someone whose eyes seemed different. When I looked deeply into them, I felt like I could see shared experiences from the past," said Caroline.

"Ah, that is good. I can't say what role this man may play in your life. Still, your ability to look at him and see deeply into his spirit is a good sign that you are applying the knowledge you have gained here."

"I haven't peered into the Akashic Record to see who he might be, said Caroline sheepishly.

"Your roles are still evolving because the future is unwritten."

Next, they discussed astrology, as this was an important subject. Caroline suddenly remembered some of the older books Serena had in strange languages. "Serena, I was curious about some of the oldest books. I've seen you reading them, but I can't. How did you learn the languages?"

"Most of the older books are written in languages that are dead. Only Greek and Latin are still taught and would be good languages for you to learn."

Caroline groaned. She knew she had to take a language, but she had hoped for something more modern and valuable, like Spanish.

"Caroline, you will be learning for the rest of your life. Suppose you want to read the older books. In that case, you will have to learn how to decipher dead languages like the ones spoken on Atlantis or Old Britannia. These books come from all the old worlds where seeing a wood nymph was more common," Serena said with a slight smile.

"I plan to study mythology even if I know that what I learn aren't necessarily 'myths,'" Caroline said with a wink.

"I feel this college experience will be good for you. Anywhere there is higher learning is a positive place. It would help if you tried researching the lost lands and beliefs from places like Egypt. In time, you will find people who are open to your knowledge. Eventually, you will find a mystical family here on Earth similar to your soul family," Serena said as she picked up the plates and cups from their lunch. She had provided Caroline with protein from nuts and meat to help restore her strength for the trek back down. Then, Serena looked at the light and said, "You should get started on your way."

"Serena, does the man I might marry have to come from this mystical or soul family?" Caroline asked as she strapped on her snowshoes, not wanting to look at Serena's face.

"I expect you would like to find someone special at last, and, no, they don't have to practice the metaphysical arts. They do need to be supportive of your work and . . ."

"I know," said Caroline, "and keep me on my path. Speaking of which, will it be easier if I follow the same one down? It's always a delight to spend time with you, Serena. Our moments together are truly precious." Caroline started to leave, unaware of the sorrowful expression in Serena's eyes.

Meg's parents took Caroline to the station, where she grabbed a local bus to reach her grandparents' house. She loved having them all to herself, and her grandmother allowed her to help more in the kitchen. Caroline finally moved up to cutting vegetables. Her grandmother also taught her how to make a pie. Her grandfather sat in his rocking chair, watching their activities and saying little, as usual.

On the phone, Caroline spoke to her mother, who sounded tired. During the holidays, Edward had paid them a visit, but Caroline's mother remained tight-lipped, only expressing her happiness at seeing him. Edward had plans to relocate to Kansas City, which stirred a tinge of jealousy in Caroline, especially because he'd have the opportunity to spend time with Grandmother Howard. However, Caroline reminded herself that jealousy was an emotion best left unattended. Instead, she decided to reach out to her grandmother, hoping she would relish the chance to get better acquainted with Edward and perhaps even understand him.

Just before Caroline left to return to Boulder, her mother called again. She had received Caroline's report card and was pleased that Caroline had earned a 3.8. Caroline was surprised and happy that her hard work had paid off. She warned her mother that the next semester would be more challenging. Her mother said to keep studying, and all would be well. Caroline was glad she could give her mother this happiness. Even Grandma Andersen mentioned how pleased everyone was at Caroline's progress at CU. "I know it's hard to have your parents so far away. I am hoping your mother will spend time here this summer. I worry that she is under a lot of stress." For the first time, Caroline realized her grandparents saw through all her mother's attempts to hide her father's drinking.

Caroline stuck with the code they were using. "I agree, Grandma, though I know she'll be busy with real estate. If she can get away, I'll try to come see her." Caroline had told her grandparents she planned to work at Keystone again that summer if they would hire her.

As Caroline journeyed on the bus back to Boulder, her thoughts were consumed by the upcoming semester. She anticipated the cold weather and envisaged the possibility of quieter weekends, as those with skiing plans would be absent. Meg's family had intentions of returning for spring break. Nevertheless, Caroline couldn't shake her curiosity about Daniel. Would he grace the coffeehouse stage once more, and how could she stay informed about his performances? She resolved to make an effort to socialize more during the weekends, even though her funds were dwindling. She had thought about working over the holidays but didn't have a place to stay in Denver. Also, she had wanted to see her grandparents. But she might work at Keystone next year during the break. Then, she could practice her skiing. She was pleased to have her grandpa's two twenties in her wallet.

As Caroline expected, the math class gave her difficulty. She was embarrassed and didn't want the other freshmen to know. Finally, she went to the professor and asked if he had any suggestions. He mentioned free tutoring. That was a relief. Caroline's other classes were going well. She didn't like her English class as much. She felt the professor needed to be more challenging. But her papers got As once she learned what topics her professor preferred. She couldn't believe that included the Muppets. She focused on songs sung by Kermit the Frog. She loved "Rainbow Connection" and often hummed it as she wrote.

Scott had become a social butterfly. He was always going somewhere. He had moved into the frat house, and Caroline wondered if that was good for him. She occasionally went to the house to see him.

Seeing her gazing around their cafeteria, he said, "Daniel doesn't live in the house. He has an apartment with some other SAEs up on The Hill."

Caroline looked down at her food.

"Caroline, I've never seen you look at any guy like you did that night at

The Coast," said Scott. "Have you seen him again at Penny Lane? I don't think he's a regular. And it's ski season, so he's typically away on the weekends."

Caroline was learning how ski season changed the nature of the campus. Amanda had gone up several times to attend parties. "We might be having formal up there," said Scott. Caroline looked at him and thought about asking if she could go as his date but realized Scott would probably have a date, so she left it alone.

Caroline still went to the coffeehouse and dragged Scott with her one night. She wanted him to see the local performers. One time, she saw Kathy sing. Her voice had improved, but her style needed to fit Penny Lane's vibe. That made Caroline even more determined to find the nerve to perform there. She mentioned this to Scott as they left.

"I don't have time to play the piano for you, Caroline. I'm busy. Speaking of which, I have a party to go to. Where do you want me to drop you off?"

"So, I guess this isn't a party for me," she said.

"No, not this time." Scott was becoming very secretive, and Caroline didn't understand why.

"Just drop me at the dorm."

"Oh, Caroline, how boring. Why don't you at least have a beer at The Walrus before heading home?"

"Alright." The Walrus was a big hangout and a place she could go by herself.

Caroline walked in and looked around to see if she knew anyone. To her surprise, Meg and Cindy were there. Caroline rushed over and squeezed onto a chair. Old Sixties music was playing, and as Caroline looked around, she felt as if she were in a scene from "Animal House." One of the boys at the table invited her to dance, and she accepted the offer. They danced energetically to a James Brown tune, and then a slow song started playing. Instead of politely asking, the boy embraced Caroline and began to sway with her. While she tried to enjoy the song "My Girl," she soon became aware that the guy was attempting to slide his hands into her pants.

"Hey," she retorted and pushed him away.

"What's your problem?" he replied.

"I don't have a problem," Caroline responded as she returned to the table.

She had started to sit down when the guy grabbed her arm. "Look, calm down. Let's keep dancing."

"I think you have me confused with girls who like groping," said Caroline tensely.

"Frigid bitch," the boy responded.

"I think I'll be heading home," Caroline told Meg and Cindy. She grabbed her purse and pushed through the crowd to the door, trying not to cry. Running down Walnut Street, Caroline practically fell into another group of people coming out of the Rio Grande Mexican Restaurant. "Oh, I'm sorry," she said in a quavering voice.

"Are you OK?" said a male voice that sounded familiar. She looked up into Daniel Portnoy's eyes.

Caroline stood utterly still, gazing at him, and then tore her eyes away. "Yes, I'm fine. I needed to get away from a jerk at The Walrus."

"You have to be careful of jerks in Boulder," said Daniel, smiling. "But you really shouldn't be walking about alone. Where are you going?"

"Just back to the dorm," she said.

"Hold on. Let me say goodbye to my friends, and I'll escort you."

*Escort,* Caroline thought. *Who talks like that?*

Daniel buttoned up his navy peacoat and asked, "Which way?"

Caroline pointed toward Baker Hall.

As they began walking, Daniel asked, "Would you be interested in getting a cup of coffee?"

Caroline laughed and said, "I've already been to Penny Lane tonight. But I don't recall having a cup of coffee there."

"How about we stop in at Boxcar? Have you been there?"

Caroline hadn't, and they headed toward it. Fortunately, it wasn't too crowded on a Saturday night, and they could get a table quickly. Then, Caroline realized she would have to make conversation with this man. She started with the standard safe topic: "What are you majoring in?"

"Business," he said. "My father owns a company back in St. Paul that he wants me to take over."

"Oh," Caroline said, realizing he would be going home and maybe soon. "What year are you?"

"I'm a junior, and I guess you're a freshman," he replied. "And have you decided on a major?"

"I'm thinking about something in English. I enjoy writing, and my professors seem positive about my work."

"I think that's a major you can never go wrong with. Do you want to be a professional writer?"

"I'm not sure about that. It seems like a tough road, and I need a career that provides enough to take care of myself. But eventually, I might try it."

"You plan to be a career woman?" he asked.

"I'm not certain that's a choice. My parents live in Branson, Missouri now. My oldest brother is in Chicago, and my other brother is in Kansas City. I'm not afraid of a career. I want to be certain I can afford to live."

"And where do you plan to live," he asked.

"In a perfect world, I would live in Summit County, but I'm not sure it's possible. I'll probably look for a job in Denver."

"The mountains! I would love to live in the mountains, too, but I don't think my dad would be too pleased."

They continued talking about the mountains, Daniel speaking of his love of skiing, Caroline talking about her winter vacation and working for Keystone in the summer. Talking with Daniel was easy. When they'd had enough coffee, Daniel asked if she wanted a ride home.

"You have a car?" she asked.

"Yes, it's just out back," he said.

Caroline laughed. "Then, why were you *walking* me back to the dorm?"

"I like walking. It gives me more time to talk with you."

Caroline smiled and then followed him behind the building. He walked up to a brown Volkswagen Rabbit. "Sorry, it'll be cold. We need to let it warm up a bit," he said.

"I understand. I've lived in Colorado all my life," said Caroline through chattering teeth.

"Well, it's not as cold as St. Paul," he said, shivering.

"Really? I bet the mountains are colder."

"Probably about the same. And it's more fun to be in the Rockies." He put the car in gear and started to drive, but he wasn't heading toward her dorm.

"You like music, right?" he asked.

"Yes, very much."

"I thought we might stop at my place and listen to some new albums I got."

"Really? You're using the line about 'listening to my new stereo," Caroline said, looking directly at him.

"OK, it's lame, but I'm not ready for the evening to end, and as you like the coffeehouse, I thought you might enjoy listening to music."

"I'd enjoy listening to you play," she said. "Alright."

The drive to Daniel's house took a while. It was dark. "My roommates are up in the mountains," he said. Inside, the house had that unmistakable college hand-me-down vibe. Yet, in the living room, a piano and a guitar beckoned. Caroline settled onto the sofa, spotting a homemade afghan draped over the top. She reached for it, cocooning herself within its warmth. Daniel asked if she'd like a drink. "Just water," she replied. He nodded and got her a glass. He had a small glass of dark liquid.

Then, he sat on the piano bench. "Any requests?" he asked with a smile.

"Play whatever you want. Just nothing from a musical."

He laughed and started playing an old Beatles tune, one of her favorites.

I give her all my love

That's all I do

And if you saw my love

You'd love her too

Caroline adored the song, but she wondered why he had chosen this particular one for her. It was a love song more suited for a romantic partner.

However, she scolded herself, urging herself to stop overthinking and simply immerse herself in the music. As he strummed another melody, her eyes gently closed. Gradually, he set the guitar aside and joined her on the sofa, his hand tenderly cradling her chin. "I don't need to tell you how beautiful you are. You already know that," he said in a whisper.

"Some women might know that, but I'm not one of them. It's OK if you say it."

"You seem older than a freshman."

"It's my soul that's older," she said.

"Ah, a wise woman," he replied against her lips.

"Yes."

And Daniel kissed her. It felt like no other kiss, though she hadn't had many to compare it with. It was firm, warm, and tingly. Yet, in some way, it was familiar, which made her feel safe. Warm and safe. The kissing continued, and she fell further into it. Suddenly, he lifted her and carried her to the bedroom. She stiffened when he laid her on the bed, and he immediately noticed. "We won't do anything you're not comfortable with. You're in charge."

She had never heard words like these. It was as if he already knew her fears. They continued kissing as her clothing peeled away without her noticing. When she realized she was almost naked, she stopped and looked around. She grabbed her shirt to cover herself.

Daniel looked at her eyes so she wouldn't see him look at her body. "I apologize for moving so quickly. If you want to stop, it's fine. We can just sleep." He got up and grabbed a T-shirt from a drawer. He kept his back to her as she slipped it on. Then, she crawled under the covers. He turned off the light, slipped off all his clothes except for his boxers, and slid in beside her. He reached his arm out and pulled her next to him. "It's warmer this way, don't you think?"

She looked up into his eyes. He smiled warmly, his face bathed in the dim light of the room, and she took a moment to observe his handsome visage. It possessed a captivating charm, and she couldn't help but appreciate its beauty. Nestling her head gently against his chest, she noticed the firm, muscular contours beneath her cheek, with just the right amount of hairiness to exude masculinity.

As she lay there, she tuned in to the reassuring rhythm of his steady heartbeat, the sound of which brought her a sense of comfort and security. His hand moved soothingly along her back, and gradually, the tranquility of the moment lulled her into a peaceful slumber. As the sun began to rise, Caroline awoke. She looked at the sleeping Daniel.

He was kind. He hadn't pushed her to do anything she didn't want to do. She found herself reaching out and tracing the lines on his face. His eyes opened, and he smiled at her. She moved toward him and kissed him. He wrapped his arms around her, and their passions rose together. He was ready to enter when she looked at him with panicked eyes. "Is it alright?" he asked.

"I'm not on any protection," she whispered.

He nodded and turned over, reaching into a drawer. In a minute, he turned back and asked, "Are you sure?"

This time, she nodded.

He kissed her and stroked her body. He checked to see if her body was ready and entered her. He moved slowly, trying to help her meet his rhythm as if he were playing a duet on the piano.

She was frightened about how her body was responding. It was a completely new feeling inside, which scared and intrigued her. He began to move faster, and she moved with him. He finished, and she felt a small explosion inside. She made a noise and laid back on the bed, her body fully relaxing. He smiled and kissed her. Then, he got up and went to the bathroom.

When he came back, he asked if she wanted to go. She nodded, and he directed her to the bathroom. It was a typical guy's bathroom, far from pristine. She swiftly used the toilet, washed her hands, and assessed her reflection. Grabbing a tissue, she wiped her face clean, revealing her large, expressive eyes. She felt different. She tried not to think about the times her father touched her. She hated that those memories were still inside her. But now she had better memories, and she tried to use what had happened with Daniel to cover up the old, ugly ones.

Entering the bedroom, Caroline found Daniel fast asleep, accompanied by a faint snore. She made her way to the window, where the morning sun was starting to stream in. As she gazed outside, her eyes settled on an elm tree reminiscent of the one from her previous home. Perched on a branch, a male bluebird began its melodious morning serenade. At first, Caroline could barely hear it through the window, but she focused her senses, and the song became clearer and more distinct.

Without hesitation, Caroline joined in, her soprano voice harmonizing with the bird's tune. It was a magical moment. Then, a memory stirred in her mind, and she recalled a song by Paul McCartney.

*I'm a bluebird, I'm a bluebird, I'm a bluebird Yeah, yeah, yeah*
*I'm a bluebird, I'm a bluebird, I'm a bluebird Yeah, yeah, yeah*

"And what's the reason you're not majoring in music with a voice like that?" she heard Daniel ask.

Caroline turned her head. "No, I've already played that game. It's not for me."

"Now I understand why you go to Penny Lane. How come you've never performed?"

"I not a good enough pianist to accompany myself, and I don't play the guitar." She held up her hands. "Having tiny hands makes playing anything difficult." Her clarinet flashed in her mind, but that was something from the past. It was better to look forward. She was getting cold, so she jumped back into bed and snuggled down into the blankets.

"I could accompany you," Daniel said.

"Caroline sat up quickly. "Would you? Really?"

He smiled at her and said, "Yes. But we'll have to find the right song."

"That would be fun. Scott and I used to spend hours doing that. I loved it. We'd try out different numbers. He always said I was born in the wrong era. I should have been a singer in the Thirties and Forties. I would have loved singing with a big band." She hummed a few bars of "Boogie Woogie Bugle Boy."

Daniel laughed. "It's a bit early for a Sunday morning, but how about some coffee and then breakfast?"

Caroline smiled. "That would be very nice."

Caroline sat at the kitchen table while Daniel scrambled some eggs.

She decided it was better to ask the question and know the answer. "For some reason, I don't think you're single. Do you have a girlfriend?" she asked tentatively.

"Hmm. I didn't want to discuss this topic, but you have a right to know. Yes, I've been dating someone for a while. But we're having some issues. She doesn't want to move to St. Paul. She wants to move to Denver or preferably back to LA, where she's from. That's not an option for me. I'm afraid the relationship will die a natural death. What happened between us wasn't planned. But it's a happy surprise."

Caroline smiled at him, appreciating his honesty. "I would prefer that you were free before we continue what happened in your bedroom," she said, looking down at her hands. Then, she looked at him, "But as for singing, we can do that regardless of any attachments."

"Good. As no one is here, perhaps we can practice before I take you home."

Caroline smiled with heartfelt approval, nodding in agreement.

She was pleasantly surprised by Daniel's invitation to the SAE formal in Breckenridge. Caroline asked Scott whether she should wear her blue sapphire prom dress, and he gave the green light. Caroline still needed a dressy coat, which meant either borrowing one or finding one at a second-hand store. Amanda, who was attending the Sigma Chi formal, eagerly offered her help and support. Unfortunately, Amanda had more of a figure than Caroline, so she couldn't borrow anything. Plus, Meg was going to a formal on the same night.

Caroline and Amanda went shopping on Pearl Street. Amanda kept trying to get Caroline into the lovely boutiques, but Caroline knew she couldn't afford their merchandise. Her mother had offered a bit of money. Caroline wished she were here. She could have made the perfect coat. For once, Caroline wondered if it was time for her to learn how to sew. But there was a better time.

They went inside the Buffalo Exchange. They needed help finding anything that might work. Most of the clothes were too casual for Caroline's requirements. Suddenly, Amanda said, "What about this?" She held a thick, sparkly black scarf in her hand.

Caroline walked over and tried it on in the mirror. It would keep her shoulders warm but not her whole body. The store manager mentioned something she had in the back and came out with a long black sweater. "You could probably glue some sparkles on it if you want to dress it up. Or you could put the scarf with it," she said. Caroline tried them both together, and Amanda nodded enthusiastically. Caroline negotiated the price to 20 dollars.

Upon their return to the dorm, Amanda asked about Caroline's hair styling plans. Caroline told Amanda how she had done it the last time. "That would be nice. But you could put it up to better show off the pretty scarf," Amanda said.

Caroline borrowed Scott's car and went to the mall with Amanda. They went to a store that sold a bunch of prom accessories. Amanda showed Caroline sparkly clips and different ways to put up her hair. Caroline spent another 15 dollars. It was all she could afford. She prayed to her spirit guides, particularly Anne, that she would look pretty enough to make Daniel glad he'd asked her.

Caroline had directly asked Daniel about his relationship status, and he confirmed it was over. They rode to the Breckenridge Hilton Hotel with another couple, and Daniel mentioned they had separate rooms due to their being gentlemen. Caroline proposed hiking on Sunday, and Daniel readily agreed.

The night of the dance was magical for Caroline. While putting up all her long, curly hair had been burdensome, she thought she had done a decent job. The pretty clips had helped the messy updo look intentional. The smile Daniel gave her made her worries go away. He complimented her outfit several times.

Scott was there with a date from one of the sororities. He seemed to like the girl, but Caroline found her snobby. She was from Virginia and spoke as if she came from old money.

Caroline had one dance with Scott, "You're even prettier than the night we went to prom. And I bet you're having more fun!" he said.

She blushed, unused to the positive attention. She didn't notice anyone from A-West, and for the first time, she wasn't afraid. She wasn't that girl anymore.

Caroline spent the night with Daniel. It felt right to Caroline, and it allowed them to leave early the following day for their hike. Daniel saw that Caroline had all the gear necessary for hiking this time of year. They made a pit stop at the Sunshine Café in Silverthorne, a place Caroline had frequented with her family. They ordered breakfast scrambles and shared a delicious cinnamon roll. Caroline pointed out the trail's entrance to Daniel. Although she didn't intend to linger, she couldn't resist sharing her good news with Serena, who could easily navigate the trees to see Daniel if she wished.

When Caroline and Daniel reached the rock, she explained that he needed to wait there for her. He didn't understand and didn't want her to go on by herself. She finally had to be firm and said, "Daniel, I've done this since I was a girl. I need to do this next portion of the trail alone. I can't explain why now. Perhaps someday I can, but I don't want to waste time arguing with you. Enjoy the beautiful view of the Williams Fork Range. I'll be back soon." Something inside Caroline was urging her up to the cave. Something awaited her there. She ascended swiftly, hoping Daniel wouldn't trail behind.

Caroline scrambled as fast as the snow would allow. It was spring, so the snow was soft, making it heavier to walk through. But she pushed hard, growing more frantic to reach the cave. When she came close, she felt that something was different. She stopped, her heart pounding as she looked around. What was wrong? Then, she realized it was quiet. No birds were singing. She didn't remember a time when the birds had stopped singing. She started running through the snow, calling out to Serena so hard in her mind that it finally came through her voice. "Serreena," she sang out in her unique way. A profound stillness prevailed, devoid of any energy emanating from the cave.

As she reached the opening, she felt cold. The wind blew snow and pinecones in front of the cave. It felt neglected. And there was no fire. She couldn't remember a time without a fire, as Serena always knew when she was coming. Caroline walked into the cold cave. Moving to where Serena kept the logs and kindling, she pulled out a small amount. Then, she lit a fire using the magic she had learned in this cave.

Caroline walked toward the back. All the books were there, jumbled about as always. The skins were on the floor and over the benches, but Serena's clothing was missing. Her cloak wasn't hanging in its regular place. Caroline walked to the back where Serena slept. She had never been to this part of the cave. There were linens she was sure Serena had woven to use as sheets. There were thick skins on the bed with no smell. They were old. The bed was made. She laid her hand on it and found it was as cold as everything else. *Serena, how could you go without telling me?* Caroline didn't understand. She sat on the larger bench that Serena had always used. Then, she picked up Serena's favorite skin and pulled it around her shoulders. She stared into the fire with the third eye and asked the universe for an explanation.

Suddenly, her power animals walked into the cave, followed by the chief. He folded his legs and sat by the fire. The bear lay next to her while the hare climbed into her lap. Caroline waited for the chief to speak.

"She has left for another place," he said.

"Is she gone to the heavens?" asked Caroline.

"Perhaps, but it does not matter," said the chief. "She left this cave for you. It is now the place where you will train and grow your knowledge and power. You will wear the cloak of power even when you walk among men. I am to help you put it on." The cloak wasn't something one could see, as the fabric was power. When the chief placed it on her, Caroline felt the energy go into her body, down through all of her limbs. It was the most vital golden energy that came from the universe. It was strongest in her fingers. Caroline looked at her tiny hands, which now glowed. She drove the power out from her fingers, and fire burst into the cave.

The chief said, "You must learn how to use this new energy properly. Everything you need to know is in the books here."

"Some of the books are in languages I cannot read," said Caroline.

"Ask the universe to send you a guide to help you learn the language in the books. The universe will provide all that you need."

"Will the cave be safe until I can come in the summer?" Caroline asked. "Use your power to camouflage the opening from human eyes. All will be fine," finished the chief. As he stood and approached the cave's entrance, the sun casting elongated shadows in the west, the bear and the hare followed suit. Caroline rose as well, and the animals patiently awaited her while she conjured the incantations in her mind to seal the opening from curious onlookers. She trusted her guides to stand as vigilant sentinels, protecting the cave until her eventual return.

Caroline walked down the hill back to Daniel. She followed the trail she had made but found the walking more effortless than before. The power had given her added strength. She walked toward the rock but didn't see Daniel. She pushed out her energy and saw him looking for her. *I am here, Daniel.* She sat on the rock, waiting for him.

"There you are! I was getting worried," he yelled out.

"There was nothing to fear. These are my woods. I know them well," said Caroline.

He stared at her, trying to figure out what had changed. Her hair color was different, more red but somehow brighter, too. She seemed to glow as if lit from inside. She looked more beautiful than ever. He was almost afraid to touch her.

Caroline smiled and reached out her hand. "It's time to leave." Touching her was like touching fire. It surged up his arm.

"Did you accomplish what you wanted?" he asked.

"It wasn't what I expected. Change has come. More change is coming. But that can wait until I return in the summer," she replied.

"I was thinking I might return for a week," said Daniel. She turned to look at him, and he needed to blink. The sun was in his eyes. Then, he saw her face shining through the western light.

"Indeed, that would be delightful," she said, gracefully disembarking from her perch atop the rock. With a measured pace, she descended the hill, the sun bestowing a golden aura upon the mountains, while the power radiated in her wake.

# The End

# Acknowledgments

*T*HIS BOOK WENT THROUGH many different drafts. It began as a memoir, but with a recommendation to change the genre, I transformed it into a book of fiction.

I had never written fiction, and it was recommended that I work with a developmental editor. I contacted Page Lambert. She did a yeoman's job of changing me from a journalistic writer to one who could craft a creative story. I still hope to attend one of her writing seminars, and I encourage anyone wanting to grow as a writer to do the same.

It took me a long time to learn some of the many modalities of spirituality. Several women gave their time to me, and I wish to thank them. First, I want to thank Sharon Dacotah, a woman with many spiritual gifts who took me through the medicine wheel. She taught me the importance of ethics when working in the metaphysical field, and I will always be grateful to her. Also, my beloved medium, Cynthia Rose, has done more than teach me about mediumship. She helped me resolve many questions about this life and discover my life path. Last but never least is Lisa Barnett, founder of the Akashic Knowing School of Wisdom, who trained me to read the Akashic Record. It is her shielding technique that Serena teaches Caroline. She is another ethical teacher whom I would recommend to anyone.

To write the chapter on the Korean War, I used the book "U.S. Marines in the Korean War," edited by Charles R. Smith. I learned so much from this research and wish I could have written more, but finding accurate information about the tank battalions was challenging. This work reminded me of how much I want to write a book of historical fiction one day. I look forward to conducting research and taking road trips with my brother, Randall Ward.

Thanks to my readers, particularly Dan Fristoe. Great Father sent us to our new home in SaddleBrooke to meet and develop a deep friendship with Dan and his partner Rick. Much love!

I could not take on the work of writing a book without the support of my loving husband, David. He is my knight, and I am forever grateful to my Grandmother Jensen for telling me to marry this man! My beautiful daughter, Madeline Rose, is the joy of my life. She has supported me in creating my brand and designing my websites. But even more, it is for women such as Madeline that I write stories on female empowerment. I will continue to support organizations that provide mental health to abused children. Sadly, it is desperately needed.